HOW REAL PEOPLE OUGHT TO LIVE

Reebok
SPORT

HOW REAL PEOPLE OUGHT TO LIVE

THE CASHINAHUA OF EASTERN PERU

KENNETH M. KENSINGER

Bennington College

WAVELAND PRESS, INC.

Prospect Heights, Illinois

For information about this book, write or call:

Waveland Press, Inc.
P.O. Box 400
Prospect Heights, Illinois 60070
(847) 634-0081

ISBN 0-88133-847-8

Printed in the United States of America

7 6 5 4 3 2

CONTENTS

INTRODUCTION

This book is not a traditional ethnography. It is, rather, a collection of essays written over the last twenty-five years about the Cashinahua of the Curanja and upper Purus rivers of eastern Peru (see figure 1). I lived with them for eighty-four months between 1955 and 1968; I returned for three more three-month visits in March and October 1993 and March 1994. These essays examine the cultural practices of the Peruvian Cashinahua only; I have never lived with the Brazilian Cashinahua, whose history differs considerably from that of their Peruvian kinsmen.

All Cashinahua appear to be the descendants of a group that at the turn of the century lived on the upper Muru River and its affluents, particularly the Iboiçu, in what is now the Brazilian state of Acre. In the 1870s Peruvian and Brazilian rubber barons began to exploit the rich resources of the region. Many indigenous groups were either massacred or enslaved, "adopted" as mistresses, domestic servants, gunmen, hunters, and woodsmen. The survivors spread out to a number of rivers in the upper Jurua Basin, where their descendants are to be found to this day. A major historical division of the Cashinahua occurred sometime around the mid-1920s when the Cashinahua living at Seringal União on the Emvira River "preempted their [Brazilian] neighbors, who were planning such a massacre. They killed them, took everything in their *borracão* (storehouse), and fled to the upper Curanja in Peru" (McCallum 1990:414). It was among survivors and descendants of this group that I began my fieldwork in 1955. With the exception

Figure 1: Map of Cashinahua Villages, 1993-94

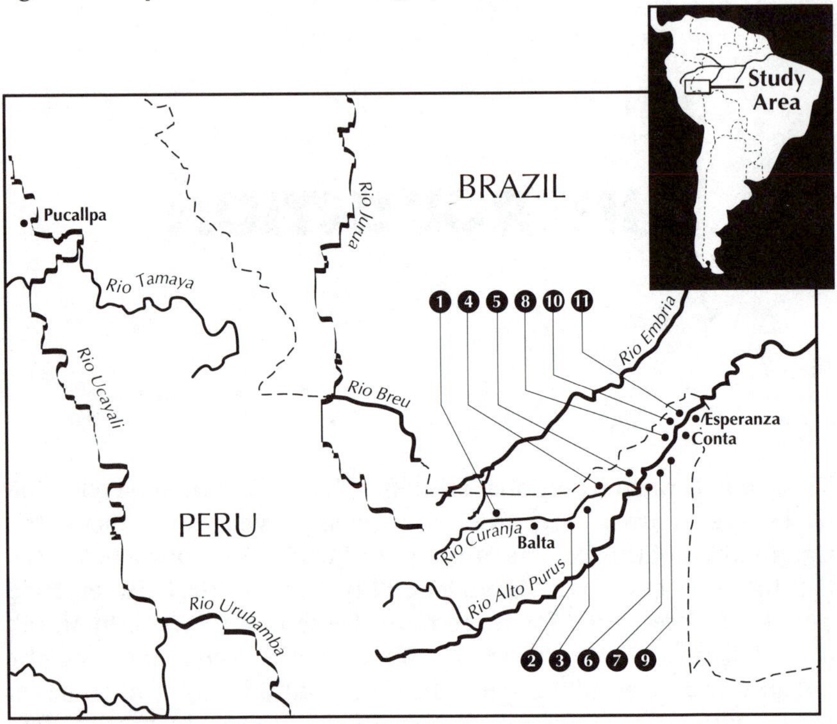

Key to Map:

1. Santa Rey
2. Colombiano
3. Curanjillo
4. Nueva Luz
5. Miguel Grau
6. Lidia
7. Cashuera
8. Bufeo
9. Canta Gallo
10. Pikiniki
11. San Francisco

of the last chapter, the ethnographic present covered by these essays is 1955 to 1968.

Among the Cashinahua groups remaining in Brazil, according to Seu Sueiro Kaxinaua, longtime leader of the Jordão Cashinahua, the adults were massacred, leaving young people and children with only a partial knowledge of traditional lore and technology, such as rituals, myths, herbal medicine, and weaving. Sueiro insists that the aim of the perpetrators of these massacres was to destroy the Cashinahua's political system and, hence, resistance to their control. In this they succeeded. The action was compounded by the subsequent further dispersion of the survivors in small family units, a dislocation required by the spatial organization of rubber production. Each tapper lived isolated at the "mouth" of a number of rubber paths cut through the forest. He went out from his settlement each day to cut the trees and collect the latex. This system persisted more or less intact until the mid-1970s when a Brazilian anthropologist intervened on behalf of, and in collaboration with, the Jordão and Tarauaca Cashinahua led by Sueiro (McCallum 1989, 1990).

Following their flight from the Emvira River to the Upper Curanja, the Peruvian Cashinahua isolated themselves, for the most part, from contact with Brazilians and Peruvians. They had limited contacts with other indigenous groups in the region, mainly during raids on the temporary camps of the Marinahua who ascended the Curanja River each dry season to hunt and collect turtle eggs. At the instigation of the Marinahua, who were tired of having their machetes and axes stolen by the Cashinahua, a Peruvian trader established ties with the Cashinahua about 1947 and their isolation came to an end. Chapter 25 provides a brief summary of their history since that date.

These essays were written for different occasions; each was addressed to a particular topic and audience. I have tried to avoid needless jargon and keep to a minimum theoretical argumentation. By doing this I do not mean to denigrate or underestimate the value of theory, without which we can make little sense of our experiences. But theories are merely the tools with which we work. It is the product of their use that should be the focus of our attention. One of my major goals has been to place into the public domain my ethnographic data, that part of anthropological writing most likely to endure (Salzman 1988).

Each chapter is self-contained. Therefore, a certain amount of redundancy from chapter to chapter has been unavoidable, but I have tried to keep it to a minimum. I have assumed, based on my experience as a teacher, that most professors will not ask their students to read the entire book but will assign selected chapters.

The orthography used throughout the book is a practical modification of the phonemic orthography. Consonants *p*, *t*, and *k* are pronounced like their counterparts in the English words s*p*y, s*t*y, and s*k*y; *b*, *s*, and *sh* as in *b*uy, *s*igh, and *sh*y; *ch* and *ts* as in in*ch* and ca*ts*; *m*, *n*, *w*, and *y* as in *m*et, *n*et, *w*et, and *y*et; *d* in word initial position is pronounced as in English, between vowels it is pronounced like the Spanish *r*; *x* is pronounced like the English *sh* with the tip of the tongue turned back. Vowels *i*, *a*, and *u* are pronounced like the vowels in b*ee*t, f*a*ther, and b*oo*t; *e* is pronounced like the English *oo* in b*oo*t but with the lips flat, as when one smiles. Nasalization of vowels is indicated by writing *n* after the vowel or sequence of vowels; e.g., *kain* is /*kãɯ*/ and *kanka* is /*kãka*/. Phonemic pitch is not written. Words have a primary stress on the first syllable; words with more than two syllables receive stress on odd-numbered syllables, counting from the beginning of the word.

No author works in a vacuum and I am no exception. These essays would not have been written without the encouragement of a small army of teachers, colleagues, and friends. I have tried to acknowledge their contributions to my learning and thinking in footnotes scattered throughout the book. Bertil Ostlinger provided yeoman service by getting all the chapters into my computer, insisting throughout the process that I explain and clarify those parts he found too dense or obscure. My greatest debt, however, is to the Cashinahua who took me into their hearts and homes and patiently, kindly, and gently instructed me in the way "real people" ought to live.

Chapter 1

AN EXPERIMENT IN CROSS-CULTURAL COMMUNICATIONS

The data obtained through ethnographic fieldwork are central to the development and testing of anthropological theory. An ethnographer's job is to observe, learn, understand, and report on the culture of a particular society. Through observation and participation, the ethnographer attempts to learn everything needed in order to behave properly in every context and the standards by which the members of the society judge their own and others' behavior to be appropriate. Thus, by its very nature, ethnographic fieldwork becomes an experiment in cross-cultural communication.

By *communication*, I mean the process of transmitting messages between individuals. Communication involves three stages: (1) the transmission of a message, verbal or nonverbal, by a sender; (2) the reception of the message; and (3) the acknowledgment of the message (feedback) by the receiver of the initial message. In order to have a satisfactory communicative act, the receiver of a message must understand the code or codes used by the sender and then be able to respond to the message if the exchange of information is to be completed.

This process can be complicated by the fact that each person is unique. No two people ever totally share the same life experiences.

Thus, although they share a common linguistic or cultural code, they may not mean exactly the same thing even when they use the same words. For example, the word *marriage* may be interpreted in a variety of ways. If the person who receives a message containing the word *marriage* is a bride on her honeymoon, she responds quite differently from two people celebrating their fiftieth wedding anniversary. If a man who has just gone through a messy divorce hears the word, he is likely to respond in yet another way and so, too, a wife who feels that she is being isolated in the home and is unable to fulfill her potential as a woman. A single person may see marriage as a trap. Each person brings to the message his or her own experiences. At the same time, each person makes a guess about what the sender of the message means by the term. If the hearer knows the sender, his or her guess is likely to be more accurate.

The problem is magnified when the factors of totally different cultures and totally different languages are added to the equation. Just how difficult the problem is became painfully obvious to me during my fieldwork with the Cashinahua. When I arrived in one of their villages, I did not speak or understand a single word of their language, while they neither spoke nor understood any language I could use, and interpreters were not available.

I began by pointing at an object and asking what it was in English, Spanish, or Portuguese (the latter two being the trade languages of the area) and trying to write down what they would say. The responses were disappointing and confusing because they often seemed to sound similar, having a common base, *men*, with other syllables attached. Obviously, the Cashinahua did not understand me and I did not understand them. Some days later I learned that in Cashinahua you do not point with your finger, you point with your lower lip. This method of pointing is just as accurate as using a finger once you learn to follow from the curve of the lip to the object. In Cashinahua society one points with a finger only when making a legal accusation, a very serious matter. The words they had given in response to my question were, "it is his finger," "his hand," "he is pointing," and so on, all of which contained the morpheme *men* meaning "hand." Once I learned the question *hawamen* ("What is it?"),[1] I was able to collect the names of all kinds of objects, but I was not able to converse with them because I needed verbs; you cannot point at verbs, whether with your finger or your lip. More about eliciting verb forms later.

In collecting the names of objects, I became aware of sound contrasts such as *paka*, "bamboo," *baka*, "fish," *taka*, "liver," *daka*, "to rest," *kaka*, "basket." Many of the sounds used in Cashinahua are similar to those in English as in the words above. However, slight differences in sound often produce striking differences in meaning, as when I referred to a woman using the term *shanu*, which I thought meant "grandmother" or "old woman." She responded with anger because I had called her a "rattlesnake" (an insult sometimes used to refer to women who gossip). The correct term is very similar to *shanu*; the initial "sh"-sound should have been made with the tip of the tongue turned back, thus, *xanu*, which does mean "grandmother."

Late one afternoon I was called to eat with the men. All of the men of the village had gathered, sitting in a circle around the bowls of food placed on the ground. I was a little slow responding to the invitation so that when I arrived, all the turtle shells, carved wood stools, and firewood used as seats were occupied and I was left with the option of squatting or sitting on the damp ground. I thought it would be better to use a palm leaf mat and turned to ask one of the women for one, but at the moment I could not remember the word. I knew that it was similar to the word for ribs, *pishi*, so I said in what I thought was good Cashinahua, *en pisi bikatsis ikai*. She stood up and went to get what I had requested, and I squatted down and started to eat. When two men across the circle started to smile, I turned to look for the source of their amusement just as something hit me between the shoulder blades. There was a popping sound, something wet and sticky ran down my back, and I was engulfed in a putrid cloud. Everybody started to shout "*pisi, pisi, min pisi haida*" at me. They spat and howled with glee. I had received what I had asked for, something foul smelling. The woman had gotten an egg that had been under a hen for six weeks without hatching. Because we were all contaminated by the fumes, dinner was adjourned while we went to the river for a bath. When we returned, the woman handed me a palm leaf mat and said, "*Pisi maki, pishin*," (it isn't *pisi, pishin*"). I was right, the word for "mat" is similar to "ribs." The only difference is that the final vowel of the word for "mat" is made with air passing through the nose and mouth simultaneously; that is, it is a nasalized vowel as opposed to the oral vowel, a distinction we do not use in English.

Verbs were more difficult to elicit than nouns. After various attempts to get them by acting out something—like "jumping"—without success, I found that it was easier to guess at the meaning of words used in situations involving actions. Someone would hand me a banana and say "*piwe*," or take me by the hand and lead me over to where food was being served, saying "*pinunwen*." I guessed that the *pi* might mean "to eat." They often gave added nonverbal clues, like putting food up to my mouth. Little by little, I was able to figure out the meaning of the parts of utterances. For example, in the following words based on the verb-stem *ka*, many recurrent forms are found: *kawe* "Go!," *kanunwen* "Let's go!," *enkai* "I am going," *kadiwe* "Go quickly!," *kaditanwen* "Go quickly, but return!," *kapa* "May I go?"

Verbs were easier to elicit once I had learned the meaning and proper usage of *min hawa wai*. I had guessed that the form meant "What are you doing?" However, when I responded to that form with a statement of what I was doing, they seemed to be insulted. When I asked a man who was sitting in his hammock, sharpening his arrows, "*Min hawa wai*?," he responded, "*En hawa maki*," the same response I got from his wife, who was grinding corn, and from his young daughter, who was playing. Several days later, I sat in my hammock watching two children playing a game of chase. One of them ran into the side of a large clay pot full of about five gallons of corn gruel. It cracked and spilled its contents onto the ground. The child's mother called out to the child, "*Min hawa wai*?" The response—"*En hawa maki*." The mother repeated her question, "*Min hawa wai*?" The child answered, "*En beyusai*," "I'm playing" (I knew this form). As I puzzled over this verbal exchange, I did not know what it all meant, but I guessed that my original hunch that *min hawa wai* meant "What are you doing?" was correct. A little later one of the men came into the house and said to me, "*Min hawa wai*," to which I replied, "*En hawa maki*." He repeated his question "*Min hawa wai*?" I replied, *En disin dakai*," "I'm resting in the hammock." He whooped and laughed, running from the house only to return with his brother, who repeated the sequence: "*Min hawa wai*?" "*En hawa maki*." "*Min hawa wai*?" "*En disin dakai*." His response was the same, and more men were called to repeat the sequence. I was mystified, but they were happy. I had learned something important. But what?

Some time later, I realized what it all meant. *Min hawa wai* does mean "What are you doing?" and *en hawa maki* means "I'm not doing anything." However, the significance does not lie in the meaning of the words, but in the sequence and the cultural rules. The question is not asked in order to find out what a person is doing. One's actions are visible to the questioner. Rather, it is a query about one's mood. If the response to the initial question is a statement of one's activity, the implication is that the individual is busy and does not wish to be bothered or is not in the mood to be sociable. A response of *en hawa maki*, "I'm not doing anything," implies "pull up a turtle shell, sit down, and talk." This sequence is not unlike our "How are you?," which usually calls for a response of "Fine, thank you. And how are you?" In general, only a doctor is looking for a detailed and accurate answer to "How are you?"

In the early months and years of my studies among the Cashinahua, I spent a great deal of time working with the men. This was necessary because I could determine the meaning of a word only if I knew the context to which it referred. Therefore, many of my days were spent hunting with one of the men. We would leave the village at daybreak and dogtrot into the jungle. The pace would slacken slightly once we were out of the area where the sounds of village life could be heard, but we would stop only to examine spoor or to prepare to stalk an animal. Occasionally my companion would pause to point out herbs used to treat illness or indications of the presence of *yushin*, "spirits." He rarely spoke, and then only in a low voice or whisper. Unless we were lucky and killed a large animal, like a tapir, deer, or peccary, or several smaller animals, we would hunt all day, returning to the village by three o'clock in the afternoon. After a bath in the river, I would have my companion tell me about the day's events. My assumption was that since we had experienced the same things, I would be able to make more accurate guesses about the meaning of sentences. I was only partly right. His rehearsal of the facts did provide me with many sentences for which I could provide translations. However, while I remembered the difficulties of the hunt, the thickets of sharply barbed bamboo, the thorns, the almost impenetrable jungle, as well as the excitement of the chase, he went into great detail about the signs of animal movements, or spirit activities, or about a tree with nearly ripened fruit. He had seen and would speculate about the amount of honey in the hollow-tree home of stingless black bees. It was years before I learned the mechanics of moving quietly through the forest and began to see the jungle through Cashinahua eyes.

My participation in the hunt resulted in my learning an important lesson in nonverbal communication. Companions in a hunt share the results, and my success produced problems. I often returned with more than ten pounds of meat. With no refrigeration, I was only able to use part of the meat, so I followed the example of my companion and generously gave most of it away. In order to show no partiality, I carefully distributed meat to every family, giving it to the women of each household. I was unaware that the distribution of meat within the village follows strict rules. A man gives meat to his wife or wives, to his mother, his mother-in-law, his sisters, or his grandmothers. Meat given to other women constitutes a proposition and with the acceptance of the gift, the woman obligates herself to arrange for a sexual exchange. My generosity resulted in increasing friendliness from the women but suspicion, anger, and hostility from their husbands. The problem was resolved when the headman started to address me as "son," and his son (now my brother) told me to whom we could give meat without arousing suspicions.

Increased understanding of their language and culture led to an increased degree of communication with the Cashinahua. After several years, I found myself thinking and even dreaming in the language. Behavior patterns that had once been studiously performed became second nature. However, no matter how fluent I became in the language, I could never become a Cashinahua because I carried in my head a totally different cultural background that I could never fully communicate to them. Good communication was possible; perfect communication was not.

Perfect communication is only theoretically possible in a situation in which the parties are identical in every respect; something that never happens. Good communication does not demand that the parties share the same values, beliefs, experiences, etc. Rather, it results from a desire for mutual understanding based on mutual respect, and a lot of hard work.

Chapter 2
SUBSISTENCE ACTIVITIES

The Cashinahua depend about equally on hunting and gardening for subsistence. Fishing and gathering provide variety to the diet and supplement the food supply, particularly when the old gardens have been exhausted and the new ones have not yet come into production.

Until recently, everything the Cashinahua used or consumed was garnered from or produced within the local setting and with locally available materials. The recent introduction of foreign goods and techniques has caused only slight modification of the traditional subsistence patterns. For example, the steel axes and machetes that replaced stone axes and bamboo knives have increased their efficiency without changing their technology. On the other hand, the introduction of shotguns, with their greater killing power, cannot but have an eventual impact on the delicately balanced equilibrium that the Cashinahua have established with their surroundings. Some of the effects of changes in Cashinahua subsistence technology will be mentioned where appropriate.

Hunting

Hunting, next to sex, is the major passion in the life of a Cashinahua male. It is through the hunt and his skill as a hunter that he makes his name as a good provider, that he gains a reputation for generosity because of the meat his wives distribute, that he lays the groundwork for his much desired sexual affairs, and that he gathers the basic data for the yarns he will spin as he sits about the fire or the bowls of food in the evening, swapping hunting tales with his kinsmen. He views himself primarily as a hunter and only secondarily as a gardener.

Ideally each adult male has a hunting territory over which he has total exploitative control but not ownership. All territory surrounding a village is owned by the two extended families; one owns the upstream area, the other owns the area downstream. These are then divided into gardening areas exploited by individual nuclear or compound families. Radiating beyond these garden areas are the hunting territories of individual males. A man may also hunt in the territory of his father or father-in-law but at least half of his catch must go to the "owner." Each man's territory ideally contains a variety of ecological niches with their varied flora and fauna, so that he has the full spectrum of exploitative options open to him; that is, all kinds of animals and wild plants, hills, valleys, streams, and so on.

Hunting is principally solitary labor; a man leaves the village with his bow and arrows or 16-gauge shotgun, hunts, and returns alone. On occasion a brother, a parallel cousin, or son will accompany him into the forest; but unless it is a young son, they separate, each one hunting alone, and then meet to share or exchange their catches before returning to the village. They usually hunt along parallel ridges or along the valley floors on either side of a ridge, so that should one encounter a herd of peccary, *yawa*, or a band of spider monkeys, *isu*, he can call the other through whistled messages so as to maximize the kill. Men frequently return to the village or to a point nearby from which word can be spread to advise other hunters of the presence of a large herd of white-lipped peccaries, *yawa kuin*, or collared peccaries, *hunu yawa*, or a wounded tapir, *awa*. All available men immediately run from the village with their weapons to join in the hunt. It is only on such occasions that partnership or group hunting takes place. Even in the large hunts connected with *eskaitubiawe*, the ceremonial food exchange that occurs during periods of short food supply when large groups of men leave the village together and then share the catch before returning, each man hunts alone.

Although hunting is a solo effort, the fruits of the task do not belong to the hunter's own nuclear or polygynous family. Rather, they are his to share with his kinsmen and fellow villagers. Only when he returns with a very small bird or animal can he expect all of it to be cooked by his wife and served to him, his spouse, and his children.

A man goes hunting at least every third day. The frequency depends on the current supply of meat in the house, the urgency of his other duties, the tranquility of his household (hunting is the best escape from nagging wives and crying children),[1] and his ambition. I have frequently seen a man go hunting the day after he had brought two peccaries into the village because all the meat had already been eaten or distributed.

If the hunt is to take him several hours from the village, a man leaves at daybreak, frequently without eating. He moves briskly, often at a dogtrot, until he is out of the range of the noises of the village. This is at least twenty minutes, since the sound of women grinding corn can be heard at that distance. He then moves more slowly, pausing often to listen for the noises produced by the moving or calling of the animals, to examine spoor along the trail, or to mimic animal sounds either to locate or to attract the game in his direction. He rarely leaves his hunting trail. Only when he hears an animal nearby, or when in hot pursuit, or when called by a companion on another ridge or in another valley does he leave his well-marked base line, and then he returns to it as quickly as possible. When he leaves his regular hunting areas, except when chasing an animal, he is careful to break over twigs or bushes or small plants or to make gashes on trees, so that should he get lost he can always find his way back to a main hunting trail.

When a new village is established, a man uses the stream beds and tapir runs that exist in his territory as his first hunting trails. During the succeeding years, he establishes several major routes (usually in or near the streams in the valley floor and along the spines of the hills) off which a network of secondary trails is developed. Although these main routes become progressively more open and better marked, great care is taken to keep the flora along the peripheral trails as undisturbed as possible, so that they are all but indistinguishable to the untrained eye.

When he shoots a small animal, a hunter either puts it in the fork of a small tree or places it in an improvised basket of braided palm fronds, *kempax*, which he then hangs from a tree along the trail before continuing in search of other game. On the return trip he collects his cached game and often butchers it before returning to the village, particularly if he has to wait for his hunting partner to rejoin him.

Large animals like deer, *chaxu*, and the white-lipped and collared peccaries may be butchered where killed. Smaller game is normally carried to the village intact. Birds are frequently plucked in the forest. All game is usually carried in the braided palm leaf baskets with a bark tumpline, both made on the spot as needed.

After shooting a tapir, a hunter normally returns to the village to seek help in butchering and carrying back the meat. Unless he shot it near the village and along good, clear trails, he needs at least four other people to transport the meat of a full-grown tapir. Those who carry the meat keep it for their wives to distribute.

After working in the gardens or village, a man often leaves his house in mid-afternoon to go for a short hunt (that is, within a 20-to-40-minute range of the village). The object of such a hunt is invariably small birds and animals and frequently involves the use of a hunting blind. Hunting blinds are small, conical palm leaf huts (about one meter across at the base), which are built near a tree that is dropping fruit or a palm with ripe nuts. The hunter waits inside the blind to shoot animals or birds attracted by the fruits or nuts. For these hunts, bow and arrows are used more frequently than shotguns. Such blinds are also used for hunting rodents that are raiding manioc fields, as will be noted later.

Only when a man goes on a short hunt does his dog accompany him. Dogs are used principally for hunting agouti, *madi*, paca, *anu*, and Myroprocta, *tsanas*. These rodents, as well as armadillos, *yaix*, are frequently smoked out of their holes and clubbed to death as they emerge.

Most meat is obtained by shooting, using either bow and arrows or 16-gauge shotguns. Each man owns several bows and a large supply of arrows. Three types of arrow, *pia*, are used; all have reed shafts: (1) *paka*: this type, used for large animals, has a long, lanceolate bamboo point fastened to a wooden foreshaft inserted into the shaft—*paka* are always feathered; (2) *bani*: this type, used for birds, monkeys, and large fish, has a thin palmwood point about 30 centimeters long with selfbarbs inserted directly into the shaft—*bani* are always feathered; and (3) *chada*: this type, used for fishing and shooting birds and small animals found on or near the forest floor, has a trident point composed of a central prong inserted directly into the shaft with the two lateral prongs attached to the central prong—*chada* are never feathered.

In 1955 only bows and arrows were used. One 44-caliber rifle existed in the village, for which the owner had only three shells. After seeing the gun being used, I understood why he was not particularly anxious to obtain more shells. After aiming, he pulled his head to the side before firing as the bolt was ejected backward

A hunter takes aim using a bani *arrow. Note that he uses his thumb and index finger to hold the arrow in place while using the other three fingers to pull the bowstring.*

out of the gun when the cartridge was fired. By 1959, four men (my principal informants) owned shotguns and divided their hunting about equally between bow and arrows and shotgun. By 1963, all of the men owned and regularly used shotguns. Bows and arrows are used now only for fishing and for shooting small birds and animals that would be a "waste" of a 16-gauge shell, or when there is no ammunition. Shells are scarce and expensive, so that possession of them or the materials for reloading them is a carefully guarded secret.

The use of shotguns has caused changes in hunting patterns. First, since they have greater killing power, they are more efficient and deadly; second, although shotgun hunting is more effective, the noise has scared off much of the game so that hunters must go farther to get the same quantity of meat; last, the shotgun restricts their choice of game. Since arrows are reused, any animal was fair game, as no ammunition was expended. Shotgun shells are too valuable to waste on small game. As a result, men using guns often return empty-handed, something which rarely happened when bows and arrows were the primary weapons.

A man learns his skill as a hunter early. As a two-year-old boy, he receives from his father a small bow and sharply pointed arrows made of the ribs of palm leaves or stalks. This is his first and principal toy and with it he learns to shoot, first at stumps, chickens, or anything lying about the village, and later at lizards, frogs, and so on. Each "catch" brings forth volumes of praise from the adults. Between four and eight years of age, he runs freely all day with his age mates, much of his time being spent at playing "hunt." By eight or nine years of age he occasionally accompanies his father and has a "real" set of arrows. In 1966 two eight-year-olds already owned and knew how to shoot shotguns. After his initiation (at from nine to twelve years of age) a Cashinahua boy hunts regularly, either alone or with a slightly older sibling or parallel cousin. The shooting of a boy's first tapir, deer, or peccary is a time of much excitement in the village and he is liberally splashed with its blood during the butchering. He is now a full-fledged hunter although he does not reach his prime until his mid-twenties.

A good hunter is highly respected and even more highly desired as a lover or as a husband and son-in-law. He is respected not only for his ability to return with a good catch, but also for his knowledge of the habitats, sounds, spoor, and dietary and movement patterns of each animal species. He is also admired for his concentration; men who think about things other than hunting while on a hunt frequently return empty-handed. A good hunter is constantly alert while in the forest—always listening, always looking. He moves through the forest like his primary enemy, the jaguar.

A man who is distracted or continually misses his shots is thought to have been invaded by a foreign substance called *yupa*, which can be removed only by his undergoing a month-long fast, abstinence from sex, and, finally, a purification ritual.

Men of all ages, whether married or single, hunt regularly. Teenaged and old men are not expected to be the most successful hunters. However, the former are praised for their developing skill and the latter are honored for long lives of success and are patiently, if not eagerly, listened to as they spin yarns about the days when their eyes were keen, their ears were sharp, their feet swift, and their hunting baskets full. For the Cashinahua *hunting makes the man.*[2]

Gardening

Although hunting is considered to be the male's principal economic activity, gardening occupies a considerable percentage of his time during any year. In certain months it is his major preoccupation. The bulk of the diet comes from the gardens and failure to clear and plant adequately reflects negatively on his ability to provide for his family. Such failure, especially during the early years of a man's marriage, puts a heavy strain on the always tenuous marriage bond.

The Cashinahua distinguish four classes of gardens: Class 1, *bai kuin*—"permanent" garden; Class 2, *hene kexa bai*—"river bank" garden; Class 3, *tama bai/mashi bai*—"peanut" or "sandbar" garden; Class 4, *hunu bai*—"temporary" garden, each of which is distinguished by a specific environmental niche, a somewhat distinctive technology, and a partially discrete inventory of crops.

Class 1: *Bai Kuin*, The Permanent Garden

Bai kuin are also referred to as *manan bai*, "high garden." They are the major sources of garden products and are often of impressive size. One garden site composed of about twenty separate gardens was, for example, approximately 800 meters long by 50 meters wide. New ones are made annually between June and October. They are located along the steep ridges of hills within a half-hour's walk of the village. This location is preferred to the flat valley floor because vegetation is less dense and thus easier to clear, and it is necessary to fell fewer large trees in order to expose a maximum area to sunlight. Also, drainage is adequate (an important consideration in manioc production), and such an area is not much frequented by certain land mammals that normally forage in the dense low vegetation near the streams, which flow along the valley floor. These ridges often rise 25 to 40 meters from the valley floor at an angle of as much as 45 degrees.

Once a ridge has been selected, those making their gardens there (generally close kinsmen) agree on the limits of each person's plot within the site. About a third of the garden sites on any given ridge, however, are exploited by only one man, who lays claim to the ridge. In any one season, he clears only a portion of the area for gardening, with a view to making gardens along the entire length of the ridge in succeeding years.

The making of a *bai kuin* is divided into five stages: (1) *sepa*, clearing the underbrush; (2) *deda*, felling the large trees; (3) *metua*, drying brush and trees; (4) *menua*, burning; and (5) *bana*, planting. Before planting begins, men generally clear out *hedenuka*, the small trash which did not completely burn. However, since no informants volunteered this term as a stage in the making of a garden, I have not included it as a separate stage.

Stage 1. Clearing underbrush is considered the most distasteful of all tasks connected with making a garden. Therefore, a man always attempts to elicit the assistance of a large number of kinsmen. All such help must be reciprocated. When large numbers of kinsmen are involved, the members of the opposing moieties work on opposite sides of the trail and compete to see which group can clean the greatest amount of area in the shortest time. All brush and trees 25 centimeters or less in diameter are cut off at ground level with machetes.

Stage 2. The chore of cutting the larger trees is normally done with a steel axe by the garden's owner. He is frequently helped by his brother, even without requesting such aid, since tree felling is the favorite task in the garden-making process.[3] Stages 1 (*sepa*) and 2 (*deda*) are done during the months of June through August.

Stage 3. When the brush and trees have been cut nothing more is done while the cut vegetation is permitted to dry in the sun for one to two months.

Stage 4. Burning of the dried area generally takes place in late August or early September and, when the garden is a large, multiple-owner tract, is a time of ceremony. In mid-afternoon of the day the fields are burned, the men who own the garden paint their faces with red-orange *achiote* (annatto) paste and leave the village carrying several firebrands from the household cook fire. They proceed with much hooting to the far end of the cleared ridge, where they make torches of dried palm leaves and palm stalks, which they then light from the fire brands and use to ignite the dried brush. Their wives and other close female kin follow the men to the near end of the garden, where they form a line and chant to the spirits, asking them to make the fire burn well and give them a fruitful garden.

When the men have ignited small fires throughout the length of the field and are certain it is burning well, they return to the village,

Women chanting to the spirits of fertility as the men burn the trees and brush in a newly cleared garden.

where the women serve food to all who have helped in the burning.[4] This is always an occasion of much shouting, laughter, and joking.

Stage 5. Nothing more is done in the garden for at least a week, so that it has a chance to cool off. Then, a man, either alone or with the assistance of his wives or brothers plants bananas, plantains, and manioc. By mid- or late September he plants maize throughout the length of the garden. During the following weeks he will plant various tubers (*pua*, *yubin*, *yuxu*), papaya, tobacco, sugar cane, chili peppers, squash, sika, and on occasion *puikama* (the last two plants are used to make fish poison). His wife plants cotton. A digging stick made of palmwood is used to make holes and for loosening up the soil.

When planting is completed, ownership of the garden shifts to the maker's wife, who has sole responsibility for the garden until it reverts to jungle. The husband always tends his tobacco and may occasionally weed the garden or aid in the maize harvest.

All cultivated vegetable products except peanuts and watermelon are planted in *bai kuin*, the permanent gardens. Maize is harvested from December through March. Tubers, sweet potatoes, squash, cotton, and chili peppers are harvested as they mature, normally during the first year to fourteen months after planting. Manioc is harvested as needed after maturing. Women often replant manioc as it is harvested, particularly if the garden is not large and they think that the supply might be depleted before a new garden will begin producing. Plantains and bananas are harvested as they develop. It normally takes at least nine months before plantain and banana begin to produce, with peak production during the second and third years. The length of productivity depends on the amount of weeding and the speed at which reemerging forest growth chokes out the light. Some plantain patches have been in production for seven to eight years, particularly those close to or immediately surrounding a village.

Class 2: *Hene Kexa Bai*, The River Bank Garden

Gardens of Class 2, *hene kexa bai*, "river bank garden," differ from gardens of Class 1 largely in location and original plant cover. (Many informants considered *hene kexa bai* to be a variant of *bai kuin*.) Class 2 gardens are located along the banks of the river in areas that occasionally flood. These areas are heavily covered with balsa, reeds (*caña brava*), Cecropia, and several species of Helaconia. The soil is rich, sandy loam, well suited to manioc production. The garden is cleared by cutting the vegetation with machetes during the months of June to October. Since the cut plants dry faster than those in Class 1 gardens, Class 2 gardens can be burned and planted sooner, and Stage 2 is generally eliminated. The process is otherwise identical, except for the types of manioc planted.

Class 2 gardens are normally nearer the villages than Class 1 gardens. This location is considered important in that the noise and movement of people in and out of the village tends to lessen the animal predation that would normally be expected in the ridge area. However, in those occasional rainy seasons when the river floods these gardens, there is a good chance that the entire crop will rot in the ground.

Class 3: *Tama Bai/Mashi Bai*, Peanut or Sandbar Garden

Tama bai/mashi bai, as implied by the alternate names, are peanut patches planted on sandbars, either along the Curanja River or the larger of its tributaries. Not all sandbars are useful, only those flooded during the rainy season and thus "made strong" are used. The receding water leaves a thin, mineral-rich soil deposit on the top of the sand. If this deposit is too thick, it dries into a hard crust that cracks and is therefore not suitable for cultivation. A man stakes his claim to a sandbar or portions of various sandbars within one hour's travel up- or downriver from a new village and continues to use the spot(s) annually until the village is relocated to a new area. His wife or wives, however, own the produce of the garden.

Tama bai are prepared by clearing the vegetation cover as soon as the floods have receded at the close of the rainy season, usually in May or early June. They are rarely burned. Normally the trash cleared off the patch is thrown over the edge of the bank into the river or into a pile where it can be burned. Peanuts are then planted by the man and his wife with a digging stick. Along the edges of the patch watermelon and squash are also planted. Manioc or maize is occasionally planted at the ends and back of the garden or as a border between the gardens of different families. Watermelon and squash are harvested as they mature until the patch is washed away by the first floods of the new rainy season about November or December. Peanuts mature by late September, October, or early November and are harvested by the husband and wife together. The stalks are pulled out of the ground and tied together into bunches;

afterward the drying leaves are cut off. The bunches are then stored on a rack suspended under the peak of the house roof.

If the harvest has not been adequate to last until the next year's crop begins, a man frequently prepares a patch in a section of an old *bai kuin*, permanent garden, where manioc production has ceased and plants a new peanut crop during December or January. Production in both quantity and quality in these patches is always inferior to that of the sandbars, and only seed from sandbar gardens may be used for planting *mashi bai*.

Class 4: *Hunu Bai*, Temporary or Hidden Garden

Hunu bai are small garden plots cleared in the virgin forest or along the river with a view to supplementing a *bai kuin*. They can be made at any time of the year, but normally are made during the rainy season when the trees and brush do not burn well and thus are hidden (*hunu*) as opposed to *bai kuin* which are wide open, bright, clear (*xaba*).

They are normally the work of one man and are strictly confined to one crop, maize or, on rare occasions, manioc. They are never weeded and, as soon as the crop has been harvested, are allowed to revert to forest. Although a man is proud of the added abundance a *hunu bai* gives him, he will rarely talk about it, and even more rarely show it to a person when he is taking him on a tour of his gardens. When he talks about his garden, it is always about his *bai kuin*, his permanent garden.

Fishing

Fishing, unlike hunting and gardening, is not a principal source of food for the Cashinahua, who view it as a means of supplementing or providing variety in the diet. Its contribution to the family food supply is highly variable, depending on the season of the year, the availability of fishing materials or equipment, the supply of meat, and personal ambition.

The Cashinahua recognize four major classes of fishing, two of which are further subdivided. They are: Class 1, *bakawakin*, "poison fishing" with subclasses (a) *puikamawen* and (b) *sikawen*; Class 2, *baka xeamakin*, "hook and line fishing"; Class 3, *baka chachikin*, "harpoon or spear and grapnel fishing" with subclasses (a) *hashiwen* and (b) *betantiwen*; and Class 4, *baka tsakakin*, "shooting fish." Classes 1 and 3(b) are essentially group activities, while Classes 2, 3(a), and 4 are individual efforts. All are indigenous methods, but Classes 2 and 3 have increased efficiency due to the adoption of foreigners' goods, namely metal fishhooks and harpoons.

Class 1: *Bakawakin*, Poison Fishing

Fishing of Class 1, *bakawakin*, (literally, "to make fish") involves the use of fish poisons. The subclasses differ in terms of techniques, locale, and type of poison used.

Puikamawen bakawakin, "to make fish with *puikama*," subclass 1(a), is the most common form of fishing. *Puikama*, a low bush that grows to be a height of a meter or less, is planted near each house or in *bai kuin* gardens. When a person wishes to fish, he or she (often with the assistance of spouses, siblings, or children) strips the large leaves, flowers, and seeds from the plant and pounds them in a special mortar used only for that purpose until the finely ground material forms a firm, moist mass called, *tunka*, "ball." Several such balls, each about one quart, are needed. When the poison is prepared, the organizer and those who are to join him or her load the balls into banana-leaf-lined baskets and go off to a small stream within an hour's walk of the village. There they select a deep pool (its size being determined by the amount of poison available) and one or more persons begin to squeeze (*mutsa*)[5] the poison into the water at the upstream end of the pool, chanting to the fish as they do so.

Within five minutes, the fish begin to swim crazily to the surface of the pool, often swimming out onto the bank, where they are grabbed by hand, hit with machetes or clubs, or caught in dip nets. When the frantic activity along the banks and on the surface subsides, the members of the fishing party swim along the bottom of the pool looking for fish that were stunned by the poison. The effects of the poison are temporary on most fish, generally lasting an hour or less, although very small fish may die. Some of the fishermen follow the poison as it invisibly moves downstream until it becomes too diluted to be effective, often as far as 300 to 400 meters when large quantities of poison are used. At that distance only small fish are affected. When all available fish have been gathered, larger fish are gutted and their scales removed. Small fish are not gutted. They are wrapped in helaconia leaves preparatory to roasting. A good catch for a three-ball effort includes ten to twelve packages, each holding approximately 1 kilogram of smaller fish, 15 to 20 *ipu* (small armored catfish), and 4 or 5 *mexku*, a black fish which is highly valued for its sweet, oily flesh and is 20 to 30 centimeters in length with a large mouth lined with razor-sharp teeth.

While both men and women may organize *puikama* events, those organized by women tend to be smaller, involving a few other women, usually siblings and/or co-wives as well as children. The male-organized fishing parties are often small, though not as small as those of the women, but may be large enough that they include most of the members of the village, and involve twenty or more balls of poison prepared by several of the households represented in addition to that of the organizer.

Each person keeps the fish he or she catches. Only rarely is the catch shared among all members of the party. On occasion, a person not going fishing, but who assists in the preparation of the poison or prepares a ball of poison to send along with the organizer or another member of the party, receives one or more packages of fish.

There is a personal alternate to *puikamawen bakawakin* called *main puta ikai*, "to go bait fishing." A man or woman may take a small ball of poison (about 150 to 250 grams) and a stalk of peanuts, a ripe plantain, cooked lima beans, or chili pepper leaves, which are used for bait. After a little poison is rubbed on a small piece of bait, it is thrown into the pond. When the fish swallows the bait, the same results described above follow as the fish begins to swim frantically and erratically until it is finally caught by the fisherman. This is always an individual effort, and the results are limited. *Puikama* fishing is normally done only in the dry seasons when the streams are low, as a rapid flow of water dissipates the poison before it can be effective.

Sikawen bakawakin, "to make fish with *sika*," subclass 1b, is relatively uncommon. It involves the poisoning of small lakes or still-water ponds with *sika* (Lonchocarpus nicou). Sika differs from *puikama* in that its roots, not its leaves, are used, so that any plant may be used only once. It is pounded at the fishing site, is slower acting than *puikama*, and is positively lethal to all fish or reptiles in the water. Walkways made of willow or cecropia trees are built out over the pond, and there the men carry the poison for pounding. The roots are dipped into the water and then laid on the walkway where they are pounded with a small wooden mallet. The white, milky sap thus released drips down into the water, and frequent stirring of the water with the partly pounded roots spreads the poison throughout the pond. At least twenty-five to thirty plants are needed for a pond ten meters by thirty meters and approximately 1.5 meters deep. Within one hour the fish begin to swim erratically and the smaller ones begin to float on top of the water, gasping for breath. After several hours, usually at dusk, the fishermen all return to their homes or hunting camp, allowing the poison all night to work. They return to dive to the bottom to scour it for dead fish, caiman, or turtles. A good catch for 25 stalks of *sika* is 30 to 35 kilograms of fish, 4 to 5 turtles, and 1 medium-sized caiman.

A *sika* fishing party is always organized by a man (only men own sika) and always involves at least two households or a single large-household cluster. The number of persons involved depends on the size of the body of water to be poisoned. The larger the pond, the more *sika* needed and the larger the likelihood that more than one man's *sika* crop will be used. The fish caught, however, belong to the person who removes them from the water. I have never observed any sharing of the catch before it is cooked, and informants deny such activity. *Sika* fishing is done only during the height of the dry season, generally not before late August and rarely after September, when the lakes or ponds are at their lowest level.

Class 2: *Baka Xeamakin*, Hook and Line Fishing

Baka xeamakin (literally, "fish cause-to-swallow") is fishing done traditionally by men only, using a large hook carved out of the fused ulna and radius of a mature armadillo, fastened to a bark rope line and baited with a small fish. Mainly large catfish were caught in the deeper holes of the stream or river. Success was infrequent, but the possibility of catching a 5 to 15 kilogram fish was a sufficient incentive to motivate a man to try, particularly if he was not a good hunter.

With the introduction of metal fishhooks and nylon line by the traders, fishing with hook and line has become more profitable and frequent. Large hooks are used mainly in the widely separated deep holes where large fish tend to be concentrated during low water. Small hooks are used principally by younger boys anywhere the fish will bite. The large hook is used mainly in the dry season; small hooks are used throughout the year.

Hook-and-line fishing is a male activity and generally is a solitary activity. On occasion, however, a man will be joined by a sibling or another kinsman for a night of fishing. Success is rare, so that *baka xeamakin* provides no reliable supplement to the normal diet.

Class 3: *Baka Chachikin*, Harpoon or Spear and Grapnel Fishing

Class 3 fishing, *baka chachikin* (literally, "fish stab"), includes two types, based on the use of different tools and different techniques, (a) *baka hashiwen chachikin*, literally "fish spear-with stab," spear or harpoon fishing, and (b) *baka betantiwen betankin*, literally "fish grapnel-with grab/catch," grapnel fishing. Not all informants agree that the two types belong in the same class, some arguing that grapnel fishing (b) should be included with *baka achikin*, seizing fish (see below). I have decided to treat the two forms as a single class because my older informants combine them and because most informants consistently use the form *chachikin* when the instrumental forms *hashiwen* and *betantiwen* are deleted.

The translation of *baka hashiwen chachikin* depends on the particular tool being used. Prior to outside contact, *hashi* meant a barbed spear, 80 to 120 centimeters long, made of palmwood. At present, these spears are rarely made, and then only for ceremonial purposes. *Hashi* now primarily means a detachable, barbed metal harpoon point fastened to one end of a 180- to 220-centimeter palmwood pole by a rope stretched taut and tied to the other end of the pole. The remainder of the 10 to 15 meters of nylon rope is coiled and held in the hand that throws the harpoon. A balsa wood float tied to the end of the rope serves as a drag on the fish and as an aid in retrieving the apparatus from the river. The old method, performed by a lone man, involved spearing fish from the banks or in the shallow water of the river or stream and was done only when the water was clear, that is, in the dry season. Currently, harpooning is done from a canoe during any season and involves two men, one to steer the canoe, the other to wield the harpoon. Men rarely make a special trip to harpoon fish; rather, they take their harpoon with them any time they travel on the river for any distance further than the beginning of their hunting trails. Only large fish are harpooned, and most men are rarely successful in making a catch.

Class 3(b), *baka betantiwen betankin*, grapnel fishing, can be done only during the height of the dry season, when the river is low and clear. Men, always in a group and carrying machetes and *betanti*, go to a place in the river where the water is deep (2 to 3 meters) around submerged or partially submerged logs and trees. A *betanti* is a kind of grappling hook (or grapnel). Nowadays, a large metal fishhook is firmly lashed to one extreme of a hardwood shaft, and the line is nylon. Formerly, it consisted of a piece of fresh hardwood about 30 to 45 centimeters long with a hook on one extreme formed by carving and shaping a tree crotch and a short section of one of the two attached branches, and fastened to a balsa wood float by about 6 meters of bark fiber rope. Holding the *betanti* in one hand, a man takes a deep breath and swims down alongside a log to the river bottom. If he sees a fish, turtle, or a caiman, he grapples it with his hook and then rapidly surfaces and pulls his catch to shore. If he manages to hook his prey but loses hold of the rope, he can follow his catch by keeping an eye on the balsa float.

Grapnel fishing is often successful. A good catch for a group of men is one large fish per man. On one occasion I observed fourteen men take thirty-seven fish, averaging 12 kilograms per fish, from a pool in less than two hours. However, the lower Curanja River and the Purus River where the villages are now located are often too deep, even in dry season, for this method to be very successful.

Class 4: *Baka Tsakakin*, Shooting Fish

Baka tsakakin (literally, "fish shoot") properly belongs in the section on hunting rather than fishing. Anything that is shot (*tsaka*) is considered to be hunted. Only men shoot fish, just as only men (including boys) hunt. Until the advent of the shotgun, men never set out specifically to shoot fish; they went to hunt, and any fish they came across were fair game, particularly if no game animals had been seen. The trident, unfletched arrow was used most frequently for shooting fish, but the barbed, hardwood-pointed, fletched arrows were also used, mainly for larger fish. Catches were usually small, rarely more than two kilograms.

In addition to the four major classes of fishing, fish are on occasion caught by men, women, and/or children with a machete or by hand. For example, small armored catfish are frequently pulled by hand from their holes in the stream bank. This method is termed *baka achikin*, literally, "fish seize."

In summary, fishing is a highly seasonal activity that both men and women enjoy. The catch is always appreciated because it adds variety to the diet. It is not, however, a reliable source of food, and no prestige is gained through fishing.

Gathering

The fourth and least important source of food in the Cashinahua diet is gathering, an activity shared about equally by both sexes.

Only during "times of hunger," *bunitian*, the periods when old gardens have become exhausted and before new ones have begun to produce, does gathering become a significant food source. Gathering is rarely the primary objective of a trip into the forest, and men only gather food on the return trip to the village after an unsuccessful hunt. Women, however, often leave the village to gather cane shoots, *tawa*; and bamboo shoots, *paka*; a wide variety of fungi; and *nawanti*, a spinach-flavored green leaf that is cooked with manioc. Nuts, berries, palm nuts, and various fruits are picked when ripe. The collection of most fruits requires cutting branches from a tree or felling the whole tree and therefore is usually carried out by men and women together. Palm heart, usually eaten only in times of hunger, is always gathered by men. Turtles are picked up whenever encountered and are frequently kept alive for up to six months under the house. Turtle eggs are highly prized and are avidly sought along the rivers during the months of July to September.

When a bees' nest with a large quantity of honey is found, the finder and a group of close kinsmen go to collect it. Much of the honey is eaten as is or mixed with water and drunk at the site. The remainder is placed in bowls and taken to the village, where it is stored in bottles or lengths of bamboo until used.

Summary

The Cashinahua have had an abundant food supply. Their technology was based on the use of tools made locally of local materials. The introduction of metal tools and shotguns has increased efficiency. However, contact with outsiders, particularly missionaries with their medicine, school, and airstrip, has disrupted the normal pattern of moving the village every four to six years, so that it is becoming increasingly difficult to maintain their dietary standards. Fishing and gathering are becoming more important, but at least one fishing technique, grapnel fishing, is not very effective in the present locales. Gardens are further from the villages than in pre-missionary days and thus more difficult for women to care for and harvest. Game has been depleted and frightened off, requiring the men to go on long treks to hunting grounds five or six hours away from the village. Although machetes, metal axes, and shotguns represent an advance in technological efficiency, they cost the Cashinahua infinitely more than the prices charged by the

Peruvian and Brazilian traders. The cost for the Cashinahua is their independence and isolation from a world that threatens the continuation of their way of life.

Hiba, on left, with the tapir he shot the previous day. His brother-in-law, right, and son, center, helped him butcher it in the forest and carry it to the village.

Eusebio, a successful young hunter, with his bow and arrows in 1957.

In 1994, Eusebio, now an old man with grandchildren, is still an active and successful hunter. He now uses his bow and arrows only when shotgun shells are scarce.

Chapter 3

HUNTING AND MALE DOMINATION

Hunting is the quintessential Cashinahua male socioeconomic activity. It is highly valued because it produces a commodity, meat, which is perceived as scarce, despite an apparent empirical sufficiency. Sex, specifically female sexuality, is also highly valued and perceived as scarce. Furthermore, there is a link between meat and sex in Cashinahua thinking, a link that has been a recurrent theme in the Amazonian literature. Janet Siskind (1973a) has argued that the scarcity of female sexuality is an artificial scarcity created by culture; Robert Murphy (1977:19) has argued that the value of women involves "supervision and control of the sexuality of the female by others, usually men." In this chapter I shall argue that the high value and scarcity of meat parallels the high value and scarcity of female sexuality, and that it is based on male efforts to control women; and furthermore, the apparent domination of women by men in Cashinahua society is just as artificial as the scarcity of meat and the female sexuality on which it is based.

Although horticulture provides the bulk of the Cashinahua diet, hunting is viewed by both males and females as the single most important economic activity because meat, the product of the hunt, is the most highly valued component of their diet. The low value given to all other foods, whether produced by women exclusively or by both men and women, corresponds to males' assertions of their natural superiority over women, a superiority based on the fact that men hunt and women do not. Hunting is the only economic activity exclusively pursued by males. Its significance varies with the life cycle of the village. When a new village is established, approximately every five or six years, and before gardens have come into full production, hunting is more significant as a source of food than at any other time in the life of the village. This is also the period when hunting is most successful because animals have not yet moved away from the vicinity of human habitation. As a village ages, garden produce becomes more readily available, whereas game becomes increasingly difficult to find, requires that men go farther afield, and becomes more valuable. With more vegetable food available for guests, there is an increase in ceremonial activities during which there is an emphasis on the exchange of meat, requiring special hunts with a concomitant focus on the efforts of males. Decisions to move a village are based on both the reduced availability of game and the lack of sites for new gardens within reasonable proximity to the village. What constitutes reasonable proximity to the village depends on the age of the children within the family. Mothers of nursing infants complain if it takes them more than two hours to go to their garden, harvest manioc and other vegetables, and return to the village.

Only during the rainy season, when men are prevented from hunting by successive days of rain, is there likely to be a day when no meat is available. At that time parched maize and/or toasted peanuts are substituted for meat. Following meals that had left me sated with quantities of maize and plantain gruel, boiled or roasted manioc, toasted peanuts, and so on, informants frequently complained that they were hungry, *en bunihaidaki*. Queries regarding the reason for this complaint always elicited the response, "*En pinsihaidaki, nami yamaki*" ("I'm hungry [for meat], there is no meat"). Hunger for meat, *pinsi*, contrasts with *buni*, "hunger for food," *piti*, which includes both *nami*, meat, and *yunu*, vegetables. Women often attributed children's crying and irritability to their being *pinsi*, and men cited the same cause for their wives' nagging. Even when meat was available, the same complaint could be heard unless the quantity of game brought to the village by hunters exceeded their craving for meat. Most informants insisted that they desired about one kilogram of meat per day, a quantity well above the amount needed for adequate nutrition. My impression is that it is a very rare day when adults consume less than 300 to 400 grams of animal protein. Although I never collected quantifiable data on food consumption, I did eat most of my meals with the

Cashinahua, and I have clear impressions of the quantities of food consumed. I would argue, on the basis of these observations, that the Cashinahua experience no real insufficiency of meat despite their frequent assertions to the contrary. This perceived scarcity of meat in the face of an apparent sufficiency or abundance has been reported by other researchers in Amazonia (Carneiro 1982; Johnson 1982).

I have argued elsewhere (Kensinger 1983) that there are multiple causes for the perceived scarcity and the high value of meat. Meat is highly valued by the Cashinahua because (a) it is part of a cultural tradition ("We eat meat because our fathers and grandfathers ate meat"); (b) it is considered good to eat ("Meat tastes good"); (c) it is used to create, to maintain and/or facilitate social relationships; and (d) it is the product of the hunt. Hunting serves three important functions for the hunter:

1. It is the central feature of male identity. To be a "real man" is to be a successful hunter. The extent of a man's extramarital pursuits and the tranquility of his household are directly related to his success as a hunter.
2. It provides a release from the tensions resulting from social life. A man may leave the village "to go hunting" even when there is a good supply of meat. This is particularly true if his relationship with his wife or in-laws is strained. They would complain if he left to visit his parents' or siblings' households, but never if he went hunting.
3. It gives pleasure. I would submit that some Cashinahua hunters are "addicted" to hunting in the same way that some joggers seem to be addicted to jogging because of the pleasure obtained from the release of endorphins. This argument is, I admit, highly speculative, but I offer for consideration the statement of one old man that "good hunting causes good pain" (Kensinger 1983:129).

To these three motives, I shall now add the argument that the importance of hunting and the high value placed on meat are also related to the apparent domination of females by males. In making such an argument, I must not impose my view of the situation on the Cashinahua. To what extent and in what ways do Cashinahua males actually dominate females? Do Cashinahua females feel that they are dominated by males? To attempt to answer these questions, it is necessary to examine how the Cashinahua view masculinity and femininity, gender roles, and the behaviors associated with them.

There is some possible bias in my discussion of gender since my principal informants were men. Although I got data from most of the women throughout my fieldwork on a wide range of topics, there were several topics about which most of my female informants refused to talk. These topics were what both men and women called "women's knowledge," that is, birth, menstruation, menopause, female physiological disorders, and to a limited extent sex. When I broached any of these topics, the women's usual response was, "When you bring a wife with you, we will tell her those things. Of course, she won't be able to tell you what we teach her because they are women's secrets." There is no comparable body of men's secret knowledge; male knowledge is public information. Children were a significant source of information; their knowledge, often somewhat limited, was generally very accurate. Although not yet sexually active, they provided graphic and detailed descriptions of adult sexual activity. Their play and discussions of gender roles provided me with information on how men and women were supposed to act and stories about how specific men and women acted. They often told me about extramarital affairs before I heard of them through the adult gossip network.

Gender: Concepts and Behaviors

The Cashinahua believe that the difference between males and females is primarily biological. A male has a penis; a woman does not. When a baby is born, the older women assisting with the birth call out either *hinaya*, "It has a penis," or *hinauma*, "It is without a penis." (I have never heard them say in this context *xebiya*, "It has a vagina." The alternate phrasing is *hinauma, xebi hayaki*, "It doesn't have a penis; it has a vagina.") Some informants said that women could not be like men because their penis (i.e., their clitoris) was hidden, *hunu*.[1] When queried about the apparent contradiction in their statements that women do not have penes and their reference to the hidden penis, or clitoris, my informants assured me that the clitoris is not a *real* penis. They quickly pointed out that both men and women have breasts, but only women have real ones. A real penis gets erect and penetrates vaginas; real breasts enlarge and produce milk. The penis, or the lack thereof, is the central feature around which notions of masculinity and femininity and definitions of gender-specific roles are constructed. The penis (and he who possesses one) is active and assertive, but the vagina (and she who possesses one) is largely passive and restrained. Males are expected to be aggressive and assertive; women, in their dealings with men, are expected to be relatively passive. Men are ambivalent about women who are sexually aggressive, either in the seduction process or in sexual intercourse. They have, say the men, an erect or hot penis (clitoris) that causes them to be aggressive and, like jaguars, they are exciting and dangerous.

Women, unlike men, menstruate, a physiological process which according to the Cashinahua has its origins in a curse placed on women by an incestuous male who had been fatally cursed by his sister before going on a raid. His severed head, with the telltale black paint on its face, cursed all women as it climbed into the sky to become the moon, and each month both men and women are reminded of the consequences of incest.

Menstrual blood is dangerous. At worst, it can cause a man's death through a slow deterioration of his strength and energy. At the very least it results in a loss of his hunting ability by infusing him with a substance, *yupa*, that causes him to miss his shots, makes him inattentive to the dangers of the forest while engaged in sexual fantasies, or gives him a strong odor that drives animals away. The debilitating effects of menstrual blood can be counteracted through a month-long fast that requires abstinence from meat or fish, sweet gruels, any seasoned foods, and from sexual activity, followed by a brief but highly purgative purification ritual.

Menstruating women are not permitted to go into the forest beyond their gardens. To do so would drive the animals deep into the forest. Some informants say that there are spirits that are attracted by the smell of menstrual blood and which may kidnap or kill menstruating women who wander into the forest. Others argue that all vaginal fluids have the same potential. In fact, even women who are not menstruating seldom venture into the forest without a male kinsman. Menstruating women are not segregated; they continue to carry out their normal activities, taking care to prevent menstrual blood from getting onto anything with which men may come in contact.

The fact that males have a penis and females menstruate provides the basis for the division of labor in Cashinahua society. Female tasks are defined as those appropriate for the village and the surrounding region including the gardens, that is, the area in which menstruating women can move freely without threatening the game supply. Men, however, are free to penetrate the deep forest, the locus of the activity that provides the primary defining ingredient of masculinity, hunting.

Most informants are explicit about the symbolic link between masculinity and hunting: a man's penis is his arrow by which he causes women to die (that is, to have an orgasm) and his arrow is his penis by which he kills animals. A man who is incapable of having an erection is one whose arrow is broken. Women, having no penis, are incapable of hunting and of protecting themselves. Men, on the other hand, cannot menstruate and therefore are incapable of bearing and nursing children. Notice here the primacy of menstruation rather than childbearing as a defining characteristic of femininity. Because premenarchal and postmenopausal females do not menstruate, they are incapable of bearing or nursing children and as a result are not fully female.

Both male and female informants state that the division of labor by gender is to be explained by these biological truths. All tasks are classified as either men's work or women's work, and certain tasks are defined as exclusively men's or women's. Men hunt, protect women and children from spiritual and nonspiritual dangers, clear new garden areas from virgin forest, and assure a tranquil village through their political and ritual activities. Women bear and care for children, care for and harvest gardens, cook vegetables and meat, plant and harvest cotton, make hammocks, and so on. Fishing and foraging are primarily defined as men's work, but women may join in fishing expeditions and may forage on their way to and from their gardens. Chopping and carrying firewood and carrying water are primarily defined as women's work, but men may assist their wives, mothers, sisters, and mothers-in-law with these tasks without a loss of manliness. The manufacture of all objects is gender linked (Kensinger et al. 1975).

My female informants provided me with essentially the same reasons as did men when I asked them whether women ever hunt, and if not, why not. Women cannot hunt, they said, because they do not know how to hunt. Even if they knew how, they could not go deep into the forest because it is too dangerous for women since spirits might molest them, or because animals would flee from the smell of their vaginas. Also, nursing mothers could not leave their infants alone that long and, if they took them along, their crying would scare the animals away. The only reason cited by men but not by women was that women lacked penes.

The identification of men with hunting rather than horticulture reflects, in addition to the symbolic content of hunting, the time and energy expended by men on these activities. Hunting is a year-

A woman peeling manioc, the starchy tuber that is an important ingredient in every meal.

round activity. Most men spend at least one day in three hunting. Although gardening is also a year-round activity, men's participation in it is seasonal.

No Cashinahua man identifies himself as a horticulturalist although he takes great pride in the gardens he has created. A *man* is a hunter all the time; making gardens is just one of the things a man does as part of the annual routine. To be an indifferent gardener is no reflection on his masculinity, although it makes him less desirable as a husband and son-in-law; to be an indifferent hunter makes him something less than a real man. Surplus garden produce is no substitute for meat as a gift for one's lover. Furthermore, since the products of the garden are a wife's possession, it is she who distributes them.

Although most Cashinahua men complain about the onerousness of making gardens, they never gripe about hunting. Gardening is enervating, hot, and dirty work; hunting is energizing, cool, and cleansing work. Hunting frees a man to pursue his amorous interests; gardening binds him to a wife or wives and her/their mother(s). Hunting is an expression of his manliness; gardening is a responsibility of a married man. The measure of a man is his skill as a hunter, not the size and number of gardens he makes.

Men and Hunting

As soon as a boy can walk unassisted, and sometimes before, his father or paternal grandfather gives him a small bow and arrows with which he learns to shoot banana trees, papayas, leaves, insects, lizards, and the like. His successes are lauded, his failures are either ignored or gently responded to with instruction. By the time he is five or six, he and his peers are shooting at just about anything that moves in the garden surrounding the village, cooking and eating any birds, lizards, and rodents shot during these expeditions. By the time he is ten, he occasionally accompanies his father or another adult on short hunts in the forest, where he learns to read animal spoor, to identify animals by sound and smell, and to locate animals as they move through the forest. He also learns how to identify those things, both natural and supernatural, that pose a threat to the hunter and to avoid them or neutralize their potential danger. By thirteen years of age he has learned how to site and build a hunting blind and begins to hunt independently within or just beyond the radius of the village where women are free to move. By fifteen or sixteen he is generally able to hunt like any adult male. Although he has no obligation to provide meat for his family, his catch is widely acknowledged and praised. Women openly talk about what a fine son-in-law he will make, and men joke about his desirability as a lover. With the killing of his first tapir, he is recognized as an accomplished hunter, and he proudly supervises its butchering. The greater his success as a hunter, the wider the swath of his amatory pursuits and the greater his chances of arranging a marriage.

The Cashinahua distinguish three styles of hunting, which I translate here as real, regular, and play hunting.[2] Real hunting is distinguished largely by its intensity. A man leaves the village at daybreak or shortly thereafter and moves quickly, often at a dogtrot, into the forest. He maintains this pace at least until he is beyond the range at which sounds of the village can be heard; at this point he has reached his hunting territory and is following one of his hunting trails. His eyes constantly scan the forest, and his ears are attuned to any signs or sounds of animal movements. A real hunt demands a hunter's full concentration and frequently leaves him exhausted but euphoric. He relentlessly pursues his prey, ignoring the pain from thorns in his feet or insect bites while in the heat of the chase. He pauses only when he has completed his hunt or, after catching an animal that does not satisfy his self-imposed quota, to stash it safely until his return to the village. If he kills a large animal, he returns to the village directly. If not, he hunts until he has reached his quota or becomes discouraged. He may choose to sit and rest during the heat of the day when there is little animal movement in the forest and the chances of scoring a success are minimal, waiting for signs of the resumption of animal movements, or he may forage as he makes his way back to the village.

Following a real hunt, a man generally rests for a day or two, spending most of the time swinging in his hammock or repairing or sharpening his arrows, while recuperating from the physical toll of the hunt. A man rarely returns from a real hunt without having suffered some wound, generally a thorn deeply imbedded in the sole of his foot. Numerous minor to moderately severe injuries occur while hunting, and a few days of rest are needed for them to heal before a man can effectively hunt again (thus explaining some ethnographers' observations that men spend much time just sitting around while their wives work; e.g., Siskind, 1973a, b; Murphy and Murphy, 1974; Henley, 1982). Real hunting is hard work. But, for a real man, a Cashinahua, it is more pleasurable than any other activity, except perhaps sex.

But not all hunting is real hunting and not all hunters are real hunters. All Cashinahua are regular hunters, at least part of the time, and the majority of hunts are regular hunts. Regular hunting shares most of the characteristics of real hunting, differing from it mainly by being less intense, less arduous, and less prey specific. The pace of the hunt is more leisurely. The hunter may allow his concentration to lapse, thinking about things other than the hunt. When he sights game, however, he will (unless he is not a good hunter) immediately focus his attention on making the kill. A man generally returns from a regular hunt less battered and tired, and, of course, with less game than from a real hunt. Regular hunts are also less pleasurable. Several men compared the difference between real and regular hunts to that between the excitement of sex with a new lover or wife and sex with a wife of many years.

Either a real or regular hunt may be transformed into the other if the mood of the hunter or the circumstances of the hunt change. Some informants said they always leave the village expecting to have a real hunt; that is the way a real hunter is. Others admitted that they were often reluctant to hunt unless there was a shortage of meat or a need to kill enough game to provide for the needs of their wives, with enough extra to make gifts to their lovers. Such men were said to be regular, *kayabi*, hunters rather than *kuin*, real. Such an admission would never be made in public because real men are supposed to be real hunters.

Play hunting contrasts with real and regular hunting primarily in terms of intent or motivation. It is the hunting a man engages in when he wishes to escape from the nagging of his wife, wives, or mother-in-law, or from the whining and crying of his children, or when he wishes to disengage himself from social interaction in the village. He takes his bow and arrows or shotgun and leaves the village. He may make a hunting blind or use an old one; he sits there and watches for animals to come to eat fruit or nuts in the trees toward which the blind is oriented. Or he may saunter through the forest, pausing frequently to sit down or to bathe in a small stream. This pattern also occurs among the Mehinaku (Gregor 1977:218–219). Such a hunt is rarely transformed into a real or regular hunt. Should he encounter game, he shoots it, an unexpected bonus, but the object of play hunting is therapeutic. The pace is always leisurely. Play hunting generally takes place in the afternoon and may occur after a man has hunted in the morning without success. All my male informants agreed that such hunting, even if it does not produce a catch, allows a man to relax without incurring the disapproval of his wife or mother-in-law.

No man announces his intention to play hunt. If asked, he says that he is going hunting, leaving ambiguous his intention as to the kind of hunting. All are aware that he would have started shortly after daybreak if he were really serious about the hunt. Furthermore, since such hunts are frequently the pretext for meeting a lover at a prearranged location, most onlookers assume that his target is sexual, not animal. (This contrasts with marital daytime sexual activity in which husband and wife leave the village together, saying either that they are going to the garden or that they are going to the forest to defecate, a statement that normally elicits understanding smiles and/or ribald comments.)

Cashinahua males, and I suspect this holds true for those of other Amazonian societies, have created a perception of meat as a scarce commodity by defining hunting as an exclusively male activity, by excluding all women with reproductive potential from hunting territories, and by elevating the social and cultural significance of meat while at the same time denigrating, or at least giving a reduced value to, garden products. They have relegated to themselves control over and access to the resources of the forest beyond the gardens.

Scarcity of Sex

Like meat, female sexuality is seen by the Cashinahua as a scarce commodity, even though female as well as male members of the society find sex pleasurable. While men are more verbal about the subject, all my female informants who were willing to talk about it indicated that women enjoy sex as much as men do. Both males and females exhibit considerable ambivalence about sex; males fear the pollution of vaginal fluids and menstrual blood, and females fear an unwanted pregnancy. Among both sexes there was some disagreement about how much sex is too much. Some of the men, especially older ones, argued that too much sex could be enervating, particularly for youth, citing the debilitating effect of the intense and frequent copulation of couples "working" at making a baby. The women's arguments focused on the reduced ability of a woman to manipulate men if she made it too obvious that she liked sex.

Both sexes agreed that there is a scarcity of sex. Men spoke of women as sexually insatiable once aroused but complained that they withhold their sexual favors in order to manipulate men. Most women said that males are assertive and demanding, opportunistic, and predatory, promising more than they can deliver and more concerned with their own satisfaction than with that of their partner. All informants agreed that mutual satisfaction was desirable. Women reward a sensitive lover with bites and scratches, marks that men wear proudly as insignia of their virility. Males who are inattentive to the desires of their lovers soon find their services no longer in demand. Women often complain that a man talks a better game than he can play, whereas the men say that a woman talks a better game than she is willing to play. Moreover, all women fear an unwanted pregnancy, which could result in a painful abortion or in infanticide of the newborn. It is unlikely that any serious scarcity of sex would result from the preceding factors. Other factors, however, like polygyny, female (but not usually male) infanticide, and an incest taboo that excludes, for both marriage and sex, all persons but members of the kin class opposite-sex-cross-cousins could result in a scarcity not of sex, but of wives.

Scarcity and Domination

We return now to the relationship between the high value and perceived scarcity of meat and the apparent male domination of women. The Cashinahua clearly have an objective sufficiency, if not an abundance, of meat (Johnson 1982:415). The perceived scarcity is rooted in cultural rather than biological needs and parallels a perceived scarcity of female sexuality.

The link between food and sex in Cashinahua thought is evident in the way they use language. The vocabulary of eating and drinking, of the hunt, of gardening, and of flora and fauna are all sources of blatant and subtle sexual puns. The fact was brought home to me one day after I had spent several hours transcribing song texts recorded at a dance some days earlier. I was sitting with some Cashinahua and absentmindedly began to sing the songs, which were replaying themselves in my mind. The men guffawed, the women giggled embarrassedly, and I was confused, since the words of the songs seemed to be about vegetables and fruits. They were, but these products symbolize sexual organs, as the men quickly informed me after their laughter subsided. My mistake was in singing the songs outside the proper ritual context.

The link between meat and sex has been a recurrent theme in the literature on Amazonian peoples. Allan Holmberg, in his now classic monograph on the Siriono, stated that "food and sex go hand in hand" (1969:126) and that "while the drive of sex is seldom frustrated to any great extent, it is mobilized largely through the drive of hunger" (225). Thus, for the Siriono food was the scarce commodity, and males gained access to female sexuality through gifts of meat.

More recently, Siskind (1973a) and Murphy (1977) in related papers have discussed the link between sex and meat. Siskind states that:

> an artificially or culturally produced scarcity of women provides a density-dependent mechanism that functions to disperse groups of hunting-and-gathering or hunting-and-agriculture populations in accordance with the availability of game, where game is the limiting factor (1973a:226)

and that "the exchange of meat for sex is an economic system, a system in which men strive to be good hunters in competition with other men in order to gain access to women" (235). Siskind further argues that her hypothesis applies "to hunting populations in which women provide the bulk of the food supply and where it can be established that protein resources are the limiting factor and their procurement the responsibility of men" (226–227).

Thus, according to Siskind both protein, particularly meat protein, and female sexuality are scarce, but the scarcity of female sexuality is artificial, whereas that of meat is not. Although her argument, based as it is on the assumption of protein deficiency, may not stand up, her attempt to link the shortage of female sexuality and the scarcity of meat has considerable validity. It appears that Sharanahua women are competing for what they perceive to be a scarce commodity, meat, while men compete over another item they perceive as scarce, female sexuality.

The ongoing debate between those arguing that there is a protein deficiency in Amazonia (e.g., Gross 1975, 1982, and 1983; Harris 1974; Divale and Harris 1976; Ross 1978)[3] and those arguing the contrary (e.g., Aspelin 1975; Beckerman 1979; Berlin and Markell 1977; Chagnon 1983; Chagnon and Hames 1979; Hames 1980; Hames and Vickers 1983; Hurault 1972; Johnson and Behrens 1982; Lizot 1977; Vickers 1978) has not demonstrated to my satisfaction that there is, for the most part, any real shortage. Allen Johnson (1982:414) has argued that "native Amazonian communities typically obtain more than twice as much protein as recommended for minimal health maintenance." He concludes that "despite an objective 'sufficiency' or even an abundance of food, we find that a perceived scarcity exists that influences individual behavior" (415). Robert Carneiro (1982:419) states that "among many Amazonian tribes, the physiological need for protein may be satisfied, and yet people clamor for more meat."[4]

In the same paragraph in which Siskind asserts that "the exchange of meat for sex is an economic system" (1973a:235), she adds,

> I know of no real evidence that women are naturally or universally less interested in sex or more interested in meat than are men. On the contrary, in terms of the reality of hunting societies a more natural exchange would be hunted game for vegetable produce (234).

This is precisely what Donald Pollock (1985) has argued for the Culina.

Are women less interested in sex or more interested in meat than men? Not among the Cashinahua, if one is to believe their statements. Is it possible that the exchange that takes place is not meat for sex but meat for something else?

Robert Murphy, like Siskind, points out that for sexuality "to be used for social purposes, it must have a certain value placed upon it; in short, it must be a scarce supply" (Murphy 1977:19). He also sees this scarcity as artificially created.

> The value placed upon women is in all societies reinforced by a series of norms that may include, with varying emphasis, the ideal of premarital chastity, a sense of personal modesty, the institution of marriage as the approved outlet for sex, the exclusiveness of sexual rights in marriage, *supervision and control of the sexuality of the female by others, usually men*, and the basic injunction that a woman should withhold access of herself except under defined and sanctioned circumstances. (Murphy 1977:19–20, italics added)

He further points out that in contrast to the culturally contrived shortage of female sexuality, "In nature . . . male sexuality is in short supply" (21). This cultural inversion of nature has its roots in the masculinization phase of ego development, "which is an escape from early identification with the mother and the assertion of an autonomous ego. Beyond that, it is a denial of passivity and an attempt to assert active dominance over the maternal sex" (22). In the process of trying to allay their fears and anxieties, rooted in childhood and reinforced by constant reminders of their potential inadequacy, by establishing their control of, or at least dominance over, women, men have created a scarcity of female sexuality and thus have given a high value to it.

Must we conclude that in the Amazon basin, men dominate women in an attempt to get even with their mothers? Or, are meat and sexuality kept artificially scarce by males as a part of a grand design to subordinate females? Or, are men and women coconspirators in an eternal confidence game based on the exchange of two commodities, meat and sex, the values of which are inflated through culturally created shortages?

The psychosocial aspects of male ego development as they relate to the relationship between males and females fall outside the scope of this chapter. (For an excellent discussion of this problem, see Gregor [1985], particularly his chapter 9.) I am less interested here in the psychodynamics of the situation than in the shared perceptual myths that foster the ongoing battle of the sexes, a battle that characterizes Cashinahua, and I suspect most Amazonian, male-female relations.

Cashinahua males readily proclaim the superiority of their masculinity and the inferiority of women: "She is only a woman; she doesn't have a penis." Cashinahua females, however, do not seem to feel inferior. One older informant, in response to a man's taunt that she was "without a penis," said, "What is he talking about? He has never given birth to a child, and he cannot always produce semen." Although they do not agree on the natural superiority of males and inferiority of females, both men and women do agree that meat and sex are scarce and valuable.

Is Siskind correct, then, in arguing for an "economy of sex," wherein men are motivated to hunt in order to gain access to female sexuality and females withhold their sexual favors unless rewarded with meat? I have said elsewhere that "if we limit our attention only to extramarital affairs among the Cashinahua, the answer would be affirmative. Men are expected to reward their extramarital sexual partners with gifts of meat, beads, perfume, etc." (Kensinger 1984). However, extramarital sex in Cashinahua society seems to be less a case of reciprocity, as postulated by Siskind, than a case of market exchange based on the law of supply and demand. While it is true that the best hunters have, or can have, the most extramarital sex partners, the most sexually active females do not seem to have either a larger cache of trinkets or a more reliable supply of meat. Thus, the initiative is with the male since a female who makes herself readily available lowers the value of her sexuality in the extramarital meat market.

If, however, we focus on the relationship between husbands and wives, Siskind's postulated exchange of meat for sex is not sustained among the Cashinahua, even though the wives of successful hunters generally own more luxury goods and preside more regularly over the distribution of large catches of game than those whose husbands are less successful. Both male and female informants agreed that husbands give wives gardens; wives give husbands cooked food. Husbands give wives a house in a peaceful village; wives give husbands a tranquil, orderly household. Husbands give wives meat; wives give husbands sons, a matter of no small importance in a patrilineal system. Husbands give wives sexual pleasure; wives give husbands sexual pleasure.

Wives do, of course, sometimes withhold sexual favors to motivate their husbands to hunt, but they do the same for other reasons. Moreover, men may withhold sex from their wives, may refuse to hunt, or may give their game to a co-wife, sister, or mother as a way of showing displeasure with their wives. And men, at least, seem to see a connection between their wives' sexual response and the amount of meat they had eaten. I have argued, however, that these responses represent not economics, but domestic politics (Kensinger 1984:3). Within marriage, sex is self-reciprocal, and meat is exchanged for sons. We must now ask whether men and women are starting from positions of equal strength or whether the deck is stacked in favor of men. What is the nature of power and authority in Cashinahua society?

Within the context of the village, no individual or group of individuals has the authority or the power to force any other individual to do anything he/she does not wish to do. Those individuals known as headmen, *xaneibu*, have power by virtue of their ability to persuade others to follow their lead. The same holds within the family. Although a man serves as spokesman for his family within the discussions of the men's circle, he may neither make a commitment on behalf of his wife or children nor coerce them to support the position he takes there. Women, who have the greatest responsibility for childcare, are expected to persuade their children to do what they wish them to do. Resort to physical force by anyone, male or female, adult or child, is considered a graver offense than the behavior that precipitated the action. The Cashinahua are uncomfortable with voices raised in anger. Commands (verb forms with an imperative inflection) are best seen as requests or suggestions, and although the speaker expects compliance, there is little he or she can do if ignored. Despite, or perhaps because of, this state of affairs, Cashinahua villages are neither disorderly nor chaotic. Males and females operate in and have responsibility for different spheres of activities and between them they share the responsibilities for a more or less orderly social life.

For the most part, a man does not interfere with his wife's/wives' domestic activities. He may help by chopping or carrying firewood, getting water, butchering game, taking care of a child, and so on, if asked or if he thinks that his wife is not feeling well or is overburdened with work. A husband rarely intervenes in a disagreement between co-wives; they are left to settle it themselves.

The failure of a wife to fulfill her responsibilities rarely results in comments from her husband unless he is greatly inconvenienced by it, but he is equally unlikely to speak approvingly to her if she does her job well. The way a wife carries out her responsibilities is more likely to elicit comments from others, particularly other women, than from her husband. Only when there are considerable strains on a marriage will a man comment openly about his wife's inadequacies as the manager of the house and gardens. How, when, and how well she carries out her tasks are her problem, not his.

Cashinahua women also control their own sexuality and fertility. A woman is free to have extramarital affairs so long as she is discreet about them and does not refuse her husband sexual access. If he provides her with gardens and game, she is expected to be sexually available to her husband unless sex is interdicted by menstruation, the later stages of pregnancy, birth, or other taboos, and during the early infancy of their nursing child. There is disagreement among and between men and women about how often is often enough. Women have a right to expect to have sex with their husbands; wives, often co-wives, frequently complain that their husbands are ignoring them sexually. They have the right, of course, to seek sexual satisfaction with other men, and many do. But as they get older and are less attractive to other males, or if they do not want to bother with the problems of arranging and carrying out an extramarital affair, they are likely to take steps to seduce their husbands.

A woman has the responsibility for deciding whether to terminate an unwanted pregnancy or to kill the unwanted newborn should she carry the fetus full term. A husband may refuse to accept as his own a newborn child and demand that it be killed, but ultimately the decision is hers. Differences of opinion between husband and wife, particularly when the wife acts in opposition to her husband's wishes, can produce considerable tension between them, resulting in alienation and ultimately divorce.

Women have the responsibility for childcare, and men rarely intervene in conflicts between mother and child. When tensions develop between a woman and her offspring, other women intervene, frequently the child's maternal grandmother. A man may, but has no obligation to, take care of his child if his wife is busy, sick, or harried, or if it is clear that the mother is exasperated with the child. If there is a disagreement between husband and wife over their child's behavior, her wishes prevail. If he disagrees strongly enough with his wife, he may ask one of his female kinswomen to intervene; he rarely does so himself.

In addition to their economic obligations to provide their wives and immature children with meat and fish and to make the houses, the gardens, all tools used by them and their female kin, and the ceremonial regalia (except for woven objects), men are responsible for maintaining social order within the village, for defending the interests of the village in its relationships with external groups or

A child with her mother in 1956. Note babricot to left with curassow and other roasting meat.

The child as an adult in 1994 peeling a plantain. Her daughter and son-in-law sit in the background.

individuals, and for maintaining harmonious relations with the spirit world.

The men's circle serves as the symbolic, if not the actual, locus for the public phases of these activities, thereby excluding women from participation. It is not, however, the only place where matters of interest to the village are discussed, nor is it the site where most issues are resolved. Rather, it is where matters of interest to the entire community can be and sometimes are discussed. For the most part, conversations in the men's circle are inconsequential, dealing mainly with the weather, hunting, and idle chitchat about the day's activities.

Most disputes are settled outside the men's circle by the parties themselves, with or without the help of close kin, including women. When they are not settled at this level, there generally is a period during which both sexes use informal methods such as gossip, exhortation, or shaming in order to bring the miscreants into line. Only when the problem is seen to pose a serious threat to the health, safety, and/or tranquility of the community at large is it discussed in the men's circle. Although formally excluded from the men's circle, women can and frequently do make their views known from their own circle nearby.

Although women control their fertility and are free to enter into extramarital affairs, men are supposed to take the initiative in arranging both marriage and sexual affairs. These matters are not generally discussed in the men's circle unless they result in either an intravillage dispute which the principals and/or their close kin are unable to settle or in intravillage hostilities. For the most part men try to ignore the sexual escapades of other men, and even of women, unless the behavior becomes so outrageous as to threaten public order. Women play a more significant role than men in social control through gossip, and, if that fails to have the desired effect, through public scorning and scolding of the miscreants. Although both men and women gossip, it is considered by the men to be primarily a female practice. Men who gossip are sometimes called women.

Men are responsible for scheduling the public rituals designed to maintain harmonious relations with the spirits. Men are frequently loath to initiate these rituals because they require large quantities of meat and thus additional, intensive, hunting. Women, therefore, frequently become the instigators by taunting, cajoling, or trying to shame the men into carrying out their responsibilities. But men make the decision to hold the rituals, schedule them, and play the major roles in them. Even the timing of the subsidiary rituals for girls within the initiation rites for which women are responsible, but from which men are excluded as participants but not observers, is determined by the larger ritual process controlled by males.

Although both males and females may interact with spirits and both may become shamans whose power and knowledge is gained largely through dreaming (see chapter 18), only males may drink the hallucinogenic beverage *nishi pae* in order to communicate with the spirits on behalf of the community. Women are also not permitted to use tobacco snuff or alcoholic drinks, both of which are viewed as recreational drugs associated with the spirits.

Finally, men are responsible for external relations with other Cashinahua villages, other tribal peoples, and foreigners. Except when other villages are invited to participate in public rituals, at most twice in a year, most contacts between Cashinahua villages are contacts between individuals or families. Contacts with non-Cashinahua are infrequent and are always between small groups of men or, less frequently, a family when traveling up- or downriver to hunt or trade.

Cashinahua males clearly dominate the public arena and assert their right to do so based on their superiority over women. However, even in those areas over which they acknowledge male control, women exercise substantial influence on the course of events from behind the scenes. Men frequently discuss important matters with their female kinswomen, particularly their wives and mothers. At the same time, women have virtual autonomy and control over significant areas of their lives. They own and control their houses and gardens. They control their fertility and, within certain limits, are as free as males to engage in extramarital affairs. And, finally, they are responsible for and have control over their young offspring. Thus, it would appear that like the shortage of meat and of female sexuality, male domination in Cashinahua society is a myth, an artifice.

Discussion and Conclusions

In this chapter I have been concerned with understanding the importance given to hunting in Cashinahua society and have argued that the key is to be found in the relationship between men and women, specifically in men's attempts to assert their domination over women. Meat, the product of the hunt, is defined as both scarce and valuable. Women are prohibited from hunting and thus dependent on men to provide meat for them. But hunting is hard work, and men could adequately provide for nutritional needs simply by planting larger gardens (see Johnson 1982 and Johnson and Behrens 1982). Motivation for hunting is provided by linking success at hunting with a highly desirable good, female sexuality, which is also defined as scarce and valuable and made so through rules of exogamy, incest, and female restraint. Furthermore, tasks are divided by sex, with men responsible for hunting, politics, and religion and women responsible for gardening and caring for house and children; childbearing of necessity is a female responsibility.

And therein lies the problem. Although men can define themselves as indispensable as hunters and can attempt to control women through controlling their sexuality, men cannot reproduce themselves. Thus, they substitute the appearance of control for that over which they have no control.

That does not mean that these artifices have no effect on the way the Cashinahua behave and on what they believe. Both men and women believe that meat is scarce and valuable; both accept, at least for others, the regulation of sexuality; and for the most part people behave as they are supposed to. However, there is a price to pay.

Males must hunt. Their sense of identity and worth as men is intimately tied to their success as hunters and hunting is at best a gamble. They have no control over the availability of game or of its movements. And the price of losing is a lack of sons, because in their exchange with women, they give meat for sons.

Women must bear children and are responsible for their care for at least four years. A barren woman has little status and, once she has gone through menopause or has lost her desirability as a sexual partner, she must do the tasks no one else wants to do in exchange for food and a place to hang her hammock. Furthermore, unlike men, women are spatially restricted to the village. They leave the village only in the company of their husbands or other women and cannot visit other villages without a male escort. They are excluded from hunting and from formal decision making. And finally, although they are free to have sexual affairs, they are supposed to exercise restraint, waiting for the male to be the aggressor. Women who instigate affairs and are brazen about it are beaten by their husbands, fathers, or brothers.

Do Cashinahua women feel dominated? What does it mean when they on occasion refer to their husbands as *xanen ibu*, the term used for headman? I suggest that for the most part the term conveys for them what it means when a man refers to another man as headman, namely, that he is a person whose judgment one trusts and whose leadership one trusts for the time being. Should circumstances change, one's relationship to the leader may change. When a woman is unsatisfied by her relationship with her husband, she may terminate her relationship by putting his possessions outside their house. She keeps the house and the gardens and has custody of their children until they are old enough to leave her care. Her husband does not own her. And, should he order her to do something, he has no assurance that she will acquiesce. Theirs is a reciprocal relationship, a relationship between opposites but equals. As her *xaneibu*, he is but the first among equals. Thus, within the context of mutual interdependence characteristic of Cashinahua male-female relationships, the high value given to meat and hunting becomes the symbol of and the justification for male leadership but not male domination. And it is males' attempts to dominate rather than lead that fuels the ongoing battle of the sexes in Cashinahua society.

Chapter 4
BAWDY RITUALS AND CASHINAHUA SEXUAL STEREOTYPES

During ritual activities, male-female interactions often exhibit considerable sexual antagonism, using stylized behaviors that represent male and female stereotypes of maleness and femaleness. Both the rituals and the sexual stereotypes tend to depersonalize the conflict and thus, in a society where the verbal or physical expression of anger, hostility, and frustration are severely repressed, they become socially acceptable ways of releasing the tensions that build up during cross-gender social interactions within which the participants' perceptions are shaped by conflicting gender dogmas. That the Cashinahua are aware of the distancing and depersonalizing functions of the stereotypes and rituals was demonstrated by their reactions to real, as contrasted to ritualized, cross-gender conflicts between individuals with real personal grievances that erupted within ritual contexts. This chapter examines two such cases.

Case 1: The Angry Mother-in-law

Background Material

The marriage of Kuxi and Disi had been terminated, despite considerable reluctance on the part of both, about four months prior to the *nixpu pi* initiation rituals, largely as a result of hostility between Kuxi and his mother-in-law. Disi's mother, Chana, strongly disliked Kuxi and had opposed the marriage from the start because she thought him fresh and impudent (and he was), and because he had only recently moved to the village and she was not certain that he intended to stay. Should he leave with Disi, she would lose her only daughter and the support that a co-resident daughter and son-in-law assured. A further reason was that she wanted Disi to marry another man, one her daughter disliked. Although Kuxi was a clear economic asset to the household (he made a very large garden for Disi and, being a very successful hunter, provided an abundant and steady supply of meat), Chana continuously bad-mouthed him both to her daughter and to anyone who would listen. While Kuxi was absent from the village on an extended hunting expedition, Chana convinced Disi to terminate her pregnancy. On his return, Kuxi was outraged; he very much had wanted the now aborted son. He verbally assaulted his mother-in-law, accusing her of being an interfering slut, behavior that all agreed was highly improper despite the clear provocation. Chana threw him and his belongings out of the house, thus terminating the marriage unless Disi chose to follow him. She did not.

The Ritual Context of the Event

During the mid-morning rituals on the fourteenth day of the initiation rites the men form two groups composed of those who have children already initiated, the *epabu* (the fathers), and those who do not, the *bedenbu* or the *bakebu* (the sons or the children). The women form two parallel groups, the *ewabu* and the *bakebu* (the mothers and the daughters).

The "mothers" form a line facing the dance ground where they dance three steps forward and three back, waving carefully selected large ears of old corn with the husks pulled back to expose the kernels, while singing chants lauding the corn's length and firmness in comparison to the puniness of male genitalia. The chants are punctuated by ululations when the dancers shell off kernels and spasmodically "ejaculate" them onto the dance ground.

The "fathers" respond to these insults by breaking out of the open circle in which they have been dancing on the margin of the dance ground to the left of the "mothers" while chanting songs insulting of female genitalia, and by individually dancing backward while pulling the cheeks of their buttocks apart to expose their anuses

Initiates are paraded in the village plaza.

brightly painted with red achiote and chanting "dirty, bloody, gaping, dripping cunts."

The "sons" launch an attack with bows and arrows, from which the points had been removed, against the "daughters" who were standing in the middle of the dance ground chirping like birds or hissing like snapping turtles. They attempt to shoot their arrows through the women's skirts between their legs. The "daughters" counterattack the men, jabbing them with sticks or scratching or pinching them and trying to knock them off balance so that they fall to the ground, where they are mercilessly attacked by all the women.

All of this is done with mock seriousness, punctuated by peals of laughter from the audience of nonparticipating adults and children. This continues until the leader of the men's chant yells "hii, hii, hii" and the leader of the female chant yells "huu, huu,

huu'' and the whole group laughs raucously as they go to the river to bathe, men and women separately.

The Event

When the "sons" attacked the "daughters" with bow and arrow, Kuxi accidently shot Disi on the arm, breaking the skin slightly, a not infrequent consequence of the attack. Disi screamed that he had intentionally tried to hurt her. Chana, standing on the sideline, grabbed a large piece of firewood and began to beat Kuxi about the head and shoulders with no little vigor. Close kinsmen quickly intervened, arguing that Kuxi's action was not personal, that minor injuries are a normal and expected consequence of the ritual. After the combatants retired to their hammocks, the ritual resumed, but with less intensity.

The Aftermath

Tension was high between the kinsmen of Kuxi and Disi. Disi's kin argued that Kuxi was too good a hunter for the shot to be accidental, while Kuxi's kin argued that he had been shooting "daughters," as appropriate within the ritual, and Disi just happened to be one of them and thus received the not unprecedented injury. All agreed, however, that (1) Chana's behavior was both uncalled for and unacceptable, (2) that she was angry with Kuxi because she knew he was trying to convince Disi to leave her parents and join him, and (3) that although Kuxi's taunts during the rituals about "mothers'" vaginas were perhaps overly zealous, Chana should not have taken them personally because he was insulting all mothers-in-law. Kuxi, following his older brother Musu's advice, left the village in order to give passions time to cool. Four months later, Disi married Musu against her mother's wishes, but that's another story.

Case 2: The Spurned Wife

Background Material

When Dutu abandoned his wife, Huxu, for a younger woman, she was upset but not angry. Four previous marriages had ended in the

An albino woman, who is called a spirit child, attired for the fertility rites.

same way, and being a spirit child, *yushin bake*, she knew that men saw affairs or marriage with her as a temporary convenience for them and was resigned to her fate. But Dutu was not content just to abandon her; he frequently insulted her in private and public.

The Ritual Context of the Event

Kacha nawa, the fertility rite, is performed several times a year to attract to the village the spirits of fertility. Men organize and lead most performances, although both sexes participate. Occasionally, however, females play the traditionally male roles and vice versa. The ritual is boisterous and raucous, filled with bawdy joking between same-sex cross-cousins and between the sexes generally; a man may slur, *xebi ichai* ("vagina insult"), any woman, including

Women dancing around the kacha *log in anticipation of the fertility rites.*

Men dancing around the kacha *log.*

his mother-in-law, (but not his actual mother); and a woman may insult, *hina ichai* ("penis insult"), any man except her actual father, with impunity. Following a meal that consists of drinking copious quantities of gruels, men and women join to dance around the *kacha*, a hollowed-out palm log. As the dancers continuously circle the log, they become nauseated; the women leave the dance line and go to the bushes to vomit, but the men simply lean forward and aim for the log. After several hours, the women leave the dance line, usually to get the children settled in their hammocks for the night. When they return, they form a circle ten to fifteen yards away from the men dancing around the log. While they dance, they chant songs that insult male genitalia and sexuality; the men's songs insult female genitalia and sexuality. The women's circle slowly drifts toward the men and when the two circles collide, the women run screaming and yelling to grab dried palm leaves they have stashed nearby, ignite them at the hearth, and attack the men with the burning torches, beating their legs and backs until the flames are extinguished. The men must keep dancing and try to prevent the women from breaking the unity of their dance line.

The Event

Huxu was angry. She felt that Dutu had aimed his insults at her, and so when the women attacked the men with torches, she grabbed a firebrand and attacked Dutu furiously. When he fell to the ground, she thrust the firebrand into his groin, seriously burning his genitalia.

The Aftermath

The other men grabbed Huxu and threw her to the ground. Several suggested she should be burned in like manner, but when they went to grab a firebrand, they found themselves surrounded by the women already armed with firebrands. After several tense minutes, somebody farted loudly and the tension was broken by laughter. All informants agreed that Huxu's behavior was inappropriate, that she should not have taken the insults personally: "He was insulting vaginas." Many, including men, told me later that Dutu probably deserved his burn since throughout the ritual he seemed to have targeted Huxu for his most nasty insults.

Bawdy Rituals and Sexual Stereotypes

Although there is considerable implicit sexual symbolism and language in Cashinahua ritual, much verbal and nonverbal behavior is explicitly sexual. And, whether implicit or explicit, it expresses women's stereotypes of maleness and their own femaleness and men's stereotypes of femaleness and their own maleness. And, like their disagreement over the men's dogma of their superiority, males and females disagree about the stereotypes. [Note: My understanding of these stereotypes is based on discussions with informants, confirmed by offhand comments like "*Habiaskaki, huni keskaki*" (That's the way it is, just like a man).]

Gender Stereotypes

According to women, the typical (but not the ideal) male is pushy, demanding, over-sexed but not sexy, and self-centered. Unless he wants something from a woman—usually sex, he is an indifferent hunter and lover. During the day he struts about the village like a bull tapir, sniffing the air for food or sex, but at night he scurries about like a raccoon looking for sex. And, when a woman is available and willing, he talks a better game than he is able to play, being more interested in his own, rather than mutual, satisfaction.

Males define maleness somewhat differently; their stereotype is more idealistic. A male is assertive but quiet spoken, forceful but restrained, concerned about the welfare of others but a fierce defender of his image, a caring and considerate father and husband, a good and generous provider, one who loves women but is not ruled by his gonads, a skilled and enthusiastic hunter. He moves with the quiet cunning of his archenemy, the jaguar.

According to men, the typical (but not ideal) woman is an enigma. She is shrill and whining; when she gathers with other women, their talk sounds like the chatter of a flock of parakeets or a tree of nesting orioles. She walks with the ponderousness of a tapir or a capybara and the awkwardness of a turtle. Despite all this, she is alluring and sexually insatiable but stingy, using her sexuality to get what she wants. She is a disrupter of male unity. Her vaginal fluids, particularly menstrual blood, are dangerous and polluting and she thus has the power to destroy men and to decimate the forest's game animals. At the same time she and her offspring are like a

A woman dressed for the fertility rites epitomizes the grace and beauty of the ideal woman.

nest of wide-mouthed baby birds noisily chirping for meat, the culturally most valued part of the diet.

Women's definition of femaleness sharply contrasts with what they consider to be the misogynistic male view. The stereotypic woman is strong and hard working. She is a good manager of her household and gardens and generous with the products of her labor. She is a caring and devoted mother and, like an ocelot, she vigorously defends her children. When not pregnant or burdened by baskets of food or firewood or by children, she walks erectly with head held high, her steps agile and graceful. She is sensual and seductive, but although she enjoys sex, she fears an unwanted or untimely pregnancy. She is the giver and sustainer of life. She is proud and outgoing.

Expression of Stereotypes in Ritual Behavior

Aspects of these images are explicitly or implicitly expressed in ritual behaviors. Since males organize and control most rituals, male stereotypes of maleness and femaleness tend to be expressed more frequently. However, in those aspects of the rituals in which socially approved expression of intersexual antagonism occurs or in those rituals where women are in control, women's images of themselves and of males are expressed.

During the segment of the *nixpu pi* initiation rites described in Case 1, the demeanor of the women dancing with ears of corn is a parody of the male gait with his pelvis thrust boldly forward. Note that a man is acutely embarrassed if his penis slips from beneath its restraining belt or if he shows signs of sexual arousal other than in private intimate situations. Thus, the women's belittling men's genitalia and flaunting of what is normally private is highly provocative.

When the women as birds seize the shooters' arrows, they assert their equality with and autonomy from men, denying men's right to dominate them with the arrow/penis. While the males with their red-painted anuses verbally insult vaginas, they are at the same time asserting that it was they, not women, who gave birth to the initiates.

Thus, within this ritual, there is role reversal. The "mothers" act out their stereotype of maleness while their "daughters" act out their stereotype of femaleness; the "fathers" respond as the stereotypic female and their "sons" act as their stereotype of males. While the performances are carried out with mock seriousness and there is considerable boisterous laughter, the tension between the sexes is palpable throughout the performance.

The cross-gender stereotypes are less obvious within *kacha nawa*, the fertility ritual, where for the most part they are expressed verbally in the genital insults. However, on those occasions when women lead the morning inviting-the-guests phases and the evening greeting-the-visitors phases of the rituals, males and

A man carries two of his children and a woman's basket in a parody of female behavior during the fertility rites.

females trade roles, and their performances are gender parodies that give expression to their opposite sex stereotypes. Female dancers strut, pelvis thrust forward, and are boisterous and assertive. Some tie to their dance belts overripe or roasted plantains that hang at groin level, slowly dripping juices. Male dancers, wearing old, soiled, well-worn skirts, plod along with a partially filled basket on their back, carrying a child in a sling and talk in high voices, either shrill or whining. Men taunt women with penis insults and vice versa. The atmosphere is festive and largely without tension. The mood changes in the evening, the context of Case 1, when the actors resume their normal gender roles and the genital insults are for real, that is, men as men against women as women.

Discussion

Yolanda and Robert Murphy, in their delightful book *Women of the Forest*, describe Munduruсu intergender relations in terms appropriate to the Cashinahua situation: Munduruсu men proclaim their superiority and dominance over women and women "investigated the secret source of men's power—and found absolutely nothing" (1974:167); "the separation between the sexes and the domination by the males is less an inter-personal matter than an intergroup question"; and "the battle of the sexes is not carried on by individual gladiators, as in our society, but by armies (136)."

Cashinahua intergender hostility is defused through the use of sexual stereotypes expressed in verbal and nonverbal behaviors. Within rituals men and women are pitted against each other as groups, not as individuals.

Thus, when Chana physically attacked Kuxi for injuring Disi, people assured Chana that Kuxi's injury was not without precedent; they too had received such injuries in previous rituals. They also argued that Kuxi did not intentionally shoot Disi; he, like the other men, was shooting women. Women used their stereotype of women to justify Chana's inappropriate behavior, saying that in coming to Disi's defense, she was just acting the way a woman acts when her child is threatened.

In Case 2, people were appalled by Huxu's vicious attack on Dutu, but they immediately tried to depersonalize it. The women calmed Huxu by assuring her that Dutu was not insulting her personally but merely insulting all women and, therefore, he was just behaving like a man. Meanwhile, the men were trying to convince Dutu that what had happened was an accident; Huxu, being a woman, is clumsy and she lost her balance and thrust the hot firebrand into his groin by accident. Although neither Dutu nor Huxu were convinced by these arguments, they got the message: further hostile behavior between them as individuals was unacceptable.

Cashinahua sexual stereotypes and their verbal and nonverbal expression in ritual contexts serve to reduce the anger, frustration, and hostility that emerge in the course of daily social life by depersonalizing the offense—"that's just the way men/women are"—and by generalizing the expression of real emotions to a group rather than an individual. Although many informants agreed that provocation existed in both cases, they argued that by publicly holding Kuxi, Chana, Dutu, and Huxu blameless, they prevented a wider conflict of all against all.

Kachanawa *in 1994. The building behind the dancers is the old primary school. To the left is the new primary school under construction.*

Chitima with his wife and three of his four sons.

Boys gathered around the kacha *log in 1956. Chitima is standing to the left.*

Chapter 5
HARDFACED HUSSIES AND FLACCID FELLOWS

Robert F. Murphy, in his classic studies of deviance and social control in Mundurucu society (Murphy 1974), demonstrated how the Mundurucu use informal mechanisms to modify the behavior of two deviants, Waru and Borai. Although the cases were not resolved before Yolanda and Robert Murphy left the field, they permit us to see at work the informal processes the Mundurucu use for dealing with socially disruptive behavior. Waru expected to have to flee for his life when his father and protector died; Borai faced the prospect of gang rape once her protectors, the Murphys, left the field.

It is these informal mechanisms for dealing with socially disruptive behavior in Amazonian societies that is the focus of this chapter. What are they? How and why do they work and what happens when they fail to produce the desired results? What role do shame and shaming play? In this chapter, I will examine how the Cashinahua males and females use shaming as part of the ongoing battle of the sexes.

I argued in a previous paper (Kensinger 1989:26) that "it is males' attempt to dominate [women] rather than lead that fuels the ongoing battle of the sexes in Cashinahua society." Although males consider themselves to be superior to females by virtue of having penes, females do not consider themselves to be inferior. Furthermore, no Cashinahua, male or female, can order another to do or not do anything and know for certain that the order will be obeyed. Compliance usually follows because the order is deemed to be appropriate to the occasion and/or to the relationship between the parties. Noncompliance with an appropriate order may be ignored or may result in one or more of a series of responses, among them criticism, ridicule, scorn, gossip, insults (generally genital in character), shunning, and ostracism. The miscreant is rarely confronted directly. The use of physical force to obtain compliance is considered a more serious offense than the failure to comply. Each of these mechanisms is intended to cause the miscreant to feel shame.

Cashinahua Concepts of Shame, Shaming, and Shamelessness

The Cashinahua do not have a specific word for shame. Rather they have a series of expressions that can be translated as "to feel ashamed," "to shame (cause to be ashamed)," and "to be shameless."

A person who is ashamed is said to be *besu kuai haya*, "face hot has," and will say of him/herself "*En besu kuai tenei*," (I face hot feel). If the feeling of shame is acute, the person is said to have a hot body, *yuda kuai haya*. To shame another person is *besu kui wai*, "face hot make," or *besu kui tenemai*, "face hot feel-cause."

These same terms are used in the sense of embarrassment. Shaming is the result of verbal or nonverbal disapproval of one's behavior by others, *hatun en besu kui-mai* ("they my face hot-cause"); embarrassment is shame one causes one's self to feel, *eandan en besu kui-mai* ("I my face hot-caused"). Another person's misbehavior cannot cause one embarrassment or shame. It may cause one to feel anger, distress, or fear, based on the possible personal or social consequences of the misbehavior. One can only feel embarrassment or shame for one's own behavior. This is wholly in keeping with the Cashinahua emphasis on personal autonomy and interdependence. (Only infants who cannot walk or talk are considered dependents.)

A person who is shameless is one who *besu kuxi haya*, "face hard has." He/she is unresponsive to all attempts to cause him/her to be ashamed. One whose behavior and demeanor is beyond reproach is *besu babu haya*, "face soft has."

Response to misbehavior is variable, depending on the seriousness of the offense and whether one will be directly affected by it. Much misbehavior is simply ignored. However, if one should choose not to ignore the offense, a range of responses is available: criticism, ridicule, scorn, insults, gossip, or shunning. Ostracism is a group response (chapter 14). These responses rarely involve direct face-to-face confrontation between two parties. Criticism involves a statement about the inappropriateness of the behavior spoken loudly enough for the miscreant to hear but aimed at a present or absent third party: "he shouldn't have done that." Ridicule is a statement made with the intent of making the miscreant look silly: "did you see the stupid thing he just did?" Scorn focuses on the response of the observer to the misbehavior and the character of the miscreant: "how could he have done such a nasty thing?" Insults are statements which are intended to offend the miscreant: "he behaves just like a raccoon" (he steals). Gossip involves comments to other persons about the behavior and/or character of another person who either is not present or cannot hear what is said: "did you hear about what so-and-so did?" Cashinahua men insisted that only women gossip; men, they said, use the other mechanisms. However, they were not reluctant to talk with me about other people's misbehavior and faults if we were alone. They assumed, and rightly so, that I would not pass on what they said. Such is not the assumption about women's gossip, which both men and women expect to make its way around the village. Shunning treats the miscreant as if he/she does not exist.

Shaming in the Ongoing Battle of the Sexes

The Murphys characterize Mundurucu male-female relations as follows:

> The antagonisms between the sexes are very real and evident, ritualized by the men and verbalized by the women. (1974:163)
>
> **********
>
> The ideology of dominance of male over female runs through rite and myth, but it is not so evident in daily life. If we were struck by one feature of relations between husbands and wives

The men appear victorious after a round in a mud "fight" with the women, who have been urging the men to organize the fertility rites.

The women seem to admit defeat in their battle with the men.

The women launch another muddy assault on the men.

> as individuals, it was by the evenly modulated egalitarianism of roles, based not on dogma but on the simple fact that men and women are separated from one another. Coercion and obedience had no subject matter, and the men expressed their maleness, their need for ascendancy, their fears that perhaps their power was not real after all, in the public fantasy of ritual. (186)

It is within the context of "the public fantasy of ritual" that I wish to examine how the Cashinahua use shaming as a weapon in the ongoing battle of the sexes.

The Cashinahua usually celebrate the fertility ritual, *kacha nawa*, twice a year around the time of the planting of the two major types of gardens, *bai kuin* and *mashi bai*. The ostensible purpose of *kacha nawa* is to attract the spirits of fertility to the village and the newly planted gardens in order to assure good harvests. As planting time approaches, discussions can be heard about the need to schedule *kacha*.

The women first raise the subject while sitting in their circle during the late afternoon/early evening meal. They speak loudly enough for the men, eating in their circle nearby, to hear them. If the men ignore their comments about the need for *kacha* and continue talking about other matters, the women begin to shame them as individuals and as a group. Men, they say, are lazy, interested only in eating, sleeping, and having sex. They are irresponsible. If the *kacha* is not held, what will happen to the crops? Do they want their children to be hungry? That one over there, he is a pathetic case. He's always looking for sex but his penis is like a hummingbird beak, and I hear that it is broken as well. They say they can't go to hunt "heads" because they are clearing new gardens. Do you hear any trees falling or the sound of the axe? What a strong guy that one is! One ant stings him, and he sits for three days in his hammock. What would he do if he had to give birth? They don't want *kacha* because they might not be able to satisfy us. They are a soft lot. What is more useless than a flaccid phallus? And on and on.

The men, for their part, look forward to *kacha* as a time when women are free with their sexual favors. They also eagerly anticipate the ritual "head" hunt that precedes the *kacha* despite the effort it takes to kill enough game so that optimally each man has a head portion for each adult male member of the opposite moiety and minimally for each of his male cross-cousins. (The leg portions of the animals are for the women.) But, the trees and brush in the new gardens must be cut so that they have sufficient time to dry in order to assure a good burn. Since most men are reluctant gardeners, their gardens are not ready to burn when the women start talking about *kacha* and the ritual hunt takes at least a week until enough "heads" have been accumulated.

The men try to ignore the taunts of the women. Those who have finished cutting their gardens assist those who have not. As an indication of their intentions to hold the *kacha*, they designate several young men to cut the *kacha*, the bulging section just below the leaves of the pona palm, hollow it out, and drag it to the village square. When they are ready to set a date for starting the ritual hunt, the men respond to the women's taunts. We are going for "heads," they say. What more do you want? You will get your gardens, and your children will not be hungry if you bother to harvest the crops and cook for them. Some of you don't know how to cook; your gruel tastes like mud. Your children have snot on their faces. You are an insatiable lot. Give me this, give me that. But what do you give in return? You grumble and whine. Your husbands are not satisfied because you give your favors to foreigners (a charge that is rarely true but elicits loud protests from the women). Some of you wouldn't be satisfied with a tapir's enormous penis. You walk around with semen running down your legs. You are a bunch of hardfaced hussies. And on and on.

The men leave for the ritual hunt between two lines of women singing chants about meat and impotent husbands and lovers. If the men return loaded down with baskets of meat, the women greet them with songs of praise. A man may secretly give special delicacies like small birds and animals to the woman he hopes will reward him with her favors during the long night hours of the *kacha*.

During the evening portion of *kacha*, the men consume large quantities of gruels before dancing around the *kacha*, which they explicitly acknowledge is a huge vaginal symbol. The continuous circling of the *kacha* produces nausea and the dancers vomit on and into it. After the log is sufficiently defiled, the women form a line and dance back and forth near the circle of dancing men. They chant songs insulting men, particularly their phalli. Their line moves progressively closer to the men and when the two groups collide, the women whoop and dash off to grab firebrands with which they beat the legs and backs of the male dancers until they force them to break their circle. They take a break to drink some gruel and then together, men and women, continue to dance until just before daybreak.

During the night, couples leave the circle and slip into the darkness to make love. At odd intervals various men leave the dance, grab an axe, and with much whooping, run to the *kacha* and beat on it with the axe until it breaks into pieces. A young man grabs a piece of the slimy bark, runs to his mother-in-law's house and throws it under her hammock accompanied by an insulting reference to her vagina, accusing her of being either promiscuous or frigid. She, in turn, throws it outside the house with an equally insulting taunt, advising him to keep his slimy penis out of her house.

Conclusion

Cashinahua men admit that shaming often works. The taunts of the women sometimes cause their phalli to go soft. But women, they say, are not easily shamed. They have soft genitalia but hard faces.

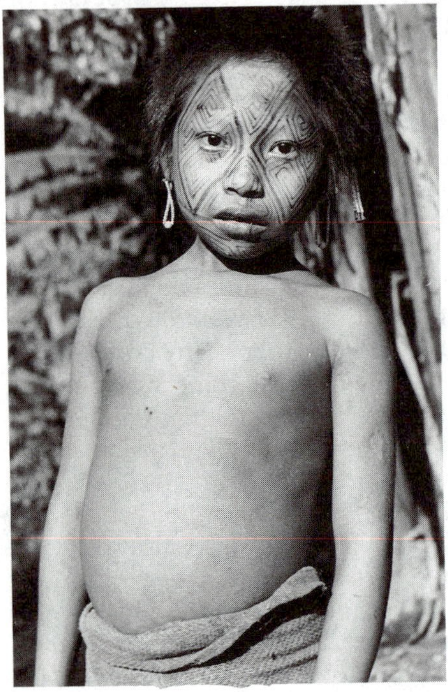

Body painting with genipap identifies this girl as a member of the inanibake *moiety.*

Face painting identifies this girl as a member of the banubake *moiety.*

Chapter 6

WHY BOTHER? CASHINAHUA VIEWS OF SEXUALITY

Various ethnographers of Amazonian peoples, most notably Thomas Gregor (1985), Robert Murphy (1977), and Yolanda Murphy and Robert Murphy (1974) have reported on the ambivalence regarding sexual matters exhibited in Amazonian cultures. The sexual ideology and practice of the Peruvian Cashinahua are riddled with contradiction and ambivalence.[1] Males proclaim their superiority over females by virtue of possessing penes and denigrate females as penis-less beings whose genitalia are smelly and polluting. But as one informant told me, "When I think of a vagina, my mouth waters." (When asked about oral-genital sex, all informants reacted with horror, saying that only animals behave that way.) Although women normally ignore the men's proclamations of their superiority, their behavior indicates that they accept neither the male dogma nor a status inferior to that of men. Nor do they accept male beliefs about the dangers of vaginal fluids. As one woman told me, "It is good that men think our menstrual flow is dangerous because for many days they are not demanding sex." In myths, rituals, and public joking, men and women treat the genitalia of the opposite sex as the objects of ridicule and derision. But in the privacy of man-to-man talks, men rhapsodize over the pleasures of women's vaginas. (I was never privy to women's conversations on these matters.)

The Pleasures of Sex

Both male and female informants talked about the pleasant physical sensations created by sexual intercourse, but males were more vocal on the topic. Both spoke of the delicious sensations, often bordering on exquisite pain, experienced during sexual intercourse; comparing them to the itching felt when you scratch an insect bite, or to the tingling felt when you bump your elbow on a house post, or to the burning felt when you accidently brush against stinging nettles, or to the warm cramps in the abdomen felt when you eat food or drink gruels (a sensation commonly experienced by those with intestinal parasites). Men also spoke of feeling a dizziness such as that when they blow tobacco snuff or drink alcohol or the hallucinogen ayahuasca and of the tension, heightened awareness, and euphoria experienced while chasing animals during a hunt.

Orgasm by the male is the focus of his sexual pleasure; all informants reported that females experience orgasm only infrequently.[2] There seem to be several reasons for this fact: (1) the physical setting is not conducive, (2) intercourse is usually hurried and furtive; there is little, if any, foreplay in sexual intercourse, particularly in extramarital sex, (3) the preferred sexual positions minimize the chances for a women to achieve orgasm, and (4) female orgasm is thought to increase the chances of pregnancy.

The Physical Setting for Sex

Most sexual intercourse takes place in the woman's garden or in the forest between the village and the gardens. Because it is considered inappropriate to enter a garden without an invitation from its female owner or her husband, gardens are one of the few places where privacy is possible, making it the preferred site for sex. However, most sexual activity, particularly extramarital sex, takes place in the forest near the village, where any attempt to clear an area of underbrush in order to enhance physical comfort during sex creates suspicion and surveillance and thus reduces the chances of privacy.

Both sexes complain that neither the gardens nor the forest sites are comfortable places in which to engage in sex because of the ubiquitous insects, many of which bite or sting. In addition, the ground is frequently damp or muddy, particularly during the rainy season; any person returning to the village with mud on his/her body other than on the feet is immediately the object of suspicion and gossip.

Some informants indicated that a sandbar or a shallow pool of relatively still water on the edge of the river or in a small forest stream is the ideal place for sexual intercourse. There one can laze in the sun, wash one's self after sex, and be free of most of the discomforts of the forest floor. Unfortunately, streams and rivers are public ways, and thus one must be wary lest one's tryst is discovered.

On rare occasions, sexual intercourse takes place within the house and then only in the dark of night. The palm bark and palm leaf thatch of which houses are made screen little from public view during the day. Even at night, household architecture and sleeping arrangements make privacy almost impossible. The Cashinahua sleep in hammocks tied less than a meter apart along the timbers that serve as major horizontal elements of the house structure. Movement in one hammock is telegraphed along the timbers, affecting all other hammocks tied to its length between vertical supports. Therefore, it is virtually impossible to have sex in a hammock without detection by other residents of the household. Lovers spending the night together slip out of the hammock where they have been fondling one another and lie or sit beneath the hammock to have intercourse. In a large household, the chances of discovery are high because it is rare that there is not someone up and about, caring for a child, stirring up the fire to dispel the chill, or answering nature's call.

The Rapidity of the Sex Act

Sexual intercourse is hurried and furtive. No couple, either married or unmarried, wants to be caught in the act—a most shameful thing because sexual intercourse is by definition an animalistic act. An oft told myth credits human knowledge of the sex act to the voyeurism of an ancestor watching capuchin monkeys copulating in the forest.

Sexual intercourse involves little, if any, foreplay. Copulation, accompanied by pinching, scratching, nuzzling, and biting, is usually vigorous and rapid, much like the capuchin monkeys who provided the ancestors with their model. Only couples working at "making a baby," a process that is thought to require frequent and repeated intercourse, or a couple involved in a torrid nonmarital affair have multiple couplings at any one meeting. It is on these occasions, according to both male and female informants, that women are likely to achieve orgasm.

Sexual Positions

Women's chances of achieving orgasm seem to be diminished by the sexual positions preferred by Cashinahua males. The most common position is for the man to kneel with spread legs in front of the woman who places her legs over his thighs; she may support herself by placing her hands on the ground behind her or her partner may grasp her firmly around the lower back. A variant of this involves both partners sitting on the ground facing each other with the woman's legs placed over the man's thighs. A less favored position but one commonly used when chance of discovery is great requires the couple to stand facing each other; the man grasps the woman by her buttocks elevating her slightly while she wraps one leg around his body. Although the prone position with the woman lying on her back and the man above her is, according to male informants, best because it permits deeper penetration, it is generally used only in the garden or stream locations.

Two further positions were described for me by two informants, both of whom seemed on the basis of gossip to be the most sexually active males. The first involves the male's sitting on the ground with his legs spread and the female squatting or kneeling astride him while she raises and lowers herself on his penis. Most male informants rejected this alternative because it gave primary control to the female. In the second alternative, the woman bends over at the waist and her partner penetrates her vagina from the rear. Most male informants dismissed this alternative; some speculated on the possibility that in his excitement the man's penis might slip out of the woman's vagina and enter her rectum, a most disgusting possibility to all of them.

Orgasm and Pregnancy

Women frequently are reluctant to have an orgasm because they believe that it increases the chances of pregnancy. They acknowledge, however, that orgasm enhances the pleasure they gain from intercourse. Although male informants said they are satisfied with simply achieving their own orgasm, they agreed that an orgasmic partner intensifies their own pleasure.

The Dangers of Sex

Men and women agreed that although it gives pleasure, sex is a source of danger, but they disagree about the source of that danger.

Men fear vaginal fluids, particularly menstrual blood, which are thought to sap men's energy and hunting acuity and can cause them to become emaciated and eventually die. Despite this danger, few men expressed a reluctance to have sexual intercourse. In fact, it often seemed that the dangers posed by vaginal fluids, other than menstrual blood, which is assiduously avoided, simply added to the excitement of a male's sexual pursuits.

For women, the danger of sexual intercourse is pregnancy, a condition that all female informants said is uncomfortable, inconvenient, and potentially life threatening in sharp contrast to their comments about the pleasure of nursing, which several informants said was more enjoyable than sexual intercourse. They frequently expressed a fear of dying as a result of pregnancy and childbirth. Male informants agreed that fear of pregnancy was a major reason why women were "stingy with their vaginas." My data on the reproductive histories of twenty-four women show that approximately 20 percent of pregnancies result in spontaneous or induced abortions; only one woman is reported to have died during childbirth or of complications during pregnancy or following childbirth.

No Cashinahua informant, male or female, told me that he or she never enjoyed or desired sex. Even old men and postmenopausal women, for whom by their own testimony sex was for the most part only a memory, spoke of sex with smiles on their faces and glints in their eyes. But it is they, the elders, who continuously warn those younger of the dangers of sex, particularly for immature males who have not yet become good hunters.

Children and Sex

Cashinahua children learn about sex early through direct observation and through what they hear. Because it is considered inappropriate for a woman to leave the village alone to go to her gardens or to answer nature's call, she is usually accompanied by another adult woman. But on those occasions when the other women are busy or if she wants to meet her spouse or lover, she takes one of her young children or young siblings with her. As a result young children often witness sexual intercourse, a fact that is amply demonstrated in their play, much to the amusement of the watching adults. In addition to what they see, children frequently hear candid and often graphic sexual language in the gossip of the women, in the ribald jesting between male cross cousins, in the verbal taunts between men and women during rituals, and in the frequently told myths. Prepubescent boys frequently gave me explicit descriptions of sexual activity they observed while play hunting in the areas frequented by lovers.

Both boys and girls are enjoined from having sex before they have completed the month-long initiation rites, which are held at roughly five-year intervals, when the initiates are between nine and fourteen years old. My data indicate that they behave as expected. Most girls marry shortly after initiation and begin having sexual intercourse well before their first menses. Boys frequently are taught the techniques of seduction and sexual intercourse by older women of the kin class *xanu*, including older brother's wife, father's father's brother's wife, and father's mother. They become sexually active as soon as their hunting skills permit them to compete for lovers with adult male hunters, but they are frequently warned to limit their sexual activity until they are older lest it inhibit both their physical growth and the development of their skills as hunters. I never witnessed nor was I informed of any masturbatory or other sexual play as described by Jacques Lizot (1985) for the Yanomami. Although the Cashinahua have terms (actually descriptive phrases) for male and female masturbation, terms they say they borrowed from the neighboring Marinahua, they insist that such practices are unnecessary because sexual partners are readily available.

Despite the ribald character of much of their conversation and their relative lack of clothing (men wear a belt under which the tip of the prepuce is tucked and women wear a skirt),[3] the Cashinahua are quite modest. Little girls are provided by their mothers with woven skirts when they begin to walk, but they are not scolded if they occasionally run about the village naked prior to their initiation, following which they are not supposed to allow males to see their vulvas except in intimate sexual situations. Little boys are given a piece of cotton string to wear about their lower abdomen under which they tuck the end of their foreskin as soon as physically possible. After three to four years of age they are teased and shamed if they allow their penis to hang free, most commonly with "Yuck, just like a worm."

Frequency of Sexual Intercourse

Men argue that there is a scarcity of sex. Women are available for sex only part time. They are unavailable for no less than ten days per month during and following their menstrual periods, when they are thought to be highly contaminating. In addition, women are expected to abstain from sex from the third or fourth month of pregnancy until the child is weaned at about three years of age. Many men and women see this long post-partum abstinence from sex on the part of women as the primary justification for polygyny. A husband who is getting sexual satisfaction from the co-wife is less likely to be philandering, with the consequent loss of meat and goods from the household to bribe or reward his lovers. However, many monogamous couples resume marital relations after the child is a year old. Women also withhold sex from their husbands and lovers in order to manipulate their behavior. They encourage their menfolk to be more diligent hunters by refusing them sexual access. They also do so for a diversity of other reasons.

Men infrequently refuse to have sex with their wives as a way of showing displeasure with their behavior because, according to many of my informants, they, the men, are the losers. Women are normally stingy with their vaginas, so only a stupid man refuses sex if his wife is willing.

Most male informants said that women, once aroused, become sexually aggressive and insatiable because they have an erect and hot penis (clitoris) which causes them to be like jaguars, both dangerous and exciting. Men fantasize and dream about such sexual encounters, but they fear them because intense sexual intercourse is dangerous and debilitating since it drains a man of energy and semen, causes him to think about women and sex while hunting, making him careless and inattentive to the dangers of the forest. By endangering his skills as a hunter, it threatens his sense of his manhood, because a *real man* is first and foremost a good hunter and not a pleaser of women.

Female informants complained about a scarcity of sex, but their concern focused on the lack of quality rather than of availability. Men, they argue, are assertive and demanding, opportunistic, always on the lookout for a quick and hurried encounter, but they are often lazy, careless, and indifferent lovers, achieving their climax almost before they begin and sometimes not achieving an erection. Women frequently taunt men about both the inadequacy of their anatomy and their techniques as lovers during the ritualized battles of the sexes that are an integral part of the fertility rituals and the initiation rites. And although everybody insisted that in these contexts women were insulting men in general and men were insulting women in general, the verbal thrusts and parries were at times highly specific and elicited cries of outrage or stinging responses from the intended target. Men say that women talk a better game than they are willing to play; women insist that men talk a better game than they are able to play.

Conclusion

When I talked with informants about the disparity between talk and action, they reminded me about the dangers of sex, of the difficulties of arranging the time and place to get together with either a spouse or lover, of the lack of privacy and danger of discovery with the consequent sense of shame, and of the usual discomfort of the physical setting. Therefore, they argued, that despite its evident pleasures, unless one is really "hungry for sex," why bother?

Chapter 7

CATEGORIES "REAL" AND "UNREAL"

Learning the language and the culture of the Cashinahua progressed at a steady turtle's pace. Communication between me and the Cashinahua improved also; by the end of three years I was usually talking "at" the Cashinahua and they "at" me. We rarely talked "with" one another, however, because I was conversing in a medium in which I was still not totally comfortable. In those cultural contexts with which I was familiar, I could converse freely without reference to the English translation and with scant attention to the grammatical forms I was using; that is, I could occasionally just sit and talk without conscious effort.

During this time, I became increasingly aware of several morphemes, *kuin*, *kayabi*, *kuinman*, and *bemakia*, which occurred with a number of diverse nouns in a variety of contexts; the meaning of these morphemes appeared to be closely related and in some cases seemed to be identical. Closer study revealed that, paired in three contrasting polarities, they are used to make important cultural distinctions. In the following pages, I will examine these polarities and the ways they are used by the Cashinahua.

Lexical domains may be divided into two major categories using one of two overlapping polarities, *kuin* versus *kuinman* (hereafter polarity 1) and *kuin* versus *bemakia* (hereafter polarity 2. Both can be glossed as "real" versus "unreal"; however, this translation is only a rough approximation. *Kuin* means real, true, known, familiar, actual, primary. *Kuinman* and *bemakia* indicate those things that are unreal, false, unknown, unfamiliar, hypothetical, secondary. The most appropriate translation is determined by the cultural domain or context being considered.

Although all informants use both polarity 1 and polarity 2, several informants, most of them older men, argue that the form of polarity 2 is incorrect; that it should be *kayabi* versus *bemakia* (hereafter polarity 3) rather than *kuin* versus *bemakia*. *Kayabi*, which can also be glossed real, true, and so on, introduces the idea of central as opposed to peripheral. Thus they speak of *hene kayabi*, the main river, in contrast to its tributaries, *hene bemakia*. These informants further argue that the polarity 1 and polarity 3 are of similar sorts. Polarity 1 establishes two contrasting and discrete categories within a domain, *kuin* and *kuinman*; that which is *kuin* can never be *kuinman* and vice versa. Likewise, polarity 3 establishes two discrete and contrasting categories; that which is *kayabi* can never be *bemakia* and vice versa. It is tempting to follow the lead of these informants in that polarity 1 and polarity 3 result in closed, fixed, and immutable categories. Patrick Deshayes and Barbara Keifenheim (1982) chose to follow this route. Their analysis is neater than the analysis presented here since it deals with the abstract ideational system. I would argue that what is lost in their analysis is an understanding of how the Cashinahua deal with the slippage between ideal norms and actual behavior. Furthermore, eliminating polarity 2 would also eliminate the problems created by the overlapping of the terms *kuin* (in polarity 1 and polarity 2) and *bemakia* (in polarity 2 and polarity 3). However, all informants, including those who say that polarity 2 is incorrect, use all three polarities on some occasions.

In order to avoid confusion in the following discussion, I shall indicate the polarity to which the morphemes *kuin*, *kayabi*, *kuinman*, and *bemakia* belong by placing the number of the polarity as a subscript immediately following the morpheme. Although *kayabi* and *kuinman* are unambiguously members of polarity 3 and polarity 1 respectively, the subscripts indicating the polarities are included to avoid confusion.

These polarities can be illustrated using the Cashinahua domain *yuinaka*, flesh or meat. Using polarity 1, we obtain the following partial listing on which there would be nearly complete agreement by all informants: spider monkey, capuchin monkey, tapir, deer, peccary, agouti, currasow, quail, and large lizards are *yuinaka* *kuin*$_1$, real meat or edible flesh. Howler monkey, owl monkey, squirrel monkey, jaguar, ocelot, snakes, opossum, anteater, sloth, capybara, jabaru stork, heron, and vulture are *yuinaka kuinman*$_1$, unreal meat or nonedible flesh.

When polarity 2 is used, the animals that were *yuinaka kuin*$_1$ in the polarity 1 classification are *yuinaka kuin*$_2$. However, of the animals classified as *yuinaka kuinman*$_1$, howler monkey, owl monkey, and squirrel monkey are almost always classified as *yuinaka kuin*$_2$; some species of opossum, some species of anteater, capybara, jabaru stork, and heron may be classified as either *yuinaka kuin*$_2$ or *yuinaka bemakia*$_2$. Jaguar, ocelot, all species of snakes, vulture, and sloth are always *yuinaka bemakia*$_2$. The important factor in deciding whether the animal in question is *yuinaka kuin*$_2$ or *yuinaka bemakia*$_2$ is whether the animal is being used as food by the person making the classification; its usage as food is contingent on the availability of those animals that are unquestionably *yuinaka kuin*$_1$, the age of the person classifying and eating the animal, or both.

Polarity 3 also produces two classes. Those animals that are *yuinaka kuin*$_1$ are also *yuinaka kayabi*$_3$ as are the howler monkey, owl monkey, and squirrel monkey. Some informants, especially those who lived in Brazil for several years, also classify capybara as *yuinaka kayabi*$_3$. The remainder of the animals listed as *yuinaka kuinman*$_1$ are *yuinaka bemakia*$_3$. Those animals that are *yuinaka kayabi*$_3$ but not *yuinaka kuin*$_1$ are animals that are frequently eaten but clearly not preferred. Their inclusion appears to be a compromise, given the reality of hunting conditions and game supply.

The Nature of Polarities 1, 2, and 3

Informants insisted that if you operate with polarity 1, you establish two categories within any domain. Those items that are not *kuin*$_1$ by definition belong to the category *kuinman*$_1$; that is, all items within domain U_1 are either A or nonA (see figure 2). The categories A and nonA are fixed, closed, and immutable. The formulation stresses the disparity between the categories, and so fails to account for the similarities which allowed the items to be lumped into a single domain in the first place. Any attempts on my part to establish the rationale for including items in the categories *kuin*$_1$ or *kuinman*$_1$ resulted in the flat assertion "that's the way it is" or "that's the way our ancestors did it."

Figure 2: Domain U_1

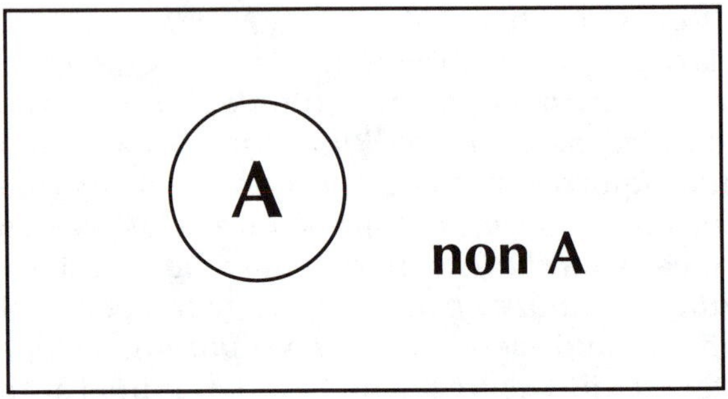

Polarity 2 also establishes two categories within any domain. Thus, within domain U_2, all items are B_1 *kuin*$_2$ or B_2 *bemakia*$_2$ (see figure 3). The unity of the members of the domain is emphasized; that is, although all items are B_1 or B_2, they are first and foremost B. In addition, categories B_1 and B_2 are not fixed and immutable. Some items that are classified as B_1 by one informant may be classified as B_2 by another informant or even by the same informant at a later date and vice versa. Pragmatic considerations affect the classification, but only in part. Those items that are classified as A using polarity 1 will always be included in B_1 using polarity 2, but non-A is not the same as B_2. Some of the items in non-A may be included in either B_1 or B_2. Furthermore, some items in both categories non-A and B_2 are potential members of category B_1. Items that are members of category A can never be members of B_2, however (see figure 4). The decisions about membership in categories B_1 and B_2 are based on individual practice rather than on cultural ideals.

Figure 3: Domain U_2

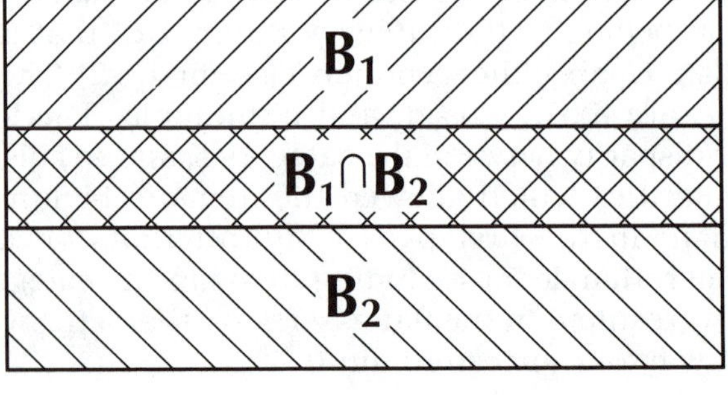

Figure 4: Domain $U_2 = U_2$

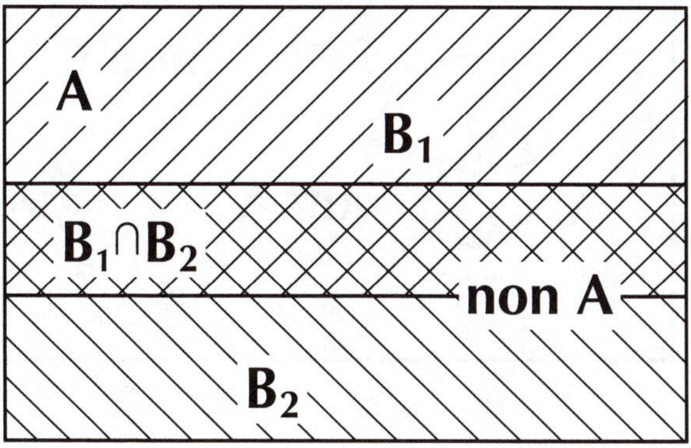

Figure 5: Domain U_3

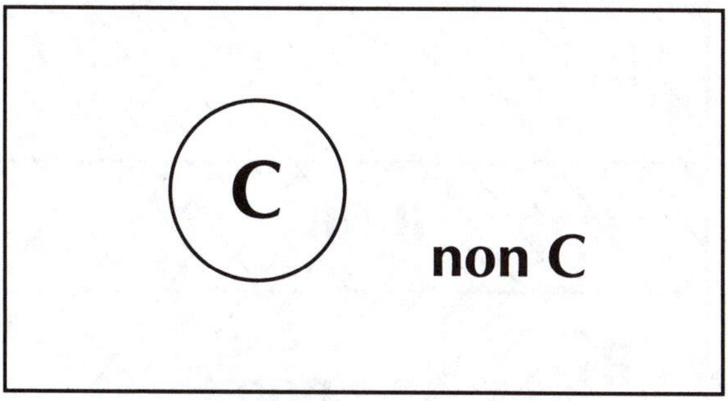

Polarity 3 divides any domain, U_3, into two discrete, non-overlapping categories *kayabi*$_3$, C, and *bemakia*$_3$, nonC (see figure 5). However, the categories are not fixed, immutable, and closed as categories A and non A. Items that are A using polarity 1 are also classified as C (see figure 6). Some or all of the items that are B_1 and some that are B_2 using polarity 2 may be classified as C, while those items that are always classified as B_2 and never as B_1 will usually be nonC (see figure 7). A few informants use polarity 3 to divide the categories produced by polarity 2 (see figures 8 and 9) and polarity 1 (see figures 10 and 11). My data on such uses of polarity 3 are inadequate or inconsistent; therefore, I will not discuss or illustrate them here. However, at any given time, categories C and non-C are treated *as if* they were fixed, immutable, and closed.

The use of polarity 3 involves a tempering of the idealism of polarity 1, without succumbing to the uncertainty of the more existential polarity 2; polarity 3 produces pragmatic categories.

Figure 6: Domain $U_1 = U_3$

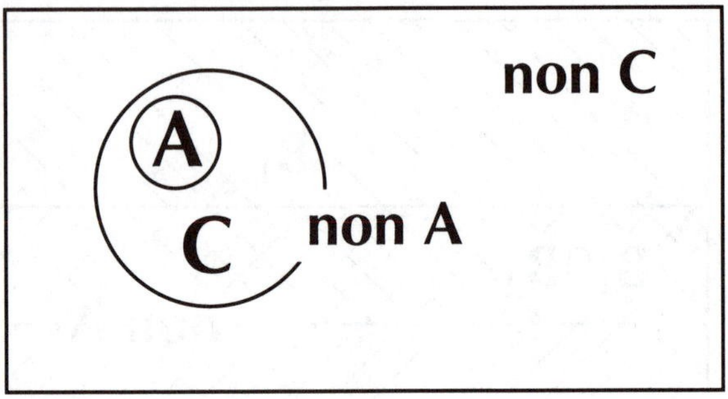

Figure 7: Domain $U_2 = U_3$

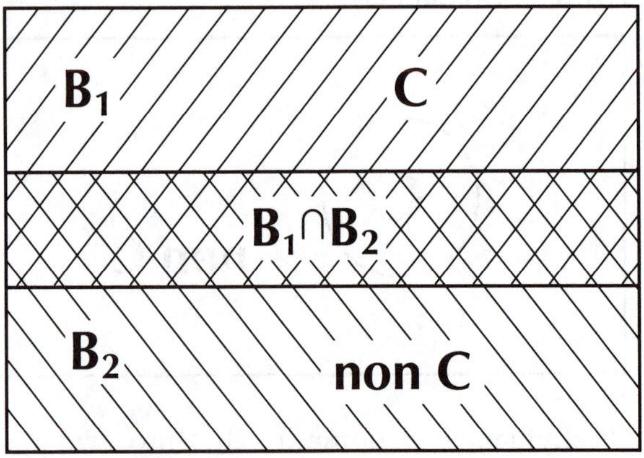

Figure 8: Domain $U_4 = B_2$

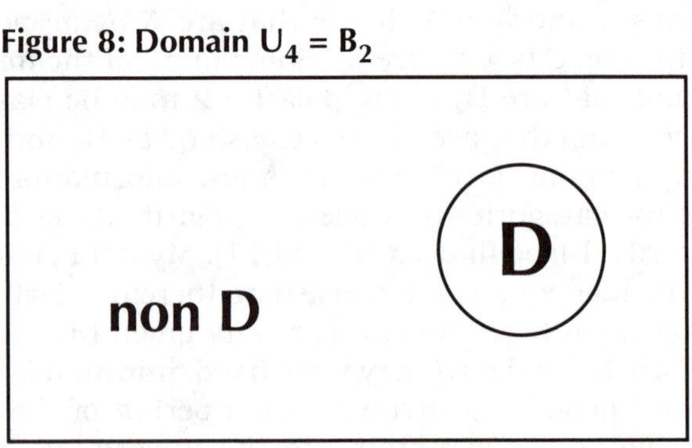

Figure 9: Domain $U_5 = B_2$

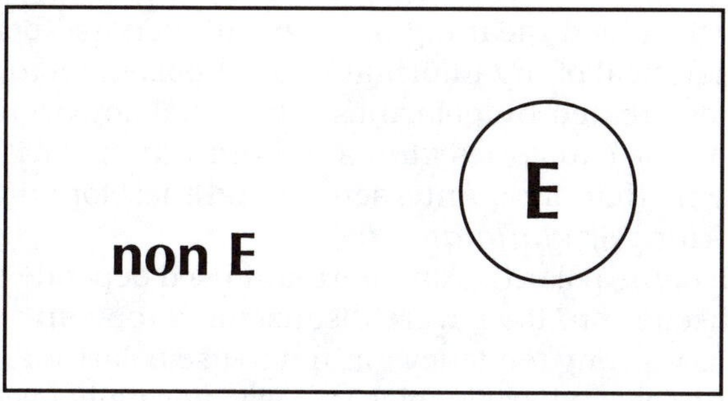

Figure 10: Domain $U_6 = A$

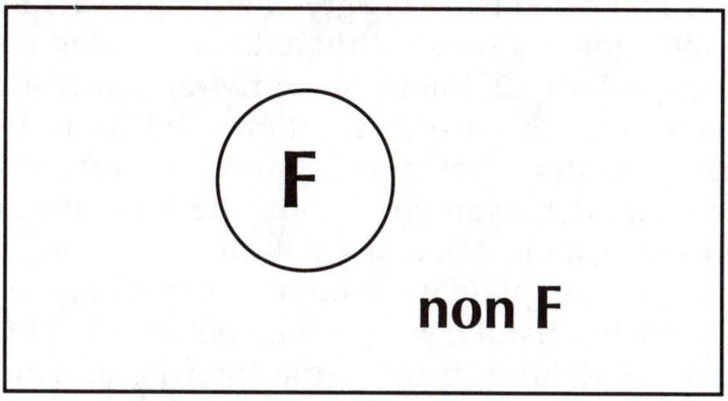

Figure 11: Domain U_7 = Non A

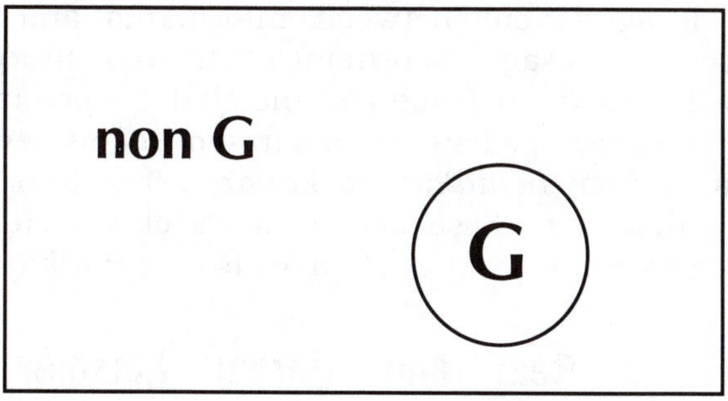

Both polarities 1 and 3 represent the norms of a group of people, much in the sense of de jure and de facto norms, while polarity 2 represents the idiosyncratic practices of individuals.

With the added meaning of "central" versus "peripheral," the more analytical of my informants used polarity 3 to subdivide the categories created by polarities 1 and 2. They argued that when applied to the categories *kuin* and *kuinman*, polarity 3 highlights those items that are quintessential and therefore indubitably and always $kuin_2$ or $kuinman_2$.

Which of the polarities an informant used depended on the nature of our discussion. If we were discussing a topic in abstract terms, there was a strong tendency for him to use polarity 1. In discussions of specific case material, polarity 2 was normally used, particularly if the situation was one in which the informant was personally involved. When an informant discussed actual cases in which he was not involved he tended to use polarity 3.

There is a high incidence of agreement between informants about the classification of items within a domain using polarity 1. Even when using polarity 2, informants are frequently in agreement on the classification of most of the items within a domain. On the remaining items, however, there is often considerable disagreement. For example, when checking the distribution of kinsmen into kin classes using polarity 1, one informant and his father were in complete agreement. They disagreed on about 25 percent of their kinsmen when using polarity 2. Three years later, I checked the data with the same informant. The results using polarity 1 were identical; there were fourteen changes in his classification using polarity 2, because he had married a woman whom, along with her family, he previously had listed as being both $kuinman_1$ and $bemakia_2$; they were now $kuin_2$. There is also a high degree of agreement between informants and between the responses of the same informant at different times when using polarity 3; for example, some of the changes precipitated by one informant's marriage had resulted in some of his new affines being reclassified from $bemakia_3$ to $kayabi_3$. The informant's father agreed with most of these changes in the classification, but he did not agree with most of the changes from $bemakia_2$ to $kuin_2$.

"Real" and "Unreal" Kinsmen

We turn now to an examination of the way in which the Cashinahua use the three polarities in classifying kinsmen. All Cashinahua are *huni kuin*, real men.[1] All persons who are *huni kuin* are also *nabu kuin*, real kinsmen or relatives. However, not everybody who is *nabu kuin* is *en nabu kuin*, my real kinsmen, the definition of which depends on which polarity is being used by each informant.

Using polarity 1, *en nabu kuin*$_1$ is narrowly defined and assumes that the ideal marriage rules have been followed (see chapter 9), most particularly the rule that prohibits marriage with persons in all but one alternating generation-namesake group and with persons who are members of one's moiety, and the rule that prescribes marriage with one's first cross-cousin, preferably a double first cross-cousin. Ideally, marriage is endogamous with reference to the village. Thus, a man's *en nabu kuin*$_1$ are his father and his father's sister, his father's father and his father's father's sister (who ideally is also his mother's mother), his siblings (half-siblings, but not step-siblings, are equated with full siblings), his son and daughter, his son's son and daughter, his first cross-cousins, his mother and his mother's brother, his mother's father, his father's mother (who ideally is also his mother's father's sister), his sister's son and daughter, and his daughter's son and daughter (see figures 12 and 13).

Not surprisingly, however, the ideal rarely occurs; of ninety-three marriages on which I have data, only five are with the actual first cross-cousin and only two of these five are with the actual double

Figure 12: Distribution of Kin Types for Male Ego in an Ideal Marriage System, Emphasizing the Moieties and the Alternating Generation-Namesake Groups.

	Moiety 1		Moiety 2	
	Male	Female	Male	Female
Alternating generation-namesake group 2	FF (EGO) B SS	FFZ, MM Z SD	MF MBS, FZS DS	FM, MFZ MBD, FZD DD
Alternating generation-namesake group 1	F S	FZ D	MB ZS	M ZD

Figure 13: Distribution of Kin Types for Male Ego in an Ideal Marriage System, Emphasizing the Patrilines.

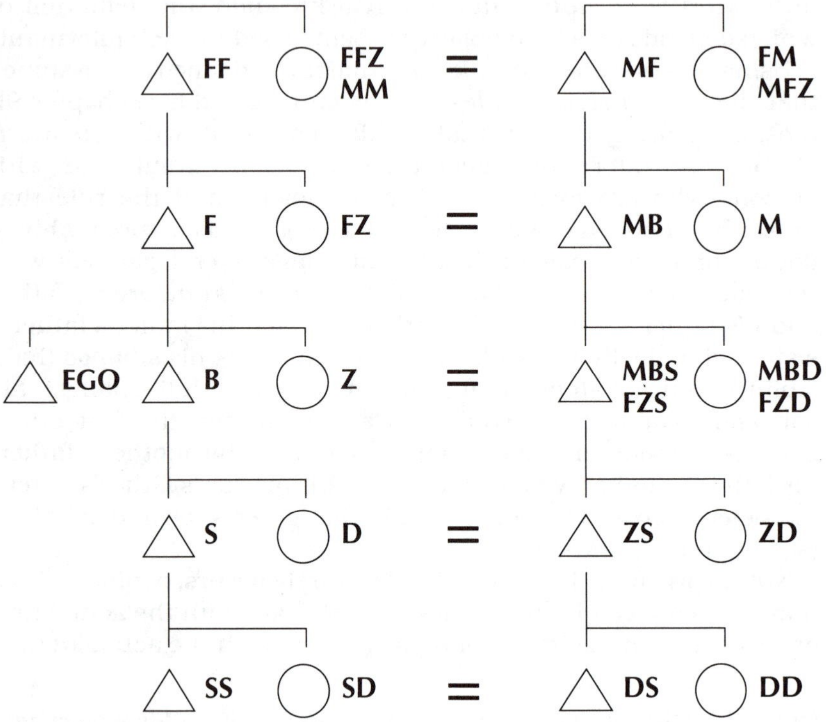

first cross-cousin. Therefore, all informants but one purist agree that a male ego's *en nabu kuin*$_1$ also includes ego's wife,[2] his wife's brothers, and his wife's father and mother. All persons who are not ego's *en nabu kuin*$_1$ are his *en nabu kuinman*$_1$.

Although ego has rights and duties vis-à-vis both his *en nabu kuin*$_1$ and his *en nabu kuinman*$_1$, because they are all kinsmen, only failure to fulfill his obligations to his *en nabu kuin*$_1$ automatically results in the imposition of negative sanctions. For example, a man may not joke about sexual matters in the presence of his *achi* (that is, a woman who is a member of his moiety, one generation senior), nor may he insult her.[3] Violations of this rule are met with immediate disapproval of all adults present if she is *achi kuin*$_1$, and an immediate apology is expected, followed by a gift of meat after his next hunt. If she is *achi kuinman*$_1$, he may be rebuked, but whether he apologizes depends on the frequency of his interaction with her and her ability to make life difficult for him. He rarely gives her meat, however.

En nabu kuin$_2$ is more broadly and vaguely defined than *en nabu kuin*$_1$, varying from informant to informant and even in the responses of a single informant through time. In addition to those persons who are *en nabu kuin*$_1$, the category includes (a) the *en nabu kuin*$_1$ of his spouse if she was not his *ain kuin*$_1$, "real" wife, before he married her; (b) the spouses of *en nabu kuin*$_1$ if they are not already ego's *en nabu kuin*$_1$; (c) any person with whom ego resides or has resided, and (d) any other consanguine or affine not already *en nabu kuin*$_1$ whom ego decides it is practical to consider or treat as *en nabu kuin*$_2$.

The decision to include or exclude a person from the category is made for practical personal reasons. For example, if a man's *en nabu kuin*$_1$ group is decreased by death, or if he is trying to increase his political power, he will attempt to extend his network of reciprocal obligations by redefining kinsmen from the *bemakia*$_2$ to the *kuin*$_2$ category. If a man is in a position where he feels that his relationship with another person is not in his own best interest—that is, he gives more than he receives—he may decide that the person is *bemakia*$_2$ and that he therefore has no further binding obligations. Notice, however, that this downward reclassification is possible only where the person being reclassified is also *en nabu kuinman*$_1$. Any person who is *en nabu kuin*$_1$ is perpetually *kuin*$_1$, and all kinship obligations are binding for life.

Polarity 3 applied to the domain *en nabu*, my kinsmen or people, produces the categories *en nabu kayabi*$_3$, my real kinsmen, and *en nabu bemakia*$_3$, my unreal kinsmen. A man's *en nabu kayabi*$_3$ includes the following: (a) those persons who are his *en nabu kuin*$_1$; (b) the *en nabu kuin*$_1$ of his *en nabu kuin*$_1$ who are not already included in the category, namely the siblings, or the children of his *en nabu kuin*$_1$, or both; (c) the spouses of his *en nabu kuin*$_1$ and the *en nabu kuin*$_1$ of his spouse if they are not *en nabu kuin*$_1$; and, occasionally, (d) other persons who are his *en nabu kuinman*$_1$ who are not included in (a), (b), and (c) above, usually persons who have resided in his village for many years. *En nabu kayabi*$_3$ is normally more inclusive than *en nabu kuin*$_1$, but less inclusive than *en nabu kuin*$_2$. Those Cashinahua who are not a man's *en nabu kayabi*$_3$ are his *en nabu bemakia*$_3$. The individuals who are included in the category *en nabu kayabi*$_3$ are those persons with whom ego frequently interacts or should interact consonant with his kinship obligations. The inclusion or exclusion of a person as *en nabu kayabi*$_3$ is to a large extent not made by ego but, rather, results from genealogical connections and frequent social interaction. The category *en nabu kayabi*$_3$, unlike *en nabu kuin*$_1$ reflects the larger reality of ego's social world, but at the same time, is less flexible and less open to manipulation than *en nabu kuin*$_2$.

The fact that the Cashinahua prefer to, and more frequently do, use polarities 2 and 3 than polarity 1 when dealing with kinship categories is, I believe, essentially a case of idealism giving way to pragmatism or existential reality. Polarity 1 provides for no ambiguity, for no manipulation of the system. It is inflexibly tied to genealogy. Polarity 3 allows for adjustments in the classification in terms of social and demographic reality. It provides a degree of flexibility without being totally existential. In contrast, polarity 2 is highly manipulative and individualistic. Thus, while polarity 2 is used by the social and political manipulator, polarity 3 is used by the peacemaker trying to resolve conflicts growing out of the manipulator's actions; polarity 1 is used by parents and the village headmen, and, at times, the entire community for instructing the young or as the basis for instituting social ostracism when the manipulator's behavior becomes too disruptive.

An understanding of Cashinahua behavior demands a knowledge of all three perspectives, the ideal, the pragmatic, and the existential. Improper behavior is condemned by the society on the basis of the *kuin*$_1$ versus *kuinman*$_1$ contrast, perpetuated by the offender in terms of the *kuin*$_2$ versus *bemakia*$_2$ contrast, and rationalized by the mediator in terms of the *kayabi*$_3$ versus *bemakia*$_3$ contrast.

Conclusion

The implications for ethnographic analysis seem to be clear. An ethnography that focuses on the cultural ideals will in all likelihood picture the society as a neat, orderly, tightly structured system, something like the pictures of homes in *Better Homes and Gardens* magazine. The pragmatic view will give us a picture which, while neat, orderly, and clean, shows the wear and tear of prolonged use. A realistic picture, however, is more likely to show how that same home looks during and after the daily round of family activity. Much behavior is understandable only if the cultural ideals are clearly kept in mind, just as the good housewife apologizes for her house not being in Better-Homes-and-Gardens condition when somebody unexpectedly drops in for coffee. Clearly, all three views are needed.

Chapter 8
CASHINAHUA SIBLINGSHIP

The Cashinahua consider the relationship between siblings, particularly those between cross-sex siblings, to be the most significant and enduring of social relationships, more important than the relationship between parent and child or between husband and wife. This chapter examines the ways in which sibling relationships are defined in both language and behavior.

In order for the discussion to be intelligible, a few comments about the structure of Cashinahua society are necessary. All Cashinahua consider themselves to be *hunikuinbu*, "real people." The second level of identity is by gender; all are either *huni*, "male," or *ainbu*, "female." Each gender is then divided by moiety membership; males are either *inubake* or *dua bake*, females are either *inanibake* or *banubake*. The moieties are further subdivided into marriage sections based on the principle of alternating generations. All persons who are members of the same marriage section, whether male or female, are said to be *xutabu*, "namesakes" or "siblings." Membership in moieties passes from F to S and from FZ to BD,[1] membership in a marriage section passes from FF to SS and from MM to DD or FFZ to BSD. Membership in both the moieties and the marriage sections determines the choice of a proper spouse and to a lesser extent lovers; otherwise, membership is for the most part significant only in the context of social rituals.

Of greater day-to-day significance is the individual's membership in a local community, *mae*. Ideally each *mae* consists of a single household composed of two focal males who are members of opposite moieties and of linked marriage sections and who have exchanged sisters in marriage, plus their male and female siblings, and the children of all the above. In practice the only requirement seems to be that both focal males marry women whom the other classifies as sister. During his/her lifetime, each individual is identified as being a member of at least two groups called his/her *nabibu*, composed of his/her parents and siblings or his/her spouse and children. Because a person's primary economic obligations are to one's spouse and unmarried children, it is possible to view the nuclear family as the basic unit of production and consumption. It is equally plausible to view the *mae* as a production and consumption unit because of the obligations for economic cooperation and sharing due to one's co-resident siblings and siblings-in-law.

Classification of Sibling Relationships

The Cashinahua use two sets of terms to talk about siblings, *betsa/pui* and *huchi/chipi/ichu*; the meaning of these terms varies, depending on the particular obligatory linguistic frame in which the terms are embedded; the behavioral expectations associated with the terms vary according to the social context to which the behavior pertains. All kin terms in Cashinahua are used within an obligatory linguistic frame minimally composed of either a possessive pronoun or a generic or both.

Using the generic *bu*, the category *betsabu* includes all persons who are members of the same marriage section, same generation or two generations senior or junior if ego and alter are of the same sex. The category *puibu* includes all persons who are members of the same marriage section, same generation or two generations senior or junior if ego and alter are of opposite sex. The category *huchibu* includes all males of the same marriage section older than ego. The category *chipibu* includes all females of the same marriage section older than ego. The category *ichubu* includes all persons of the same marriage section younger than ego. All *betsabu*, *puibu*, *huchibu*, *chipibu*, and *ichubu*, are one's *xutabu*; the primary meaning of *xuta* is "namesake," but in this context a good argument can be made for translating it as "my marriage section mates" or "my siblings."

Using a linguistic frame that incorporates the three binary contrasts, which can be translated "real versus unreal" or "close versus distant" (see chapter 7), sets up the following contrasts: *en betsakuinbu ki*, "he is my (male speaking) real brother," versus *en betsakuinman ki*, "he is my (m.s.) unreal brother," in which the latter term indicates that *betsa* is a member of the category *betsa* but not a member of the speaker's *nabibu*. Most informants also use *betsakuin* to designate half-siblings particularly if they are both members of a single polygynous extended family. If the binary contrast *kayabi* versus *bemakia* is used, the contrast would be between those *betsa* who are members of ego's *mae* and those who are not, unless the local group is split into factions, in which case the contrast would be between those *betsa* who are members of ego's political faction and all others. Co-wives, if not actual sisters, always use the term *betsakayabi* to refer to each other. If the binary contrast *kuin* versus *bemakia* is used, the speaker is saying that alter is or is not his/her real sibling of the same sex because ego chooses at that time to classify in that way, whether alter is or is not an actual same-sex sibling. The motivation for ego's choice is based on his/her current economic, political, or affective strategies. Ego's classification of alter may change as his/her motives and strategies change.

Before turning to an examination of the behavioral expectations associated with siblingship, let me add a brief footnote regarding that hoary dispute between the social categories or the extensionist theories of kinship terminology. Using the Cashinahua data, one could convincingly argue the former position. Depending on which linguistic frame is used, the terms can be viewed as social categories, including the actual siblings who by virtue of physical proximity interact more intensively with ego than others. Or, the actual siblings are the prototypes for the category to which others are added by metaphorical extension. My initial hunch was that the latter was the correct view, that in the socialization process the child learned first who were his/her siblings within the confines of his/her *nabi*, then within his/her *mae*, and later by extension to all who were *hunikuin*. However, my observations of childcare convince me that from no later than the fourth or fifth month of life, infants are often cared for by or have frequent interactions with persons other than primary kin. For example, the person tending an infant often holds the baby up to the face of another person to be nuzzled while repeatedly using the vocative kin term appropriate to the relationship between the infant and the other person. Thus, the child learns to identify all co-residents of the local group by the same terms as those who have primary responsibility for his/her care.

Expectations, Obligations, and Strategies of Siblingship

The behavioral expectations of siblingship vary with reference to both the specific relationship and the social context, that is, whether the relationship in question is between those who are *xutabu* or between those who are *huchibu/chipibu* and *ichubu* and whether the context is ritual, economic, or political.

The Xutabu Relationship

The relationship between *xutabu* is strongly egalitarian. Persons who are *xutabu* have the right to expect mutual respect, support, and cooperation from their peers. The relationship between two groups of *xutabu* linked by the exchange of spouses likewise carries the expectation of mutual respect, support, and cooperation but adds the feature of a joking relationship. Sibling-in-law interactions, unlike those between siblings, are often characterized by boisterous verbal exchanges and/or practical jokes that frequently verge on hostility. Siblings are expected to live together in what is seen as the natural state of peace and harmony and are said to be "the same as us." Siblings-in-law, who are spoken of as "similar to us, but different," should also live together in peace; this peace, however, is created, not natural. Within the context of social rituals, *xutabu* are enjoined to act as if the ideal obtains and hostilities and animosities between *xutabu* are, for the most part, suppressed both within and outside these ritual contexts. Hostility between siblings-in-law—between a male and his *chaibu* or a female and her *tsabebu*—are ritually expressed within the ritual context whether or not they exist within nonritual contexts. The extent to which the ideal behavior obtains between *xutabu* in nonritual contexts tends to be directly proportional to the closeness of actual kinship.

All informants expressed a preference for living in close proximity to as many actual siblings as possible; half-siblings, first parallel and cross-cousins are clearly perceived as less desirable, but are preferable to more distant *xutabu*. The power of a focal male as a leader is directly related to the number of primary siblings and siblings-in-law co-resident in his village who support and accept his leadership.

The *Huchi/Chipi* and *Ichu* Relationship

The relationships between *huchi/chipi* and *ichu*, like all kin relationships other than those of *xutabu*, carry an implicit and explicit notion of hierarchy, of dominance and submission, which directly confronts the egalitarianism implicit and explicit in *xutabu* and *xutabu*-in-law relationships (the model for the relationship between all who are Cashinahua).

In the relationships between *huchi* and *ichu*, between older brother and a younger sibling of either sex, there is the expectation that the older brother will care for, economically support and assist, and provide guidance and moral support for a younger sibling, who in turn is expected to obey, cooperate with, and accept the leadership of the elder brother. To a large extent the ideal obtains during infancy, childhood, early adolescence, and after both are married and settled into their respective *nabi*. During the period of late adolescence and early adulthood, however, the relationship between older brother and younger sister may be strained particularly if the brother is attempting to arrange his sister's marriage or regulate her sexual behavior to his political and economic advantage. She may be resentful, uncooperative, and on occasion openly defiant. During this same period, the relationship between older and younger brother may be strained because both are often in competition over the same women as wives and/or lovers or because the younger brother resents what he perceives as his older brother's excessive demands to work. Anger and resentment are normally suppressed and are expressed largely by a coolness and distance in the relationship. However, should they be in competition with another sibling set for a woman, brothers will join forces to assure that one of them, rather than someone from the other sibling set, can succeed. Sisters often join forces with their brothers in such a pursuit.

The relationship between *chipi* and *ichu* is characterized by warmth and affection. Older sister often bears a heavy responsibility for the childcare of younger siblings during infancy and early childhood. The bonds of affection created during this period endure for life, whether the *chipi* is an actual older sister or an older parallel cousin. Given conflicting demands or expectations, one gives preference to the obligations due a *chipi* over those due any other kinsman, including mother, father, spouse, child, or other siblings. The competition between brothers over women appears to be absent between sisters who often share a husband between them.

Discussion

What are the results of the confrontation between the ideology of the equivalence and amity between siblings and the hierarchical character of the relationship between older and younger siblings? And, what are the implications of this ideological clash for our understanding of the nature of Cashinahua siblingship?

First, if we focus on verbal behavior, the linguistic frame an individual chooses to use provides us clues to and rationalizations for his/her behavior. Thus, if the individual chooses the frame using the binary contrast *kuin* versus *kuinman*, we know that what are in focus are the moral and idealistic standards for behavior without reference to the realities of day-to-day life. If the informant uses the contrast *kayabi* versus *bemakia*, we know that the individual is taking a principled stance fully cognizant of the present state of affairs, but one that would result in maximizing the chances for tranquility and harmony in social life. If, however, the individual uses the *kuin* versus *bemakia* contrast, we can be certain that the focus is on accomplishing personal goals while actively using or ignoring the standards of Cashinahua culture in order to suit his/her purposes.

Second, the dialectic tension between hierarchy and equality provides the basis for the dynamics of Cashinahua emotional, social, economic, and political life. It provides both the stability and the flexibility which allow the Cashinahua to adapt to changing circumstances.

Third, the contradiction between the two types of sibling relationships provides the model for Cashinahua society. The relationship between the moieties is seen as the same as that between two sets of *xutabu*; all members of the moiety are siblings, and therefore are equals. This perspective directly confronts the relationship between the marriage sections within each moiety that are seen as the same as the relationship between elder and younger siblings; that is, the marriage sections stand in the same relationship to each other as younger sibling to older sibling and thus are hierarchical in character. Since the moieties and marriage sections encompass all kin roles, the conflict between hierarchy and equality characteristic of the contrasting pairs of sibling relationships becomes an implicit part of all kin relationships.

Chapter 9

AN EMIC MODEL OF CASHINAHUA MARRIAGE

In this chapter I present an emic model of Cashinahua marriage, that is, a model that takes into account what informants said about marriage in casual conversations among themselves, in the more formal discussions that took place when disputes arose about particular marriages, and in the more structured discussions with the ethnographer, and the facts of their marriage practices as gleaned from genealogies, gossip, and personal observations. The model is an attempt to account for (1) the ways in which the Cashinahua classify any particular marriage as "real" or "unreal" and as "good" or "bad," and the criteria they seem to have in mind when they classify marriages; (2) the rules implicit in their behavior and the explicit statements made about choosing a spouse; and (3) the variability within the systems of classification, and within the behavior they call "marriage," and discrepancies between the stated norms and ideals and their actual behavior. Since the analysis focuses on the social phenomena the Cashinahua label *ainwan*, to marry (male speaker), literally "wife-do/make," and *ainyan*, to be married (m.s.), literally "wife-have," *benewa*, to marry (female speaker), literally "husband-do/make," and *beneya*, to be married (f.s.), literally "husband-have,"[1] the resulting definition applies to the Cashinahua only and is not presented as having any cross-cultural applicability. However, it is hoped that this analysis will contribute to the refinement of "our etic concepts" and increase "our potential for systematic comparison" (Goodenough 1970:113).

The meaning of the terms "etic" and "emic" follows in the tradition of the linguist Kenneth L. Pike (1967), who coined the terms, and Ward H. Goodenough, who further refined the definitions as they specifically applied to ethnographic analysis, rather than in the tradition of Marvin Harris (1964, 1968, 1971, 1979). Anthony F. C. Wallace (1980:423–24), in his review of Harris's *Cultural Materialism: The Struggle for a Science of Culture*, has succinctly summarized the differences between the two traditions:

> The emic/etic distinction was originally invented and has been generally used by linguists and cultural anthropologists to distinguish between two kinds of models of discriminant behavior that the *observer* may construct for his own use in understanding what he observes. The etic model describes the behavior in categories already familiar and convenient to the observer (and ideally such categories have a "universal" scientific currency, like metric units of measurement or Murdock's "kin-types"). The subject may or may not be using the observer's etic categories, but the etic observer is not concerned with whether or not that is so. The emic model, however, sets out deliberately to describe the same discriminant behavior in the categories actually being employed, consciously or unconsciously, by the subject (which again may be the same as the observer's but usually are not).[2]

Cashinahua Marriage as Process

Four linguistic terms, *ainwan* and *benewa*, *ainyan* and *beneya*, focus on the process of establishing and maintaining a marriage, not on the act of marrying or the state of being married. These terms only roughly correspond to the English glosses "marriage," "to marry," and "to be married," used throughout the paper. The slippage in translation is further compounded by the polysemy of the English terms. For example, "marriage" can refer to the ceremonial act of marrying, as in "their marriage took place at the Church of the Immaculate Conception last Saturday," or to the relationship between the couple, as in "I have had a good marriage for thirty years." The verb forms "to marry" and "to be married," which seem to be less ambiguous referents to the act of marrying and the state of being married respectively, become ambiguous in the statement, "He was married four times." I discuss the significance of this problem further in the conclusions.

Ainwan and *benewa* refer to the totality of a series of activities that occur over a period of months and even years. They vary depending on the sex of ego, on whether it is a first monogamous marriage or a subsequent one, and on whether it is the first or succeeding marriage in a polygamous union.

Ainwan

A male generally marries for the first time between the ages of fourteen and seventeen years, although some have first married at ten or eleven. This marriage is arranged by his father or his father's brother. In the absence of these, a mother's brother speaks with the woman's father and obtains his approval. Once permission has been granted by her father, the prospective husband begins to visit her in her hammock after the rest of her family has gone to sleep or are at least settled in their hammocks for the night. These visits may last all night, but he must not be with her when the family wakens in the morning. He may also meet with her surreptitiously in the forest during the day. During these visits the couple engage in fondling, tickling, pinching, sexual intercourse, or simply sleeping in one another's arms.

About the time the boy's visits begin, he asks his father's sister to weave a new cotton hammock, which, when completed, he leaves under her hammock when he departs before daybreak. The same day he moves his possessions to where his wife hangs her hammock. This move places him under the authority of his father-in-law rather than his father. For the first month he daily leaves the village at daybreak either to hunt or to work in his or his father-in-law's garden, returning after 4:00 P.M. During this period he is supposed to be embarrassed when his peers tease him, making bawdy comments about his sexual activity. Most informants say that at the end of a month the process of *ainwan* ends. Others argue that it continues for a year, until the onset of his wife's first pregnancy, or until the birth of their first child.

If death or divorce terminates his first marriage—and this is highly likely—the process leading to any subsequent marriages is less standardized unless it is the first marriage for a man's new wife.

A kinsman of the groom seeks the father's permission only for a man's first marriage; the groom must get the agreement of the woman's father himself if it is her first marriage but not his. If both have been married before, *ainwan* refers to the period during which he is trying to convince his lover to marry him, ending when they take up residence together. In cases of polygyny *ainwan* refers to the period of courtship and the initial weeks and months of co-residence, differing from primary marriages in that there is no residential shift for the male; the wives who are added to an already established monogamous union usually join their husband at his place of residence.

The Cashinahua draw a clear distinction between *ainwan/benewa* and *atiwa*; that is, between marriage and mere sexual liaisons, either fornication or adultery; however, the point at which an *atiwa* relationship becomes *ainwan/benewa* is not sharply defined. Although both relationships involve sexual intercourse, *chuta*, only in *ainwan/benewa* is this activity ever referred to as *bakewa* ("baby-make/do"), a period of intensive sexual activity aimed at producing pregnancy. Although both *atiwa* and *ainwan/benewa* (at least in its early stages) are characterized by secrecy, privacy, and discretion, there is the general expectation that the latter will gain public recognition and approval when the couple establish co-residence. *Atiwa* relationships are often public knowledge and the topic of gossip; however, they are not publicly acknowledged, the couple never appear together in public, and the relationship is not discussed in a public forum unless their behavior becomes so scandalous as to result in public dispute and recriminations.

Benewa

Women generally marry for the first time between the ages of nine and fourteen. During the period of amatory nocturnal visits from the prospective spouse, a woman may be reluctant or even hostile and may reject a man's advances, refusing him admittance to her hammock. All informants, both male and female, told me that women never reject their suitors because of fear of the sexual act, about which even young girls are well aware. From an early age they have accompanied older sisters or parallel cousins to the forest for amorous liaisons. Women may reject suitors for failing to be sufficiently tender and loving or for being too rough or impatient. Women expect their lovers to be aggressive, but no more so than they themselves are. Cashinahua men like their women to be sexually aggressive and proudly wear scratches and bite marks as badges of honor. Whether or not the process runs full cycle depends on her satisfaction with the male; she is free to give or withhold sexual favors and all favors granted must be rewarded by gifts, which usually consist of meat sent to her through an intermediary, a younger sibling or parallel cousin of her lover. Gifts of trade goods such as beads, cotton cloth, scented soap, and perfume are signs that the romance is progressing well.

For the first month after her husband takes up residence with her, a woman is expected to stay in her house near her hearth being shy and embarrassed. When not engaged in household chores, she sits in the new hammock given to her by her new husband. She may establish a new cooking hearth near that of her mother or continue to use her mother's hearth. During the next several months she makes her own set of cooking pots, bowls, corn and peanut toaster, and water jars. If her husband has already made a garden, she becomes its owner and harvests the crops when ripe or as needed. In general, marriage brings little change to her daily routine unless there is a change in her place of residence. For example, if she becomes the new wife added to an already existing or polygamous union, she would normally be expected to move to her husband's household. Such a residential shift requires her to establish a new network of working cohorts but does not significantly change the nature of her working day.[3]

Ainyan and *Beneya*

Ainyan and *beneya* refer to the ongoing processes of maintaining a relationship between a pair of co-resident spouses. These include economic cooperation based on a series of reciprocal exchanges of services and goods, shared responsibilities for child rearing, and a continuing, but not exclusive, sexual relationship. Males are responsible for making two gardens per wife annually (see chapter 2 for discussion of gardening); women harvest the gardens and cook food. Men hunt and provide meat for their wives; women cook the meat. These reciprocal exchanges of goods and services are closely related to and support the ongoing sexual relationship between the spouses. Neither may deny his or her partner conjugal rights repeatedly and for a prolonged time except during periods of ritually prescribed sexual abstinence without risking the withdrawal of economic supports and possible divorce. Cashinahua spouses do not, however, gain exclusive access to their partner's sexual services. Both may engage in extramarital affairs as long as they are discreet and do not create a public scandal that would embarrass their spouse. This is not to say that couples never limit their sexual activities to their spouses; many do, but they can neither demand nor expect exclusive sexual services in return.

There is no single unambiguous point at which spouses refer to their relationship as *ainyan/beneya* rather than *ainwan/benewa*, but there are points before and after which it is deemed inappropriate to use the terms *ainyan/beneya* and *ainwan/benewa*, respectively. The former may not be used prior to establishing co-residence, and the latter may not be used after the termination of the first pregnancy, through either the birth of a child or a spontaneous or induced abortion.

Four Taxonomic Devices

The Cashinahua use four binary contrasts or polarities for classifying actual or potential marriage and most but not all other aspects of their life. These taxonomic devices are basic to an understanding of not only Cashinahua marriages but the meaning of kin terms as they relate to marriage rules. Polarities 1, 2, and 3 were described in chapter 7; for their application to the classification of villages see chapter 10, and of foods and food taboos see chapter 17. Polarity 4, pe_4 versus $chaka_4$, divides a domain into two categories or subdomains, those things that are good and those that are bad, each of which may be further subdivided, creating a continuum from very good, *pehaida*, to good, *pe*, to a little good, *pepishta*, to a little bad, *chakapishta*, to bad, *chaka*, to very bad, *chakahaida*. Polarity 4 establishes the relative moral value within a behavioral domain; in contrast, polarities 1, 2, and 3 establish the structural order. Figure 14 shows the relationship between the categories produced by using polarity 4 and the categories resulting from polarities 1, 2, and 3. Figure 15 shows the same relationship with the columns rearranged as a Gutman scale.

The four polarities are merely linguistic devices for labeling categories within semantic domains. The criteria by which these discriminations are made have their roots in the implicit and explicit rules that underlie Cashinahua thought and behavior. We turn now to an examination of the rules and their social context.

Figure 14: Relationship between Polarity 4 and Polarities 1, 2 and 3.

			Polarity 1		Polarity 2		Polarity 3	
			kuin$_1$	*kuinman*$_1$	*kuin*$_2$	*bemakia*$_2$	*kayabi*$_3$	*bemakia*$_3$
Polarity 4	*pe*$_4$	*pehaida*	+	–	+	–	+	–
		pe	+	–	±	±	+	–
		pepishta	–	+	±	±	+	–
	chaka$_4$	*chakapishta*	–	+	±	±	–	+
		chaka	–	+	±	±	–	+
		chakahaida	–	+	–	±	–	+

Read as follows: If an item is classified as *pe*$_4$ and *pe*, it is obligatorily classified as *kuin*, obligatorily not classified as *kuinman*, optionally classified as *kuin*$_2$ and *bemakia*$_2$, etc.

Figure 15: Relationship between Polarity 4 and Polarities 1, 2 and 3. Arranged as a Guttman Scale.

Polarity 1 (kuin$_1$ – kuinman$_1$)

Polarity 3 (kayabi$_2$ – bemakia$_3$)

Polarity 2 (kuin$_2$ – bemakia$_2$)

Polarity 4			kuin$_1$	kayabi$_2$	kuin$_2$	bemakia$_2$	kuinman$_1$	bemakia$_3$
	pe$_4$	pehaida	+	+	+	–	–	–
		pe	+	+	±	±	–	–
		pepishta	–	+	±	±	+	–
	chaka$_4$	chakapishta	–	–	±	±	+	+
		chaka	–	–	±	±	+	+
		chakahaida	–	–	–	+	+	+

Cashinahua Marriage Rules and Social Organization

Cashinahua informants often classified and evaluated specific marriages, both actual or potential. They also made statements about what they customarily do or generally expect. However, they did not explicitly formulate a set of rules regulating the choice of a spouse, list the criteria by which they evaluate a marriage, or indicate any particular order in which the rules are applied or considered. Therefore, the rules, as presented below, are a distillation of many hours of discussions with a multiplicity of informants. The order of presentation was heavily influenced by a conversation I had with one of my best informants about the selection of a wife for his orphaned sister's son, who several years later married that informant's daughter—a marriage that all informants agreed was *kuin*$_1$, *kuin*$_2$, *kayabi*$_3$, *pe*$_4$, and *pehaida*. Quotation marks set off my translations of the informants' statements from my restatement of them in anthropological terms.

Rule 1: Cross-cousin Marriage

Rule 1a: *Preferential actual first cross-cousin marriage. "He will marry his* ainkuin$_1$."[4] Marriage is preferred with an actual double first cross-cousin (FZD *and* MBD) or an actual first cross-cousin (FZD *or* MBD). (For a female ego, read: "She will marry her *benekuin*$_1$," that is, her FZS *and* MBS, FZS *or* MBS.)

This rule reflects the Cashinahua ideal model of the society, where each local group is based on sister exchange between two focal males, replicated by their sons, their son's sons, and so on. Each of these males must be a member of the opposite moiety and the appropriate linked marriage section. Actual genealogical connections are a prime consideration (see figure 16 and chapter 10).

Rule 1b: *Prescriptive "cross-cousin" marriage*. "He must marry one of his *ainbuaibu*." Marriage is prescribed with a member of the kin class "female cross-cousin," that is, with a person of the opposite sex in the opposite moiety and linked marriage section. (For a female ego, read: "She must marry one of her *benebu*," that is, any male of the opposite moiety and linked marriage section.)

This rule reflects a pragmatic version of the Cashinahua ideal model of the society, with groups of male moiety and section mates exchanging "sisters" with the males of the opposite moiety and linked marriage section; actual genealogical connections are not significant (see figure 17 and Rules 2 and 3 below).

Figure 16: Distribution of Focal Kin Types and *kuin*$_1$ Kinsmen for Male Ego — An Idealized Model of Cashinahua Society.

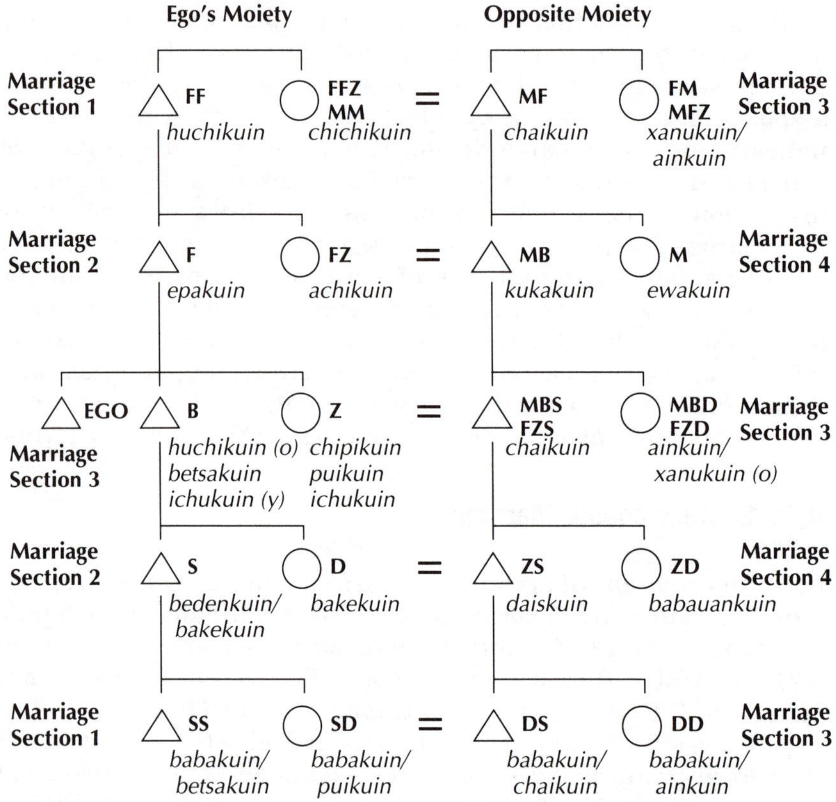

Marriage and/or sexual intercourse with women who are not members of the social category *ainbuaibu* constitutes incest. However, sanctions against incest vary depending on the degree of genealogical closeness. Incestuous relations with a *kuin*$_1$ kinswoman[5] are strongly prohibited and generally are prevented or terminated by beating and death; they are strongly disapproved and discouraged with *kayabi*$_3$ kinswomen who are not also *kuin*$_1$ kinswomen.[6] With all other kinswomen, that is, any other Cashinahua women not included in the *kuin*$_1$ or *kayabi*$_1$ categories, while technically incestuous, marriage and sexual intercourse are neither disapproved nor strongly discouraged. They are the topic of gossip, as are any illicit affairs, but they are subject to negative sanctions by spirit beings only.

Figure 17: Referential Kinship Terms Distributed by Moiety and Marriage Sections. Ego is a Member of Moiety 1, Marriage Section 2.

		Moiety 1		Moiety 2		
		Male	Female	Male	Female	
Marriage Section 1	Ol.	*epabu*	*achibu,* m *yaybu,* f	*kukabu*	*ewabu*	Marriage Section 3
	Yr	*bedenbu,* m *daisbu,* f	*babawanbu,*f	*daisbu,* m	*babawanbu,* m	
		bakebu, m		*bakebu,* f		
Marriage Section 2	Ol.	*huchibu*	*chichibu/* *chipibu*	*chaitabu,* f	*xanubu,* m	Marriage Section 4
	NA	*betsabu* (same sex) *puibu* (opposite sex)		*chaibu,* m *benebu,* f	*ainbuaibu,* m *tsabebu,* f	
	Yr	*ichubu/* *bababu*		*bababu*		

Rule 2: Moiety Exogamy

"He (a *duabake*) will marry an *inanibake*." Marriage must be exogamous with reference to the moieties.

All Cashinahua are members of one of two moieties, *inubakebu* and *duabakebu*, each of which is subdivided by sex. The female counterparts are *inanibakebu* and *banubakebu* respectively (see figure 18). A male is a member of his father's moiety; a female is a member of her mother's mother's/father's father's sister's moiety.

Figure 18: Cashinahua Moieties and Marriage Sections.

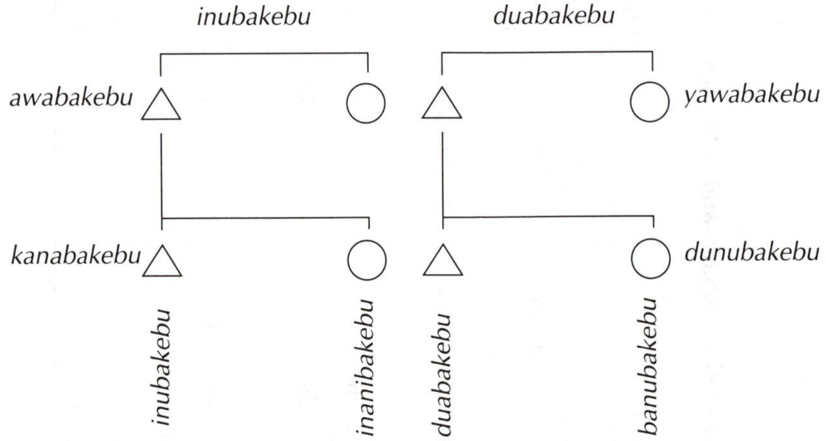

The moieties are the social structural entities that unite all the autonomous local villages into a single society. Along with the marriage sections (see Rule 3 below), the moieties provide each Cashinahua with an immediate social identity in every other community, they limit marriage choices, and they operate as social groups for ritual and ceremonial occasions. The members of the moiety within each village are the local representatives of the entire moiety; they do not constitute subgroups like localized clans, lineages, and so on (compare with Mundurucú phratries, clans, and lineages in Murphy 1960).

Rule 3: Marriage Section Prescription

"He (a *yawabake*) will marry an *awabake*." Marriage is prescribed with reference to a specific marriage section.

All Cashinahua are members of one of four marriage sections or alternating generation-namesake groups, *xutabuaibu*; they are all either *awabakebu*, *kanabakebu*, *yawabakebu*, or *dunubakebu* (see figure 18). A male is a member of the marriage section of his FF or FFB from whom he receives his names; a woman is a member of the marriage section of her MM, who ideally is also her FFZ, from whom she receives her names. Each marriage section consists of all the members both male and female of a person's moiety and generation and of those moiety mates two generations senior and junior. This group is further subdivided into two subgroups, those who are older than ego (that is, those from whom he receives his names) and those younger than ego (that is, those to whom he gives his names). The other members of ego's moiety are members of another marriage section consisting of persons one generation senior and junior to ego (that is, those who sired ego and those whom ego sires, respectively). Persons who are *awabakebu* and *kanabakebu* are members of the *inubakebu* moiety, and persons who are *yawabakebu* and *dunubakebu* are members of the *duabakebu* moiety (see figure 18). Furthermore, *yawabakebu* should only marry *awabakebu* and vice versa; *dunubakebu* should only marry *kanabakebu* and vice versa.

Under normal circumstances the rule of section prescription coincides with that of Rule 1, which prescribes marriage with a real or classificatory cross-cousin. However, in cases where there have been violations of Rules 2 and 3, adjustments must be made in the marriage sections and/or moiety membership of all female offspring; male offspring are not affected. A woman may not be a member of her father's marriage section as she would be if her father's marriage violated Rule 3. Nor may she be a member of the marriage section from which her father should have selected a spouse or of her mother's moiety, which would be the case if her father violated both Rules 2 and 3. And finally she may not be a member of the same moiety as her mother, as would be the case if her father violated Rule 2. The adjustments in group membership of a female required by the violations of these two rules are shown in figure 19. Therefore, her social identity based on her moiety and/or marriage section membership places her in kinship categories that do not coincide with her placement through genealogical reckoning, a discrepancy that can be actively manipulated by all but her *kuin*$_1$ kinsmen.

Figure 19: Adjustments in Moiety and Marriage Section Membership of Daughter Whose Parents' Marriage Violates Rules 2 and/or 3.

Moiety-Section = Moiety-Section				Moiety-Section		
Male		Female		Daughter		Condition
inu	awa	banu	yawa	inani	kana	Normal
inu	awa	banu	dunu	inani	*kana*	SV
inu	awa	inani	awa	*banu*	*dunu*	MV
inu	awa	inani	kana	*banu*	*dunu*	MV & SV
inu	kana	banu	dunu	inu	awa	Normal
inu	kana	banu	yawa	inu	*awa*	SV
inu	kana	inani	kana	*banu*	*yawa*	MV
inu	kana	inani	awa	*banu*	*yawa*	MV & SV
dua	yawa	inini	awa	banu	dunu	Normal
dua	yawa	inani	kana	banu	*dunu*	SV
dua	yawa	banu	yawa	*inani*	*kana*	MV
dua	yawa	banu	dunu	*inani*	*kana*	MV & SV
dua	dunu	inani	kana	banu	yawa	Normal
dua	dunu	inani	awa	banu	*yawa*	SV
dua	dunu	banu	dunu	*inani*	*awa*	MV
dua	dunu	banu	yawa	*inani*	*awa*	MV & SV

Read: if a male who is a member of *inubakebu* moiety and *awabakebu* marriage section marries a female who is a member of *banubakebu* moiety and *yawabakebu* marriage section, their daughter is a member of *inanibakebu* moiety and *kanabakebu* marriage section; the marriage is normal.

SV Violates marriage section rule

MV Violates moiety exogamy rule

Italics indicate the changes required.

Rule 4: Village Endogamy

"He will marry a woman from his own village." Marriage should be endogamous with reference to the village.

Rule 4 states a clear preference; it reflects the Cashinahua view of what constitutes a well-ordered society. The ideal Cashinahua village, *maekuin*$_1$, consists of a *social core* composed of two *focal males* who are members of the opposite moieties and of marriage sections of the same generational levels who have exchanged sisters in marriage—an exchange that is replicated by their sons and son's sons in perpetuity, plus the primary cognates of the focal males, that is, their *nabukuin*$_1$ (see chapter 10.) This arrangement would coincide, of course, with the ideal marriage with a double first cross-cousin.

No Cashinahua village meets the requirements for being classified *maekuin*$_1$. However, a village may be classified as proper *maekayabi*$_3$ if the two males, either actual or classificatory cross-cousins, have exchanged sisters or classificatory sisters in marriage, and have established themselves as the political leaders of their village.[7]

Only when no spouses are available in his village does a man consider going to another village in search of a wife. In such cases there is frequently heavy pressure on him to marry a local woman even if the marriage requires violation of either Rule 3 or Rule 2, or both, in that order of preference, so long as he does not marry a *kuin*$_1$ kinswoman. Such marriages would be *kuin*$_2$, *kuinman*$_1$, and *bemakia*,$_3$ but not *kuin*$_1$ or *kayabi*$_3$.

Rule 5: Residence Rules

"He will live with his *achi*." Postmarital residence is matrilocal or uxorilocal.

Under normal circumstances a man takes up residence at marriage with his wife in the household of her parents, his *achi* and *kuka*, that is, he lives with his actual or classificatory father's sister and/or his actual or classificatory mother's brother. However, if the wife's actual father[8] is dead, other residential options are open to the couple, depending on their individual circumstances: (1) they may reside with his parents, especially if the wife was residing there at the time of her marriage; (2) they may reside with the husband's older sister and her family, especially if his father is deceased, or with a brother if he has no actual sisters; or (3) they may establish an independent household near any close kinsman of either spouse.[9] The decision almost always results in their living with or near a cross-sex sibling of one of the spouses. The brother-sister bond is the strongest dyadic relationship in Cashinahua society, especially the bond between an older sister and the male siblings she cared for as a young girl. (See chapter 8.)

Postmarital residence practices also vary if either spouse has been married before or if the wife is becoming a secondary wife in a polygynous union. In polygynous unions secondary wives generally become part of the households of their husbands unless they are the last surviving daughters of their fathers, in which case the father may demand that her husband and his other wife or wives join his household. If either spouse has been married before, economic factors involving gardens and hunting territories generally influence the decision. Although marriage is entered into with the assumption of permanence, it is very fragile during the early months, so much so that the Cashinahua speak of the dissolution of a marriage as divorce (*ain puta*, "wife-to throwaway," or *bene puta*, "husband-to throwaway") only if the marriage has lasted more than a year. As a result, my data on divorce (only ten of ninety-three marriages ended in divorce) give poor indication of the residential mobility of some males and females. For example, one young male was "married" to seven different women during a sixteen-month period. None of these is counted as a marriage or a divorce in my analysis. But such affairs, whether or not the Cashinahua call them marriages terminated by divorce, do influence residential decisions.

Although Rule 5 is not a criterion in the classification of marriages, informants always discussed residential arrangements when we talked about marriage rules and classification. The reasons that residence rules play such a prominent part in these discussions of marriage are clear. First, marriage includes an actual or a potential change of locus of authority. Prior to marriage a male lives with and is subject to the authority of his father. By *authority* here I mean that he has obligations of respect, loyalty, economic, and political support, but not necessarily obedience (see chapter 14). When a man marries, he comes under the authority of his wife's father,[10] and change of residence is symbolic of this change in locus of authority. Even if a man does not change his place of residence, he still has obligations to cooperate with and economically support his father-in-law, to show him deference and respect, to support him politically except in disputes involving his primary agnatic kinsmen. Only with the death of the father-in-law, or if a man becomes a focal male, is he free from the authority of his wife's father.

Second, there may be a change in factional alignment. Until he becomes a focal male, each male is normally part of the political faction of his father and father-in-law or that of his brother and/or brother-in-law (cross-cousin). Unless he marries a woman who is part of his faction, he must align himself with the political faction of his father-in-law or brother-in-law, especially if either of them is politically ambitious and active, or he risks putting his marriage in jeopardy. (See chapter 14 for a discussion of the political manipulation of marriages.)

These are the principal rules of the Cashinahua marriage system. However, other considerations bear on the selection of a spouse, including physical attractiveness, industriousness, sexual and personal compatibility, political realities, economic advantage, and so on. Although these factors play a not insignificant part in a man's decision to marry a particular woman, they are not factors in the classification of his marriage.

Taxonomies, Rules, and Practice

We turn now to an examination of the marriage taxonomies and rules as they relate to each other and to Cashinahua behavior. Figure 20 shows the relationship between the classification of marriages using polarities 1, 2, and 3 and adherence to the marriage rules; figure 21 shows the relationship between the classification of marriages using polarity 4 and adherence to the marriage rules. Since Rule 5 is not used as a criterion in the classification of marriages, it is not included in figures 20 and 21. Figure 22 shows the frequencies of marriage by classification.

Figure 20: Relationship between Classifications of Marriage Using Polarities 1, 2, and 4 and Adherence to Marriage Rules.

		Rule 1a	Rule 1b	Rule 2	Rule 3	Rule 4
Polarity 1	*kuin*	+	+	+	+	+
	kuinman	–	±	±	±	±
Polarity 2	*kuin*	+	±	±	±	±
	bemakia	–	±	±	±	±
Polarity 3	*kayabi*	+	+	+	+	±
	bemakia	–	–	–	–	±

\+ Obligatory adherance
– Violation
± Optional adherance

Polarity 1: *Kuin₁* versus *Kuinman₁*

Kuin$_1$ marriages are those with an actual double first cross-cousin (simultaneously FZD and MBD) or an actual first cross-cousin (FZD or MBD),[11] who is a member of the opposite moiety, the appropriate marriage section, and ego's village. All other marriages are classified as *kuinman*$_1$. Five of seventy-seven marriages are classified as *kuin*$_1$, seventy-two are *kuinman*$_1$. Data are not available on adherence to Rule 4 for sixteen of ninety-three marriages.

Figure 21: Relationship between Classifications of Marriage Using Polarity 4 and Adherence to Marriage Rules.

		Rule 1a	Rule 1b	Rule 2	Rule 3	Rule 4
	pehaida	+	+	+	+	+
pe_4	*pe*	+	+	+	+	+
	pepishta	–	+	+	+	±
	chakapishta	–	±	+	–	±
$chaka_4$	*chaka*	–	±	–	–	±
	chakahaida	–	–	–	–	±

\+ Obligatory adherance
– Violation
± Optional adherance

Figure 22: Frequencies of Marriages by Classification.

Polarity 1		$kuin_1$	5/77 [a]		
		$kuinman_1$	72/77 [a]		
Polarity 2	Obligatorily	$kuin_2$	5/93		
	Obligatorily	$bemakia_2$	0/93		
	Optionally	$kuin_2$	88/93		
	Optionally	$bemakia_2$	88/93		
Polarity 3		$kayabi_3$	76/93 [b]		
		$bemakia_3$	15/93 [b]		
Polarity 4	*pehaida*	2/93			
	pe	3/93	pe_4	76/93	
	pepishta	71/91 [b]			
	chakapishta	4/93			
	chaka	11/93	$chaka_4$	15/93	
	chakahaida	0/93			

[a] No data on adherence to Rule 4 for 16 of 93 marriages.
[b] Insufficient data on two marriages.

Polarity 2: *Kuin₂* versus *Bemakia₂*

Only marriages that adhere to Rule 1a are obligatory $kuin_2$ and only marriages with an actual M, MM, FFZ (if his MM), FM, Z, D, ZD, SD, and DD are obligatory $bemakia_2$. Apart from these restrictions, ego is free to manipulate his classification of particular marriages and attempt to manipulate others' classifications in order to justify his violation of social norms and/or his failure to carry out his social obligations. Because of the highly manipulable and idiosyncratic character of polarity 2, only five of ninety-three marriages (two with actual double first cross-cousins, two with actual FZDs, and one with an actual MBD) are indubitably *kuin*$_2$. None of the ninety-three marriages is obligatorily *bemakia*$_2$; such unions would be forcibly terminated by a severe beating, resulting in death, for either of the guilty parties or ostracism of the couple from the society.

Polarity 3: *Kayabi*$_3$ versus *Bemakia*$_3$

Kayabi$_3$ marriages adhere to Rules 1, 2, and 3, and optionally adhere to Rule 4. Marriages that violate Rules 1a and 1b, 2, and 3 are always *bemakia*$_3$. Some informants argued that marriages that violate Rules 2 and 3, but not 1a and 1b, could also be classified as *kayabi*$_3$. Most insisted that since violation of Rule 3 results in confusion vis-à-vis the social status of the offspring of such a marriage, they were *chakapishta* and therefore could not be *kayabi*$_3$. Seventy-six of ninety-three marriages are classified as *kayabi*$_3$; fifteen are *bemakia*$_3$ (I do not have sufficient data on two). The marriages classified as *bemakia*$_3$ include twelve that violated both Rules 2 and 3 (six males married women from their own moiety and section, six married women from their father's section of their own moiety), and three in violation of only Rule 3.

Rule 4: *Pe*$_4$ versus *Chaka*$_4$

Marriages classified as *pehaida* (very good) are those between actual double first cross-cousins who are members of opposite moieties, linked marriage sections, and the same village; that is, they abide by the ideal rules. Only two of ninety-three marriages are classified as *pehaida*. The key to understanding the low frequency of such marriage lies in the strict requirement that actual double first cross-cousins marry. Few persons have potential spouses who meet these qualifications, since it requires a prior *pehaida* marriage, so that FZ = MBW *and* MB = FZH. An examination of my genealogical data leads me to conclude that few *pehaida* marriages have existed in the recent past, if ever.

Pe (good) marriages are those between spouses who are actual first cross-cousins but not double first cross-cousins, who are members of opposite moieties, linked marriage sections, and the same village. Three of ninety-three marriages are *pe*. Even with this relaxation of the strict ideal, most people reaching marriageable age find no actual first cross-cousins available. One informant told me that he had very much wanted to marry well or very well, *ainwan pehaida* or *ainwan pe*, but all of his first cross-cousins, his *ainkuin*$_1$, were either infants or already married.

Marriages classified as *pepishta* (a little good) are those between classificatory cross-cousins who are members of opposite moieties and of the appropriate marriage sections but who reside before marriage in different villages. Two informants occasionally classified one of the *pe* marriages as *pepishta* because, although the spouses were village co-residents, they were members of different and antagonistic factions. They argued that marrying a person from another political faction at odds with one's own faction is tantamount to violating the rule of village endogamy. The overwhelming majority of Cashinahua marriages, seventy-one of ninety-one (I lack sufficient data on two marriages), fit the category *pepishta*. Although such a marriage falls short of the ideal, it is an acceptable compromise because it often is required by demographic realities. Informants insist that although such marriages are not *pehaida* or *pe*, they are *pe*$_4$ as a opposed to *chaka*$_4$.

Many informants also used *pe* and *chaka* to refer to the quality of the relationship between a couple. Therefore, statements about marriages being *pehaida*, *pe*, and the like, are ambiguous, and intentionally so, since it allows the speaker to judge the response of the hearer before indicating whether one is making an impartial moral judgment or merely gossiping.

Marriages classified as *chakapishta* (a little bad) are those between persons who are not members of linked marriage sections, who are members of opposite moieties, who may or may not be cross-cousins, and who may or may not be village co-residents. Four marriages of ninety-three were classified as *chakapishta*. Of these marriages, one was between cross-cousins who were co-residents, but whose marriage violated the marriage section rule because the wife's father had married badly; two were between persons who were neither cross-cousins nor village co-residents; I have insufficient data on the fourth case.

Marriages classified as *chaka* (bad) are those between persons who may or may not be cross-cousins (if they are, the marriage of the wife's father and mother violated the moiety exogamy rule and/or the rule of marriage section prescription), who are members of the same moiety and therefore members of inappropriate marriage sections, and who may or may not be village co-residents. Eleven of ninety-three marriages are classified as *chaka*; none of them was between actual cross-cousins, six of them were with members of the same marriage section, five were with persons belonging to father's marriage section, and all of them involved village co-residents. One informant told me, "They say I married badly (*ainwan chaka*), but I have a good marriage (*ainwan pe*)." He agreed, however, that the classification *ainwan chaka/ainyan chaka* was appropriate from a moral perspective and speculated that his failure to realize his political ambitions was a result of his bad marriages.

Marriages classified as *chakahaida* (very bad) violate all of the marriage rules with the possible exception of village endogamy and are further characterized by being with prohibited $kuin_1$ kinsmen, namely with an actual M, FZ, MM, FFZ (if also MM), FM, Z, D, ZD, SD, or DD.[12] Strong sanctions including physical violence are used to terminate such marriages; none of the ninety-three marriages is classified as *chakahaida*.

Taxonomies, Rules, and Cashinahua Behavior

The marriage rules and elaborate taxonomies seem to have little direct impact on daily behavior. Except for those marriages classified as *chakahaida*, the Cashinahua do not shun individuals or couples whose marriages are improper; nor do they subject them to negative sanctions. Furthermore, the rules do not seem to be a serious consideration in a couple's decision to marry or not; other than arranged first marriages, most marriages are but formalizations of ongoing sexual liaisons entered into without consideration of any rules and taxonomies, except possibly those against sexual activity with prohibited $kuin_1$ kin. However, a young man contemplating marriage does take the marriage rules into consideration while surveying his prospects; he chooses to marry an *ainbuaibu* if one is available. He does so because of the supernatural sanctions he risks if he marries improperly.

The spirit world of the Cashinahua is concerned with maintaining harmony and balance in the universe including within and between society, nature, and spirits. Bad marriages, by causing social confusion, are disruptive, resulting in suspicions and claims of supernatural intervention such as unexpected illness and accidents to the members of one's close circle of kin, bad luck in hunting, the cracking of one's kinswomen's pottery during firing, strange nighttime noises, apparitions of deceased kinsmen, and so on.[13] I did not observe nor did my informants report any cases where bad marriages were dissolved to placate the spirits; instead, medicine is used (see chapter 22). Thus bad marriages, except those classified as *chakahaida*, are tolerated and are preferred to no marriage at all. Most females are married for the first time by the age of thirteen, males by sixteen. Widows and divorcées, even elderly ones, rarely remain unmarried for more than a few days; widowers and divorcés remarry as soon as a spouse is available and rarely have difficulty getting a new wife if they have a reputation as a good hunter, worker, and provider. Unmarried adults, whatever the reasons for their being unmarried, are viewed as potentially more disruptive to the society than is a bad marriage.

An Emic Model of Cashinahua Marriage

An emic model of Cashinahua marriage must account for all of the data presented above. It cannot be a mere translation or rewording of informants' statements; nor can it be restricted to such statements. It must be based both on what they say *and* on what they do; it must define marriage as opposed to nonmarriage within Cashinahua society and as compared to marriage in American, Nuer, Trobriand, or Japanese society. The elements of such a definition exist not as isolated, discrete traits but as constellations or bundles of traits that define the discrete class or classes of social behavior called marriage. In addition, an emic definition of Cashinahua marriage must indicate the range of acceptable variation, both free or conditioned, present both in actual behavior of the members of Cashinahua society and in their statements of acceptability. It must also include a statement of the distribution of the emic class or classes in larger structures of which they form a part. Thus, for example, in Cashinahua society the married pair, husband and wife, is a basic structural unit that forms the nucleus of a nuclear family or constitutes part of the nucleus of a polygynous and/or an extended family. They may also be part of an atom of social organization, the social core, or the social periphery of a village (see chapter 10).

The taxonomies resulting from the use of polarities 1, 2, 3, and 4 are not emic. Although I was prepared at first to argue that polarity 3, *kayabi*$_3$ versus *bemakia*$_3$, and/or polarity 4, *pe*$_4$ versus *chaka*$_4$, are isomorphic with an emic model, closer examination showed that they are not and cannot be so. They fail to make explicit certain factors that are crucial to an emic model of Cashinahua marriage and that all informants implicitly assume to be true but never state.

It was equally clear that polarity 1, *kuin*$_1$ versus *kuinman*$_1$, cannot be emic because it is too idealistic, restrictive, and inflexible to account adequately for much of Cashinahua behavior; only about 5 percent of the marriages are classified as proper, *kuin*$_1$. Nor can polarity 2, *kuin*$_2$ versus *bemakia*$_2$, be emic. It is too idiosyncratic, unrestrictive, and flexible to account for most of the constraints on Cashinahua marriage behavior. However, it does reveal both the range of variability possible within the system and the manner in which individuals are able to manipulate the system to their own advantage. Thus, although the four Cashinahua polarities provide us with taxonomic data essential for an emic analysis, individually and collectively they do not constitute an emic model.

My emic model of the Cashinahua marriage system consists of three emic classes—legitimate-proper, legitimate-improper, and illegitimate-improper (hereafter L-p, L-i, and I-i respectively) and a two-phase emic process. Figure 23 summarizes the defining characteristic of each emic class. Figure 24 summarizes the essential elements of the emic process; it indicates the obligatory and optional sequence of events that together define the process of Cashinahua marriage.

Figure 23: Matrix Showing Distinctive Features of Emic Classes of Cashinahua Marriage.

Emic Class	Cohab-tation	Sexual Relation-ship	Eco-nomic Cooper-ation	Cross-Cousin Class Prescrip-tion	Moiety Exog-amy	Marriage Section Prescrip-tion	Village Endo-gamy
L-p	+	+	+	+	+	+	±
L-i	+	+	+	±	±	–	±
I-i	+	+	+	–	–	–	±

\+ Obligatory presence of feature
– Obligatory absence of feature
± Optional presence or absence of feature

In an earlier formulation based on linguistic distinctions made by the Cashinahua, I viewed this process in terms of a 2 x 2 matrix that differentiated between establishment and maintenance and between first and subsequent marriages. Closer examination forced me to abandon that analysis for several reasons. (1) Although first and subsequent marriages may differ in terms of the inventory of events that occur during the establishment phase, the essential

Figure 24: The Process of Marrying among the Cashinahua.

	First Marriage	Subsequent Marriages
Establishment Phase *ainwan*	± Arrangement by proxy + Nocturnal visits/daytime trysts ± Requesting hammock ± Giving hammock to bride + Husband changes residence + Period of being ashamed + Regular hunting – catch to wife/wife's mother	+ Sexual liaison with giving of gifts to woman + Change of residence by one spouse
Maintenance Phase *ainyan*	+ Making garden ± First pregnancy and birth + Annual garden making + Regular hunting – catch to wife + Marriage of first daughter and shift from being son-in-law to father-in-law	 + Annual garden making + Regular hunting – catch to wife

features are identical, namely, the establishment of a sexual relationship and the residential shift of one partner, and the establishment of economic cooperation. The differences are a result of either conditioned variation based on the age of the partners, their marital histories, the presence or absence of significant kinsmen such as the spouses' parents, parents' marital histories, and so on, or of free variation, depending on which sequence of optional activities is selected. (2) Although the Cashinahua distinguish between the phases of establishing a marriage (*ainwan* and *benewa*) and maintaining a marriage (*ainyan* and *beneya*), they do not sharply define when these phases begin or end. For example, a male may use the term *ainwan* at the onset of marriage negotiations, with the inception of sexual activities, or later in the process. Or he may deny that he is even married, asserting that he is merely having an affair, *atiwa*. He may continue to use the term *ainwan* to describe his relationship until the birth of his first child, indicating a certain tentativeness about the relationship. On the other hand, he may begin to use the term *ainyan* as soon as co-residence and economic cooperation have been established. Others, including his parents, spouse, and siblings, tend to use *ainwan* after co-residence has been established and *ainyan* after economic cooperation has been clearly established, indicated by the husband's planting a garden and his wife's caring for and harvesting the crops. His parents-in-law tend to use *ainwan* with the initiation of sexual activity, especially if it is their daughter's first marriage, and *ainyan* only after the birth of the couple's first child.

Figure 23 includes three elements that were not discussed in connection with the informants' taxonomies and rules because they are not criteria relevant to the Cashinahua classifications, namely, cohabitation, a sexual relationship, and economic cooperation. However, they must be made explicit in an emic analysis because they are part of the behavior that defines marriage as opposed to other nonmarriage relationships.

An L-p marriage is defined as the process of establishing and maintaining a socially recognized and approved relationship characterized by cohabitation, a sexual relationship, and economic cooperation between a male and a female who are actual or classificatory cross-cousins and members of opposite moieties and appropriate, linked marriage sections. The parties to the relationship may or may not be co-residents of the same village prior to their marriage. An L-p marriage may form the nucleus of a nuclear family, and/or be part of the nucleus of a polygynous and/or extended family, and/or be part of a social core or periphery of a village. Only L-p marriages, however, may form the nucleus of an atom of social organization. All those marriages the Cashinahua classify as pe_4, $kuin_1$, and $kayabi_3$, and some they classify as $kuinman_1$ or $kuin_2$ (namely, those included in pe_4 and $kayabi_3$), are L-p marriages.

An L-i marriage is defined as the process of establishing and maintaining a socially recognized and accepted but not approved relationship between a male and a female, characterized by cohabitation, a sexual relationship and economic cooperation, by violation of the rule of marriage section prescription, and by optional adherence to the rules of village endogamy, moiety exogamy, and/or cross-cousin class prescription. Any L-i marriage between actual cross-cousins is the result of improper marriages by their parents; it results in the social identity of one or both parties, based on moiety and marriage section affiliation, being at variance with their personal identity, based on actual genealogical ties. In the classification of marriages, social identity takes precedence over personal identity. The variant forms of L-i marriages are products of the particular options followed. An L-i marriage *may* form the nucleus of a nuclear family, and/or be part of the nucleus of a polygynous and/or extended family, and/or be part of the social core or periphery of a village. An L-i marriage *may not* form the nucleus of an atom of social organization. L-i marriages include all the marriages the Cashinahua classify as *chaka* and *chakapishta* and some they classify as *kuinman*$_1$, *bemakia*$_2$, and *bemakia*$_3$, namely, those included in *chaka* and *chakapishta* but not *chakahaida*.

An I-i marriage is defined as the process of establishing and maintaining an acknowledged but socially unrecognized and unapproved relationship between a male and a female who are *kuin*$_1$ kin to each other but not cross-cousins (and who thus violate all the marriage rules with the possible exception of the rule of village endogamy), characterized by cohabitation, a sexual relationship, and economic cooperation. I-i marriages include all those unions classified as *chakahaida*, those obligatorily classified *bemakia*$_2$, and some of those classified *bemakia*$_3$ and *kuinman*$_1$. Although such unions are forcibly terminated or couples are forced to leave both their village and Cashinahua society to live with outsiders, they are defined as marriage rather than nonmarriage. And although L-i marriage can form the nucleus of a nuclear family, it cannot be part of a Cashinahua village.

Thus the Cashinahua marriage system consists of a two-phase process, taking a spouse (*ainwan/benewa*) and having a spouse, (*ainwan, beneya*) that is, the process of establishing and continuing a marital relationship, which is the primary relationship in the formation of a family unit, which in turn serves as an integral part of larger social units. The process is loosely regulated by a series of rules or understandings, and the relationships resulting from them are evaluated in terms of their adherence to and/or violation of these rules. An examination of both the taxonomies and Cashinahua behavior reveals an underlying tripartite model that reflects and can be used to generate the system but does not coincide with any Cashinahua taxonomies.

Discussion and Conclusions

The foregoing description has focused on the Cashinahua system of marriage. It is based on, but not limited to, what the Cashinahua said and what they did. These observations were informed and illuminated by concepts that are part and parcel of my anthropological training. Thus, when I write about moiety exogamy, village endogamy, marriage section prescription, and the like, I am translating informants' statements and behavior into words and concepts that are part of the ethnographer's etic tool kit. Goodenough (1970:112) has argued that

> emic description requires etics, and by trying to do emic descriptions we add to our etic concepts for subsequent descriptions. It is through etic concepts that we do comparison. And by supplementing our etic concepts we contribute to the development of a general science of culture.

What, then, are the implications of an emic analysis of Cashinahua data for the development or refinement of our etic concepts and an etic definition of marriage?[14]

(1) An etic definition of marriage must distinguish between marriage and sex. Anthropologists, like the Cashinahua, have assumed that although sex and marriage are not synonymous, a sexual relationship is an integral part of marriage. However, we need to examine how a marriage relationship differs from sexual relationships both within marriage and outside marriage.

The Cashinahua word for sexual intercourse, whether outside or inside marriage, is *chuta*; the term refers both to the act of intercourse and/or all the attendant activities. *Beyus* (play) is frequently used, perhaps euphemistically, in place of *chuta* in the sense of sexual play but never refers to the act alone. A sexual relationship outside marriage, *atiwa/atiya* (to make or have a lover), does not involve co-residence as does marriage, nor does it create the social bond that is integral to the establishment of a social unit, although it may be the prelude to marriage. Furthermore, the meat, trinkets, trade goods, and so on, given by the male to his partner in exchange for sex in an *atiwa/atiya* relationship do not constitute the economic cooperation that characterizes the marriage relationship. The reciprocal exchange of goods and services that is one of the defining features of Cashinahua marriage is expected to endure whether there is or is not an active, ongoing sexual relationship between the spouses. The termination of sexual relations does not spell the end of a marriage; the termination of economic cooperation does. In contrast, the cessation of sexual activity marks the end of an *atiwa/atiya* relationship. Furthermore, some informants classify *atiwa/atiya* relationships using the same polarities and the same criteria they use to classify marriage, indicating the structural and moral appropriateness of the lover relationships. On the other hand, they use only polarity 4 to classify *chuta*, a classification filled with semantic ambiguity. For example, *chuta chakahaida* can mean either that the sexual activity was highly incestuous or that it was very unpleasant or unsatisfactory. Thus sex as an act is differentiated from sex as part of marriage or lover relationships.

(2) An etic definition of marriage must deal with the question of the extent to which marriage limits sexual access to and/or establishes control over the sexual activities of one or both spouses.

Although the Cashinahua expect a sexual relationship within marriage, they do not expect that it will be an exclusive relationship. The husband and the wife have neither an exclusive right of sexual access nor control over the partner's sexual activities. The expectation holds both that affairs will be carried on with discretion so as not to embarrass a spouse and that the adulterous individual will not withhold sexual services from the spouse in favor of the lover. In theory, every Cashinahua has rights to sexual access to all those persons who are members of the kin class "opposite-sex cross-cousins," and every female has the right to accept or reject the sexual advances of any and all males, including her husband. However, the Cashinahua acknowledge that the economic relationship established by marriage places limits on this freedom, giving spouses prior claim but not exclusive control over or access to each other's sexuality.

(3) An etic definition of marriage must reflect the fact that in all marriage systems some elements or features are obligatory and essential while some are optional, thus creating variability within the system. The obligatory features frequently will not be mentioned overtly by informants, who simply assume their listener knows what these elements are and therefore take them for granted, just as my informants assumed that I knew that marriage included a sexual relationship, co-residence, and economic cooperation and so never mentioned them during our discussions.

(4) An etic definition of marriage must distinguish marriage from nonmarriage.[15] In most societies the expectation exists that most, if not all, individuals will marry and be married most or all of their adult lives. Unmarried individuals often are considered aberrant and potentially dangerous. The Cashinahua prefer that a person marry in violation of highly valued norms rather than remain single, since they view unmarried individuals, especially males, as potentially disruptive. Understanding why this is so often the case should contribute to a more precise etic definition.

(5) An etic definition of marriage must not imply that marriage is only an act, an institution, a state of being, or a social process; it may be one or more of these. Unfortunately, the vocabulary we

use for discussing marriage reflects our society's views. Thus my use of the noun "marriage" when talking about Cashinahua marriage does violence to the Cashinahua conception of marriage as a process, expressed with verbs rather than nouns. Given the nature of natural language, I do not know how to resolve this problem. We clearly need to develop an etic meta-language that will allow us to discuss marriage in any society with as little ambiguity as possible, while conveying whatever ambiguity exists in the system itself.

(6) Although an etic definition of marriage cannot be a legal or moral definition, since law and morals are culture specific and thus must be dealt with in emic terms, it must include provisions for dealing with the legal and moral dimensions of marriage. Like other and perhaps all societies, the Cashinahua distinguish between those marriages that are legitimate/legal and those that are illegitimate, and between proper and improper. However, if the relationship is characterized by cohabitation, a sexual relationship, and economic cooperation, for the Cashinahua it is marriage. This is not the case in American society, in which a social relationship characterized by cohabitation, a sexual relationship, and economic cooperation without the appropriate religious and/or legal rituals may or may not be defined as marriage[16] and is frequently considered amoral if not immoral.

(7) Given the complexity of all marriage systems, a valid etic definition must reflect this complexity and therefore cannot focus on one factor to the exclusion of all others even if that factor can be shown to be common to all marriage systems. Thus I suspect that an etics of marriage may in the end look something like the International Phonetic Alphabet; that is, it will be not a unitary definition but a matrix chart wherein various constellations of features can be identified as particular kinds of marriage, just as each symbol in the IPA represents a constellation of phonological features.

If we are to develop a more adequate definition of marriage, we must realize that:

> we have been the victims of our ethnocentrism, taking a functionally significant unit of our society—one that we regard as basic to society—and treating the nearest functional equivalent elsewhere as if it were, in some fundamental way, the same thing.
>
> . . . if our purpose is to develop a set of concepts to describe and compare *all* human societies—*all* distinct cultural communities—then the traditional concepts of marriage and

family are unsatisfactory, serving only as a negative standard of comparison, one that emphasizes degrees of difference from our own institutions and obscures what is common and basic to human societies generally (Goodenough 1970:5).

Chapter 10
CASHINAHUA NOTIONS OF SOCIAL TIME AND SOCIAL SPACE

The purpose of this chapter is to discuss Cashinahua notions of social time and social space by examining their classification of villages as ideal and proper. This will be done by attempting to determine why the Cashinahua insisted that certain villages were structurally identical when my observations as an ethnographer led me to conclude that there were significant structural differences between them.

The Cashinahua consider *mae*, the local community, the village, to be a microcosm of their society. In theory, each is socially, politically, and economically autonomous and is thus the local embodiment of their notion of social time and social space. This is not to argue that any actual Cashinahua village meets the ideal image informants paint for the ethnographer nor does it conform to any model created by the ethnographer by determining the statistical norms. Therefore, before discussing Cashinahua notions of social time and social space it would be useful to examine the village from both the perspective of the Cashinahua and that of the ethnographer.

The Proper Cashinahua Village

Using three polarities, the Cashinahua classify all villages as *mae kuin*$_1$ or *mae kuinman*$_1$, as *mae kuin*$_2$ or *mae bemakia*$_2$, and as *mae kayabi*$_3$ or *mae bemakia*$_3$. In each case, the terms can be translated as "real, true, or proper village" or "unreal, false, or improper village." (See chapter 7 for a discussion of these polarities.)

Although all Cashinahua informants agreed that it was highly unlikely that any village would be proper in the ideal sense, *mae kuin*$_1$, they insisted that proper villages, *mae kayabi*$_3$, could and did exist. Therefore, an examination of the distinction made by the Cashinahua between *mae kuin*$_1$ and *mae kayabi*$_3$ should permit us to isolate the ingredients necessary for classifying a village as proper.[1]

The ideal Cashinahua village, *mae kuin*$_1$, would consist of (1) two focal males (see chapter 14 for a discussion of this concept), who are double first cross cousins and have exchanged sisters in marriage, (2) their wives, (3) their sons who have exchanged sisters in marriage and are living with their respective fathers-in-law, and (4) their grandchildren. In the most ideal situation, the village would also include either parents and/or grandchildren of the focal males, assuming of course that all of these adults have married double first cross-cousins. Also, the focal males would prefer to have at least some of their brothers, each married to sisters of their wife/wives, residing with them. The social group thus formed should reside in an area where ample land is available for gardens and in which there is sufficient variety in the ecosystem for each adult male to have hunting territories that run the gamut of ecological niches used by the animal resources exploited by the Cashinahua (see chapter 2). Although the term *mae* primarily focuses on the social group occupying dwellings at a particular place, it also includes the houses, the garden sites and the hunting territories actually or potentially exploited by that social group.

In addition, the population should be large enough and contain persons with the requisite knowledge for leading rituals, for curing illnesses, and for dealing with the supernaturals. Informants were vague about just how many people were enough. If we use their notion of the ideal village, marriage, and so on, it is possible to estimate that the population would be between forty-four and ninety-two. (This estimate is derived from a highly ideal model of the society in which both focal males each have two wives, each of whom produces one son and two daughters. The sons of each focal male would exchange sisters in marriage and each wife would produce a son and two daughters, who would in turn produce forty-eight children—sixteen sons and thirty-two daughters.) If the ideal were to obtain, the focal males and their wives between them would know all of the rituals, one focal male would be *huni dauya*, an herbalist, and the other would be *huni mukaya*, a shaman (see chapter 22).

The ideal never obtains. Few marriages are contracted with persons who are actual double first cross-cousins. Persons who are not close kinsmen take up residence with them. Few, if any, village sites are blessed with ideal environmental settings, and the formal knowledge of ritual and medicine is possessed and practiced by persons other than the focal males and their wives.

Villages do exist, however, that the Cashinahua classify as proper, *kayabi*$_3$, as opposed to improper, *bemakia*$_3$. They consist of a social unit composed of (1) two males, actual or classificatory cross-cousins, who have exchanged sisters in marriage, (2) their wives, (3) their offspring, and (4)assorted other actual and classificatory kinsmen.

The Cashinahua do not consider villages where the two focal males have not exchanged sisters as wives to be real or proper, that is to say *kuin*$_1$ or *kayabi*$_3$, even in a minimal sense, until there has been a marriage between a son of one of these males and a daughter of the other, or better yet, sons of both have exchanged sisters in marriage. Prior to such marriages, the village could only be classified as *mae kuin*$_2$, a functioning village with at least two focal males, but lacking the stabilizing influence provided by marriage ties between them.

Although highly desirable, a full complement of ritual and medical specialists is not necessary in order for a village to qualify as *mae kuin*$_1$ or *mae kayabi*$_3$. Such a lack, however, results in less than full self-sufficiency for the village since it requires maintenance of ties with another village to obtain these services. Likewise, a proper village need not have equal access to adequate garden and hunting territories for all adult males. (Members of the village's social core, as founding members, have priority over members of the social appendages in their choice of gardening and hunting territories when a new village is established.) However, tensions leading to the fissioning of the village are likely to develop if some members of the village perceive the garden and hunting territories over which they have exploitative rights to be of inferior quantity and/or quality.

The social group membership of the focal males is another crucial factor in defining a proper village. In the ideal village, *mae kuin*$_1$, the focal males, as double first cross-cousins, are members of opposing moieties and at the same time members of alternating generation namesake groups linked by reciprocal marriage exchange (see chapters 7, 8, and 9). In the proper but not ideal villages, *mae kayabi*$_3$, the focal males must also be members of the opposing moieties and members of linked marriage sections. This rule holds even if they have not exchanged sisters in marriage.

In summary, a proper Cashinahua village consists of two matrilocally extended families headed by two males who have either exchanged sisters in marriage or who have arranged the marriage of at least a son of one male to a daughter of the other. Further, these two males are members of opposing moieties and have married women from the appropriate marriage section.

The Composition of Some Actual Cashinahua Villages

I turn now to an examination of the actual composition of several Cashinahua villages that I perceived as structurally different from one another. In this section, I am making no attempt to describe Cashinahua villages from the perspective of the Cashinahua themselves, but rather in terms of the categories of my own folk culture as enlarged by the categories of my professional anthropological culture (Goodenough 1970:104).[2]

In July 1955, there were three villages of Cashinahua along the Curanja River. Village A consisted of three households who had recently moved from another garden area with a single house into a new garden site where they constructed three houses (see figure 25). Household A1 consisted of (1) Awa, his wife, and two unmarried daughters, (2) his son, his son's two wives, and their two daughters, (3) the husband of Awa's recently deceased daughter and their two sons and his new wife. Household A2 consisted of (1) Noa, his four wives, his two young unmarried sons, and the son of one of his wives who was his late brother's widow, (2) his older son, the son's two wives, and two young children. Household A3 consisted of (1) Bidu and his two wives and a daughter by the older of the two wives and her daughter by a previous marriage, (2) two brothers of his wives, the wife of the elder brother, and two children, and (3) his half-brother and wife, and the wife's son by a prior marriage.

Household A1 and A2 were linked by marriage; Awa was married to a sister of Noa and Noa was married to a sister of Awa. Households

Figure 25: The Composition of Village A.

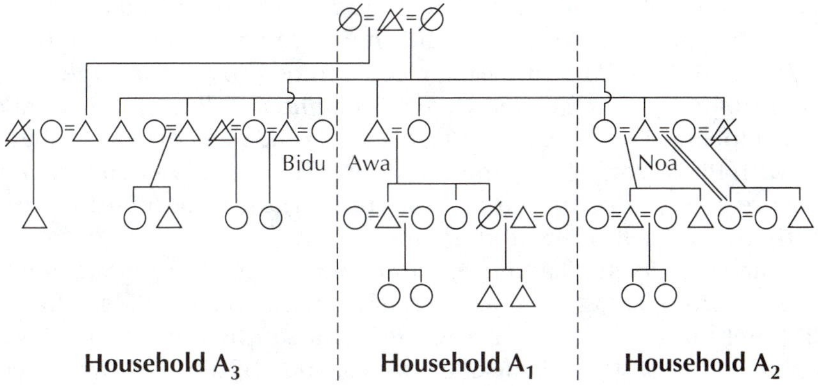

A1 and A3 were linked by consanguinity; Bidu is Awa's younger brother. Awa and Noa were the recognized leaders and focal males of the village; in addition Noa was recognized as an important herbalist, *huni dauya*.

Village B, located about four hours by dugout canoe upriver from Village A, consisted of two households (see figure 26). Household B1 consisted of (1) Pipi, his two wives and sons, (2) Tan, his wife, son, and daughter, (3) Dini, his wife, son, and daughter, and (4) Filo, his wife and son. Tan and Dini were both married to sisters of Pipi, who was married to a sister of Tan. Filo is Dini's brother and has no other consanguineal or affinal links to the household. Household B2 consisted of (1) Bimi, his two wives, three unmarried sons and daughters, his son-in-law, Ipu, who was married to two of Bimi's

Figure 26: The Composition of Village B.

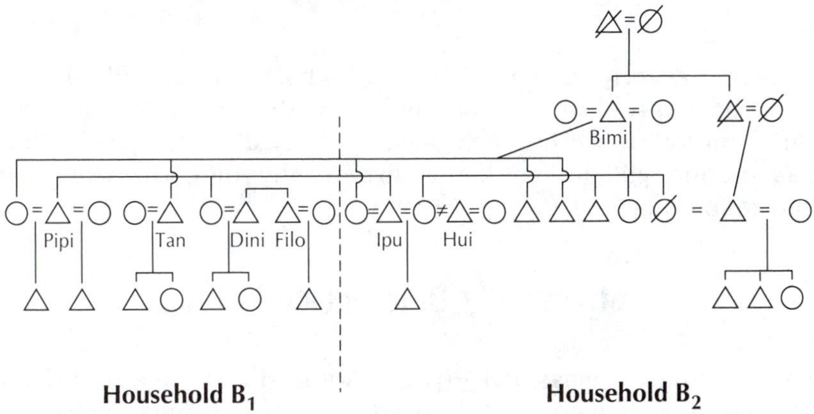

daughters, and Ipu's son, (2) Bimi's ex-son-in-law (who was also a half-brother of one of Bimi's wives) and current wife and (3) Bimi's older brother's son and wife and their two sons and a daughter.

Households B1 and B2 were linked by marriage and consanguinity. Pipi was married to a daughter of Bimi; Tan is Bimi's son. Pipi and Tan were recognized leaders and focal males of Village B, with Pipi clearly the dominant figure. Hui, Bimi's ex-son-in-law, was recognized as both a little shaman, *huni mukapishta* and a little herbalist *huni dauyapishta*.

Village C, located about an hour and a half by dugout canoe upriver from Village B, consisted of a single household (see figure 27) including (1) Toma, his two wives, a son by a prior marriage, and a young brother of one of his wives, and (2) Xiku, his two wives, three unmarried daughters, a son, the son's wife, and her son by a previous marriage. Toma and Xiku are brothers; neither was recognized as a leader.

Figure 27: The Composition of Village C.

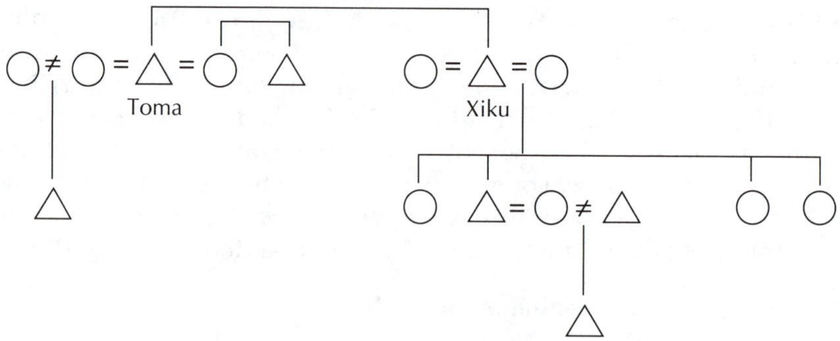

Further descriptions of other villages both similar and different from these three could be provided, but Villages A, B, and C are sufficient for answering the question "Why did I perceive certain Cashinahua villages as being structurally different while my informants insisted they were alike?"

Structurally Different or Alike?

The Cashinahua classified Villages A and B as *mae kayabi*$_3$ and Village C as *mae bemakia*$_3$. They agreed that all three villages were mae *kuinman*$_1$. Only Toma and Xiku and some of their co-residents agreed that their village, C, was *mae kuin*$_2$; most informants insisted that it was *mae bemakia*$_2$ (see chapter 7). All were agreed, however, that Villages A and B were like each other but unlike Village C.

I, on the other hand, perceived all three to be different. Village A was composed of two patrilocally extended families, Households A1 and A2, linked by the exchange of sisters between its two heads-of-family. Household A3 was an appendage to Household A1. In contrast, Village B was composed of Household B1 consisting of the nuclear families of two males who had exchanged sisters in marriage, their wives and children plus some appendages, Dini and Filo, and Household B2 consisting of a matrilocally extended family and appendages, the head of the household's ex-son-in-law and family and his older brother's son and family. In light of such evidence, I concluded that Village A and B were structurally different.

My informants' perceptions of Villages A and B led them to a different conclusion than mine because they were operating with different criteria or standards. Villages A and B were alike because both contained a social core composed of two focal males, linked by sister exchange, plus their household or households. Furthermore, this social core contained representatives of both moieties and all four marriage sections. Village C, on the other hand, did not contain appropriate male representatives of one moiety and two marriage sections. (In contrast, I had concluded that Village C differed from Villages A and B, in that it was composed of one patrilocally extended family and one nuclear family, linked by siblingship.)

Are Villages A and B structurally different or alike? If the standards used are those by which I judged them to be different, then indeed, they are different. However, in this essay I am attempting to describe Cashinahua culture and must therefore operate within the confines of their standards, and by those standards I must conclude the Villages A and B are alike.

What then are the Cashinahua views of social time and social space embodied in Villages A and B, which cause them to classify these villages as *mae kayabi*$_3$?

Cashinahua Social Time and Social Space

The ideal village, *mae kuin*$_1$, is a complete society, totally self-sufficient and self-propagating. Although no Cashinahua village is *mae kuin*$_1$ in fact, it is the ideal village that perfectly represents Cashinahua notions of social time and social space and provides the standards by which the Cashinahua judge whether or not a village is *kuin*$_1$ or *kuinman*$_1$, *kuin*$_2$ or *bemakia*$_2$, and *kayabi*$_3$ or *bemakia*$_3$.

The ideal village consists of a social core plus possible appendages. The social core is composed of two focal males and their primary cognates. Appendages would be persons who are the *nabu kuin*$_1$, the real or close kinsmen of the focal males or other members of the social core, as opposed to *nabu kuinman*$_1$, nonkinsmen.

In its ideal form, Cashinahua society, like the ideal village, is a well-defined closed social unit. People are either *huni kuin*$_1$, real men, or they are *huni kuinman*$_1$, unreal men, that is nonpeople. The ideal society is totally self-contained and exists in an area with ill-defined borders, where social activity is concentrated at the center, the village (the social core of which also is theoretically self-contained), and where little or no social activities occur at the periphery. There is an awareness that their world is not limitless but is sufficiently large so that contact between persons from different societies or villages during day-to-day activities would be unlikely.

Furthermore, the Cashinahua village, like the larger society, is divided into two male and two female moieties. The moieties are the glue that unites the autonomous units, villages, into a single society; they never function as social groups at the level of the total society. Rather, it is the local representatives of these groups who interact and intermarry. Any Cashinahua may operate as a member of his/her moiety in whatever village he/she might find him or herself. Thus, a Cashinahua's social space is defined by membership in a village, a moiety, and a society.

Social time is defined by the alternating generation namesake groups, or marriage sections, into which each moiety is divided. All members of one's moiety are either members of one's section or they are not. Each section, in turn, contains the significant moiety mates of one's lifetime. One's own section contains those from whom one receives one's name and those to whom one gives one's name. The other section of one's moiety also consists of persons who are older or younger, namely, one's father and one's son.

It is tempting to argue that social time for the Cashinahua consists of a five-generation span, consisting of the generations of one's FF, one's F, one's self, one's S, and one's SS. Such is not the case, however, because the Cashinahua do not count their own generation as a separate generation. Ego is always either the name receiver or the name giver, the one who is sired or sires, resulting in two cycles linked by paternal filiation, each consisting of only two generations. Persons who are members of ego's generation are equated with the senior generation if older than ego, and with the junior generation if younger than ego. Thus, for the Cashinahua, two plus two equals four, not five.

Social Time, Social Space, and the Proper Village

Cashinahua social time and social space are defined by and embodied in the sections and moieties. In order for a village to be classified as *mae kayabi*$_3$, it must contain all of these social units, that is, it must have persons who are members of both of the male and female moieties and all four sections. However, the mere presence of representatives of the moieties and sections is inadequate unless these persons are linked in appropriate ways. Each proper village must include (1) two focal males who are members of different moieties and different sections but of the same generational level, (2) the focal males must have exchanged sisters in marriage and produced offspring creating what for want of a better term I will call an *atom of social organization* (see figure 28), that forms the basis of (3) the social core composed of the household or households of the focal males. These are the *sin qua non* of a *mae kayabi*$_3$. However, the term implies other social conditions, namely that although all proper villages contain focal males, an atom of social organization, and a social core, they may be highly variable in other respects without changing the fundamental structure of the groups. The variability is a result of the vicissitudes

Figure 28: An Atom of Cashinahua Social Organization.

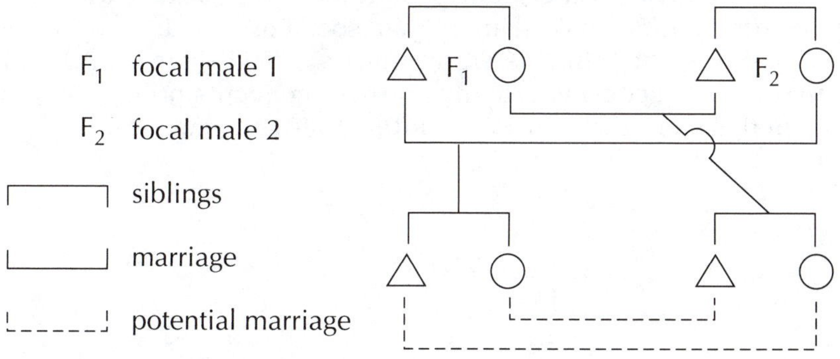

of life such as untimely death, unbalanced sex ratios resulting in the lack of an ideal spouse, and so on. It matters little if the marriage exchange has taken place between actual double first cross-cousins, or if the social core is composed of the nuclear families of the focal males or of patrilocally or matrilocally extended families, or if social appendages are absent or present in whatever form. If a village contains focal males, an atom of social organization, and a social core it is *mae kayabi*$_3$, a proper village.

Thus, when my informants insisted that Villages A and B were alike, they considered them to be conditioned variants of a single structural unit just as English speakers judge [p^h], [p] and [$p^{\cdot}$] to be conditioned variants of the phoneme /p/.

Conclusions

Joanna Overing Kaplan (1977:9–10) has suggested that ethnographers studying lowland South American societies have been ill served by the concepts and categories based on the analyses of social systems in Africa, Asia, and Oceania and has called on us "to rethink some basic problems of analysis in Lowland social organization." In this chapter, I have examined how an analysis of Cashinahua social organization based on Cashinahua criteria resulted in an answer different than the one resulting from using the categories of my folk culture and my professional anthropological culture. Ward Goodenough (1970) has argued that the conceptual tool kit, etics, used by the ethnographer must be revised continuously in light of analyses of particular societies based on the criteria used by each society, that is, emic analysis. I would suggest that my analysis of the Cashinahua village provides several potentially useful additions to that tool kit, (1) focal males, (2) social core and appendages, (3) four-generational time rather than five-generational time, and (4) an atom of social organization based on two males exchanging sisters in marriage and their offspring. It remains to be seen what, if any, of these concepts prove useful in the analysis of other lowland South American societies.

Chapter 11
THE DIALECTICS OF PERSON AND SELF

In structural theory, the structure of the psyche is universally the same, and the working of the mind involves a continual process of sorting one's perceptions into paired opposites, which are then reconciled. In short, the mind works in a dialectical fashion. In the first place, the stream of consciousness becomes broken up into discrete events and things, which are usually reducible to words. We chop up and distort the flow of reality in this process, but words and language are the only ways in which we can think of our world and by which we can communicate these thoughts to others. We fracture and break up our perceptions, but we have no choice. How we do this is where the dualism of thought comes in. Fundamentally, we arrive at our delineation and definition of objects, which we express in words and symbols, by defining what an object is not, as well as what it is. . . . Words and symbols, the very substance of our thought, are given definition by their otherness. This allows us to break up reality and reduce it to the hard, objective status of the word. At the same time, it does certain violence to the human grasp on reality. . . . the same mind that sets up these oppositions is also continually trying to mend them, to reconcile them, and to synthesize their antithesis.

Robert F. Murphy 1979:27–28

When I began my studies with the Cashinahua, I was not looking for dialectical oppositions in their social structures, worldview, and the like. I slowly became aware of these as I tried to understand what my informants meant when, in discussing their relationship with others, they said of certain persons that he is "my real father" (*en epakuin*) or "my not-real father" (*en epakuinman*). On other occasions they spoke of the same persons as "*en epakayabi*" or "*en epabemakia*," again glossed "my real father" or "not-real father." All agreed in these cases that alter was *epa* to ego. It was during my search for the meaning of *kuin*, *kuinman*, *kayabi*, and *bemakia* (see chapter 7) that I became aware of how the Cashinahua define *person* and *self*, concepts that are central to the most fundamental dialectical opposition in Cashinahua social thought, and the focus of many of the tensions of social life, tensions between society's demands and individual desires, between sociocentricity and egocentricity.

In my first attempts to define the morphemes *kuin*, *kuinman*, *kayabi*, and *bemakia*, I segregated them into two pairs, *kuin* versus *kuinman* and *kayabi* versus *bemakia*, the second element of each pair being the negation or opposite of the first. Both pairs could be glossed real versus unreal, true versus false. In other contexts they could also be glossed as known versus unknown, familiar versus unfamiliar, actual versus hypothetical, primary versus secondary, central versus peripheral, and close versus distant.

With these pairs of contrasting morphemes in hand, I systematically attempted to find out from my informants how they used the pairs with reference to kin terms. Informants were most cooperative and patient as I went through the list of people asking, "Is he/she your *kuin/kuinman/kayabi/bemakia*?" and recorded their responses. I then went through the list asking, "Is he/she so-and-so's *kuin*, etc.?,"—in other words, using a third-person frame rather than a first-person frame.

It quickly became clear that there was a high degree of disagreement among informants about how they classified kin. There was virtually unanimous agreement when the third-person frame was used with the *kuin* versus *kuinman* pair and a high degree of agreement in the third-person frame with the *kayabi* versus *bemakia* pair. However, when I used the first-person frame, responses differed widely. In fact, one informant gave me a partially different classification of his kin relationship six months after his first classification.

What, if anything, had happened in the intervening six months between his two classifications? The only significant change was that he had added a third wife to his family, a marriage that all informants agreed was a bad marriage in that it violated the rule of moiety exogamy (see chapter 9). He had married a classificatory sister. All the changes in his classification of kin were a result of this marriage. Furthermore, only he and his new wife consistently classified her as *ainkuin*, his "real wife."

It was this fact that forced me to reexamine my hypothesis that the Cashinahua were using two morpheme pairs. In fact, they were using three pairs, $kuin_1$ versus $kuinman_1$, $kuin_2$ versus $bemakia_2$, and $kayabi_3$ versus $bemakia_3$, what I have referred to in chapter 7 as polarities 1, 2, and 3, respectively. Further checking revealed that the disagreements between informants (and between the responses of a single informant six months apart) were largely disagreements about how kin were to be classified using polarity 2, rather than polarities 1 and 3.

Continued questioning and analysis led me to the conclusion that polarities 1, 2, and 3 stand in a dialectical relationship to each other. Polarity 1 represents a highly idealized view of the world. The classification of objects, relationships, behavior, and so on, using polarity 1, is based on strict adherence to this idealized model of the world, on strict adherence to the jural norms. It is sociocentric, fixed, rigid, and unchanging.

Polarity 2 is totally egocentric. Each ego classifies things largely as he/she sees fit; others may accept or reject his/her classifications. There are limits, however. For example, should ego classify his/her biological mother as *bemakia* rather than *kuin*, the classification would be rejected by all, no matter what ego's reasons for doing so.

Polarity 3 is a pragmatic alternative to polarity 1. It is based on the recognition that the ideal is often either impossible or impractical to realize. Unlike polarity 2, it is not based on the whims of ego, but represents a social consensus and thus is sociocentric. Polarity 3 produces categories that are more or less closed and fixed; some elements are obligatorily *kayabi* or *bemakia*.

Polarity 1 differs from polarities 2 and 3 in one further fundamental respect. The dualism of polarity 1 is a diametric opposition, A versus nonA. The dualisms of polarities 2 and 3 are concentric, the relationship of part to whole, or center to periphery. This same contrast between diametric versus concentric dualism can be seen in Cashinahua social structure.

Like the societies described by David Maybury-Lewis (1979) and his colleagues in *Dialectical Societies*, the Cashinahua distinguish between the ceremonial sphere and the domestic sphere. They do not, however, give this contrast on-the-ground representation in the form of a central men's house versus the peripheral domestic dwellings.

The ceremonial sphere is dominated by the patrimoieties subdivided into two marriage sections (see figure 29). The relationship between the moieties is a diametric dualism of opposition and equality. The moieties regulate ritual interaction and marriage.

Figure 29: The Relationship between Moieties and Marriage Sections.

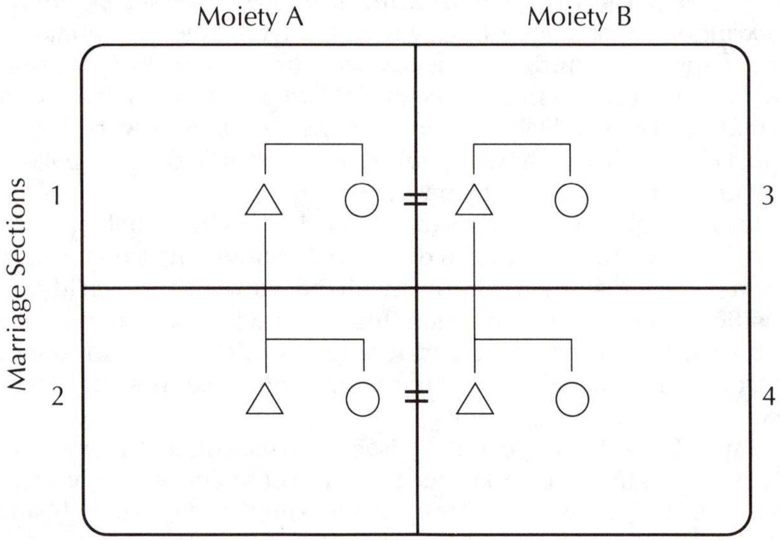

The domestic sphere is dominated by ego's bilateral network of kin beginning with ego's nuclear families of orientation and procreation, extending to the members of the uxorilocally extended families of which ego is a member and beyond to include all Cashinahua. The dualism is concentric, between center and periphery, between close and distant kin. Ego has rights and duties vis-à-vis all kin, the degree of privilege and obligation ego has toward each is defined by the closeness or distance of the relationship. Polarity 1 distinguishes primary from nonprimary kin within ego's network. Polarity 3 distinguishes ego's close (including primary) kin from distant ones. Ego uses polarity 2 to define a network of close and distant kin (which may or may not coincide with the network defined by polarities 1 and 3) as a basis for manipulating and regulating the manner and extent to which he/she will respond to the demands of, or will make demands on, others.

The domestic sphere, based as it is in uxorilocal residence, the authority of the father-in-law over the son-in-law, and the reciprocal obligations of economic exchanges, balances the power of the patrimoieties by dispersing male members, thus denying the moieties a residential base (see figure 30). At the same time, the power of the domestic sphere is limited by assigning almost exclusive control over ritual and symbols to the moieties and refusing, on the symbolic and ceremonial levels, to recognize and grant social significance to the egocentric networks and the extended families in which they are based. Against this background, we are now ready to turn to an examination of the Cashinahua concepts of *person* and *self*.

Figure 30: Cashinahua Moieties and Marriage Sections as Dispersed by Uxorilocal Residences.

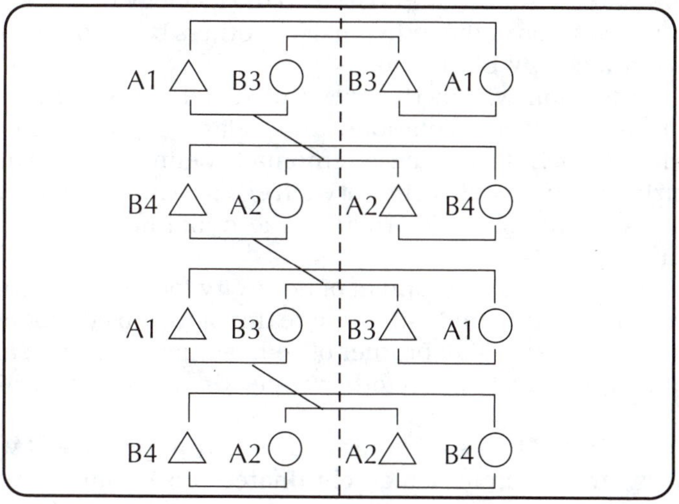

Person is defined primarily by membership in a moiety and a marriage section. From birth, each male is identified as a member of the moiety of his father and the marriage section of his FF; he also receives a set of names from FF, his namesake, *xuta*. Each female is identified as a member of the moiety of her father's sister and the marriage section of her MM (also ideally her FFZ) from whom she receives a set of names. Associated with the names ego receives is a set of designs that he/she uses for body decorations and for decorating objects ego makes. Membership in a moiety and a marriage section automatically defines ego as a member of specific kin categories vis-à-vis all other Cashinahua. This identity, unchanging for life, regulates the roles ego plays in ceremonial activities, restricts marriage choices, and ideally regulates social behavior. As such, *person* is sociocentric; all persons are equal and either opposite or same, and each *person* is expected to behave toward every other *person* in terms of that *person's* membership in a kin category vis-à-vis ego's membership.

Self, on the other hand, is defined primarily by the actual kin network established for each ego by birth and developed by each throughout life through the manipulation of socioeconomic exchanges, friendships, marriages, and so on. *Self* is egocentric, and the degree to which other *selves* are included or excluded in any ego's network depends at least in part on the intensity of social interaction between them. The freedom of each individual to manipulate the socioeconomic system to one's own advantage and to accumulate personal power based on the ideology of *self* is limited by the expectations of the individual and others based on the highly egalitarian ideology of *person*.

It is the tension within the arena of social action, the conflict between the rigid expectations and relatively inflexible rules regulating the behavior of the ceremonially defined *person* and the egocentric ambition and desires of each ego as a manipulator within the domestic sphere, that provides the dynamic of Cashinahua social life.

An examination of this conflict of necessity forces us into the real world of social action and out of the realm of idealized models. Let us look at the case of Bidi, brother of co-headman and co-focal male Awa, and cross-cousin of the other co-headman and co-focal male Noa.

Bidi was limited in his selection of a wife by a shortage of women created by an epidemic, which eliminated most eligible spouses. He therefore chose to marry two women in violation of the rules of moiety exogamy and marriage section prescription. His wives, defined by the concept of *person*, were members of Bidi's moiety, but not of his marriage section. Bidi argued, however, that they were actually the daughters of his father's female parallel cousin, that is, his father's classificatory sister, and therefore they were his cross-cousins. He argued further that he was not responsible for the fact that their mother had married badly, resulting in his wives belonging to the kin category "daughters" by virtue of their moiety and marriage section membership, rather than in the category "wives."

Some people agreed with the logic of Bidi's argument, accepted his marriages as valid and used *kuin* when referring to the kin relationships created by the marriages and in referring to the marriages themselves, but only in the sense of polarity 2, not polarity 1. When pressed on the subject, they readily agreed that Bidi had married his distant (*bemakia*) daughters, rather than close (*kayabi*) ones, making them subject to mild sanctions by the spirits, but sanctions that could be avoided by the use of appropriate medicines. However, the marriages, whether they were accepted or approved by others, did not change Bidi's *person* or that of either of his wives.

The situation created few problems in daily life. Bidi and his wives interacted with and, using polarity 2, classified people in terms of the kin roles appropriate to the nature of their interactions based on the way in which they chose to create their personal networks. Problems did arise in ceremonial contexts, however, most particularly during the initiation rites for Bidi's daughter and her age set. The conflict between Bidi's role as father, defined in terms of the *self* concept, and his ceremonial roles defined by the *person* concept, was resolved by his acting in the father role only in those aspects of the rituals where the focus was on his role as father. In all other aspects of the rituals, where the focus was on his role as a member of a moiety and a marriage section, another individual in the appropriate social category vis-à-vis Bidi's daughter served as substitute father, while Bidi operated in the role appropriate to his *person*.

A yet more serious problem arose when Awa and Noa decided to relinquish headmanship and Bidi made a bid for leadership. Despite his personal popularity and a general recognition of his leadership abilities, the community rejected his bid for formal leadership. The disparity between his *person* and his *self* created by his bad marriages prevented him from meeting the social requirements for being co-headman and co-focal male. Despite being disqualified from performing the ceremonial roles associated with formal leadership, however, Bidi continued to exercise considerable influence and informal leadership within the domestic sphere.

The case of the two males who did replace Awa and Noa as co-headmen and co-focal males illustrates the use of polarity 3. No candidates for these positions were qualified to fill the roles as defined by the ideal model, which requires two males, who are double first cross-cousins and thus members of the opposing moieties and of the linked but opposing marriage sections; who have exchanged actual sisters in marriage; and whose sons are expected to exchange sisters in marriage. Awa and Noa were double first cross-cousins and had exchanged sisters in marriage. Their sons Crow and Madi neither exchanged sisters in marriage nor married first cross-cousins. However, by the magic of polarity 3, their wives were transformed from *ainbemakia*, distant wives, to *ainkayabi*, close wives. As a result, Crow and Madi were able to fill the roles of co-headmen and co-focal males without doing serious violence to the model of Cashinahua society; all possessed the appropriate *person*.

Polarity 3 allows the Cashinahua to bridge the gap between the sociocentric cultural ideals represented by polarity 1 and the egocentric views represented by polarity 2. Not surprisingly, polarity 3 is sociocentric, giving priority to social order over personal desires. But that order is a practical order which, by mediating the conflicts that arise between the idealistic demands on the *person* and the unfettered desires of the *self*, allows for the continuity of social life.

Chapter 12
DUAL ORGANIZATION RECONSIDERED

In his classic essay "Do Dual Organizations Exist?" Claude Lévi-Strauss answers the question of his title in the negative, stating "triadism and dualism are inseparable, since dualism is never conceived of as such, but only as a 'borderline' form of the triadic type" (Lévi-Strauss 1963:151). In *Elementary Structures of Kinship* (Lévi-Strauss 1969) he held that dual organizations were expressions of reciprocity, a symmetrical relationship. In "Do Dual Organizations Exist?" he was concerned with the anomaly of societies with dual organization that have structures with an odd number of elements, for example, the presence of unilateral marriage where bilateral marriages would be expected on structural grounds.

Lévi-Strauss posits three structures: (1) diametric structures based on diametric dualism; (2) concentric structures based on concentric dualism; and (3) triadic structures. In diametric structures, the elements are separate and equal. However, these may be unequal but the inequality "does not stem from their basic nature, which is steeped in reciprocity" (139–140). In concentric systems, the elements are separate but unequal. They are characterized by one element being central, the other peripheral. "Concentric dualism is a mediator between dualism and triadism, since it is through the agency of the former that the transition takes place between the two'' (151).

Lévi-Strauss further argues that

> Diametric dualism is static . . . it cannot transcend its own limitations; its transformations merely give rise to the same sort of dualism as that from which they arose. But concentric dualism is dynamic and contains an implicit triadism . . . any attempt to move from an asymmetric triad to a symmetric dyad presupposes concentric dualism, which is dyadic like the latter but asymmetric like the former. (Lévi-Strauss:151)

Thus Lévi-Strauss solves the problem of dual organization, by defining it away.

Maybury-Lewis, in his trenchant response to Lévi-Strauss, ''The Analysis of Dual Organization: A Methodological Critique,'' sums up his objections as follows:

> 1) Much of the argument is invalidated from the start by errors of ethnographic interpretation.
>
> 2) Lack of precision in the definition of terms leads a dissertation on dual organization into a discussion of disparate dualisms, with the result that not only does Lévi-Strauss compare incomparables but he includes societies in his discussion where no dual organization, in the accepted sense, exists.
>
> 3) One of the fundamental analytical problems in the study of dual organization is that of the relation between social and symbolic dualism. Lévi-Strauss, by ignoring this distinction, confuses rather than clarifies the issue.
>
> 4) He fails to establish any adequate basis for his comparative analysis. (Maybury-Lewis 1960:40–41)

He, therefore, rejects ''Lévi-Strauss' specific hypotheses along with the evidence on which they are based'' (41).

With reference to point 2, above, Maybury-Lewis accurately points out that Lévi-Strauss neither sharply defines his subject matter nor provides a working distinction between the terms of dual organization, dual system, and dualism. The reader is left to infer Lévi-Strauss's definitions of such basic terms as ''diametric structure,'' ''concentric structure,'' and so forth, on the basis of his use of the terms. Maybury-Lewis uses the term ''concentric dualism'' in his analysis of Winnebago because it is ''an expression of a social:ecological relation, divorced from the dualism of the social system'' (20–21).

Maybury-Lewis further argues (see point 3 above) that:

> when Lévi-Strauss says that villages are actually arranged in concentric structures he is usually referring to the reflection of symbolic values. . . . rather than to any concentric dualism, involving segments of the society. (22)

He then suggests that:

> we must restrict the meaning of the term "diametric structure" to a village pattern, such that two moieties are located on opposite sides of the village circle. At the same time we must take the term "concentric structure" to apply only to societies where settlements are arranged on a circular pattern and there is a symbolic antithesis between the center and the periphery. (38)

Lévi-Strauss (1949:88, 107) sees dual organization as an expression of symmetric reciprocity. However, when he examines the content of reciprocal relations his analysis of "apparently dyadic antitheses which are found in conjunction with dual organization . . . may be represented as a point and a line, and thus considered analytically as triads and not dyads" (Maybury-Lewis 1960:40).

In contrast to Lévi-Strauss's position that dual organizations are expressions of symmetrical reciprocity and are in essence nothing but limited cases of triadic structures based on asymmetrical reciprocity, Maybury-Lewis suggests that "institutionalized reciprocity of the type found in dual organizations [is] a function of the bisection of society. Dual organization would then be thought of not as the expression of a principle of reciprocity but of a universal tendency to think in antitheses" (41–42). Thus, it appears that Maybury-Lewis finds the solution for the problem of dual organization in the psychic unity of mankind.

Maybury-Lewis concludes his paper by suggesting that since the features of social structure in societies with dual organization "may not always be rigorously dyadic and symmetric. . . . further research should investigate the possibility of a sociological as well as a formal link between dyadic and triadic structures" (43). It is against this background that I turn now to an examination of Cashinahua social structure.

Cashinahua society is divided into two patrimoieties, which are further subdivided by sex. The male segments are called *inubake* and *duabake* and their respective female segments are called *inanibake* and *banubake*. Males are members of their fathers' moiety segment; females are members of their FZ's moiety segment. An exception should be noted here: if a woman marries in violation of the moiety exogamy rule, her daughter must be a member of the opposite moiety (see figure 31).

The moieties are also divided into two alternating generation-namesake groups: *inubake* is divided into *awabake* and *kanabake*; *duabake* is divided into *yawabake* and *dunubake*. The moieties are exogamous, and are viewed as being bound in perpetual symmetrical exchange. Thus, inubake exchanges wives with *duabake*, *awabake* marry *yawabake* and *kanabake* marry *dunubake*.

Figure 31: Diagram Showing the Relationship between the Moieties (Inubake and Duabake) and the Alternating Generation-Namesake Groups (Awabake and Kanabake. Yawabake and Dunubake) and the Subdivisions of the Moieties by Gender (Inubake and Duabake—male, Inanibake and Banubake—female).

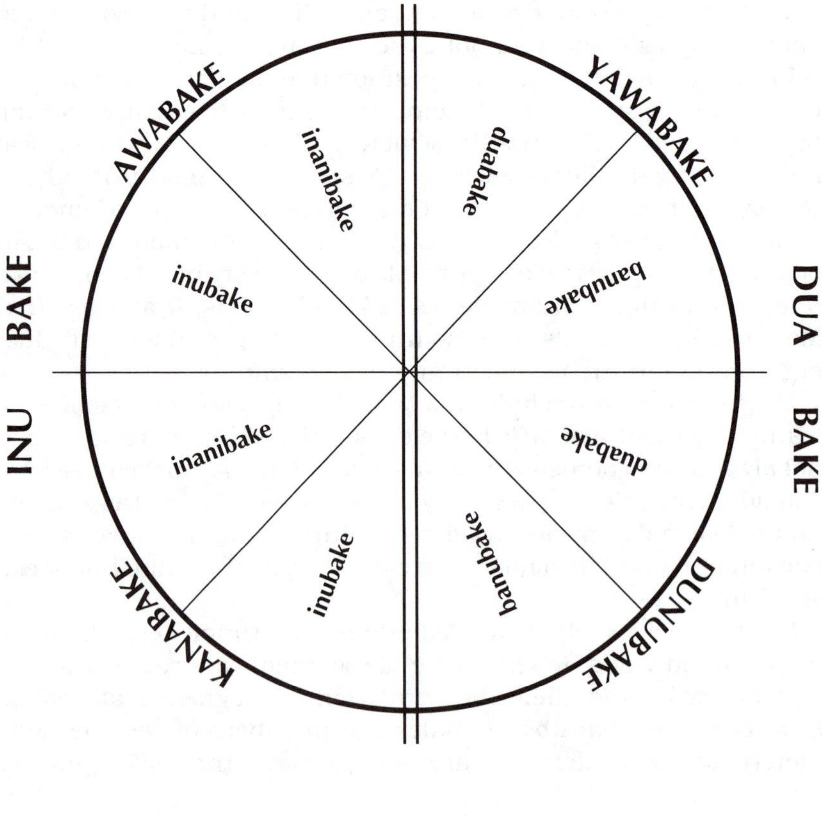

It is very tempting to attempt to analyze Cashinahua social structure in terms of A. K. Romney and P. J. Epling's 1958 model of Kariera double descent system, viewing *awabake*, *yawabake*, *kanabake* and *dunubake* as marriage sections; in fact, that is the way in which they operate. However, no social recognition is given to any social grouping based on matrilineal descent even though the rule of matrilocal postmarital residence results in de facto matrilineal groups consisting of Mo to Da to DaDa (see chapter 13 for further discussion of this point). In no case are a woman and her daughter members of the same moiety segment or alternating generation-namesake group. Furthermore, it is through her FZ that a woman receives her moiety affiliation and through her FFZ/MM that she receives her alternating generation-namesake group affiliation.

Although all of the structures above are diametric structures, only the moieties *inubake* and *duabake* constitute dual organization. Were I to follow Lévi-Strauss's lead, I could argue that the marriage sections *awabake* and *yawabake* constitute an endogamous unit and *kanabake* and *dunubake* constitute a second endogamous unit. Such an argument would do serious violence both to the ethnographic facts and the Cashinahua view of their own society. Although *awabake* marry only *yawabake* and vice versa, they do not perpetuate themselves. Their children are *kanabake* and *dunubake* respectively.

Each Cashinahua also sees the whole of the tribe from another point of view, *en nabu* and *en nabu betsa*, "my people" and "another of my people." (*Betsa* here means "other" or "another of the same sort"; as a kin term it also means "sibling of the same sex.") This view is basically a concentric structure (see figure 32). The distinction being made is that between my close kinsmen and my more distant kinsmen. The Cashinahua consider all other Cashinahua to be kinsmen; *en nabu* constitutes the core of the society from the perspective of each individual. His *en nabu* are his close bilateral kinsmen, a group which, ideally, is congruent with the co-residents of his local village. The structure of these groups is too complex to discuss in full here because rarely, if ever, does the ideal obtain. It is because of this lack of congruence between actual and ideal that it is possible to postulate a triadic structure in Cashinahua, that is, the contrast between *en nabu*, *madiabu*, and *en nabu betsa*. In every village, there are a variety of hangers-on, persons who are not part of the social core of the village. These persons are known as *madiabu*. Because they are co-residents, they are not *en nabu betsa*, but because they are not

Figure 32: The Concentric Structure of Cashinahua Society.

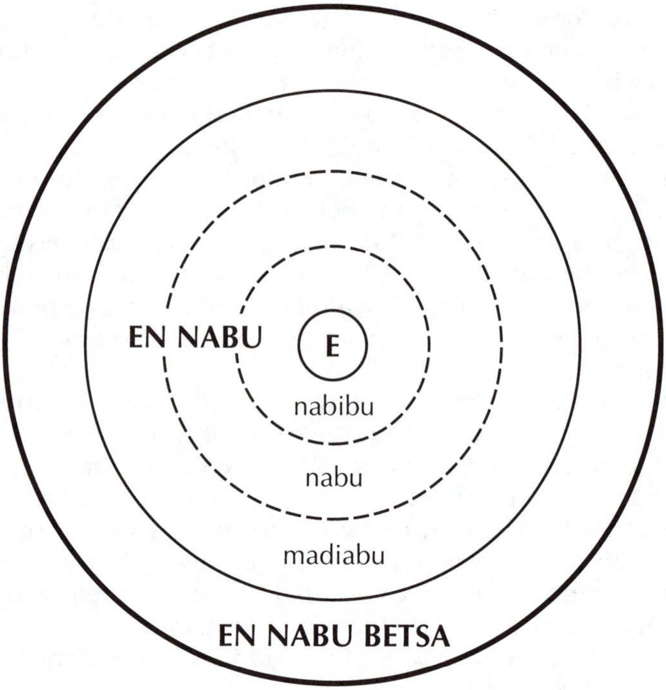

related or only distantly related to others in the village by consanguinity and/or affinity, they do not really belong.

Such an analysis, however, does considerable violence to the Cashinahua view of their society. The contrast is not between *en nabu*, *en nabu betsa*, and *madiabu* (see figure 33). Rather, the Cashinahua make a series of binary contrasts, resulting in *madiabu* being on a different contrast level in the taxonomic tree. So much for triadic structure in Cashinahua.

Returning to the concentric structure, the basic dualism is between a local village group and outsiders who are also Cashinahua. Ideally, each Cashinahua village is composed of two patrilines linked by perpetual sister-exchange, facilitated by a rule of double first cross-cousin marriage. As such, each village is an endogamous group. Such groups, however, are not and cannot be units in dual organization, because the contrast does not divide the society into two and only two groups. There are as many *en nabu* groups as there are villages.

Figure 33: A Taxonomic Representation of Figure 32.

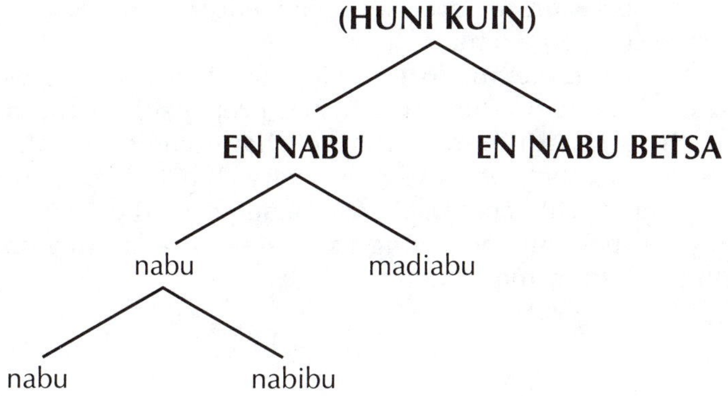

The difference between the diametric structure and the concentric structures in Cashinahua society is one of perspective. The moieties are sociocentric groups, while the local residential groups are egocentric groups.

Returning now to Lévi-Strauss and Maybury-Lewis: does dual organization exist? I would argue that for the Cashinahua society, it does exist and that to attempt to deal with it as a borderline case of triadic structure would do serious violence to the data. I would further argue that dual organization is and must be a diametric structure. The units are formally, structurally, and sociologically separate and equal. This is not to deny that inequalities might exist in such systems. I would suggest that such inequalities do not fundamentally affect the basic structure. Furthermore, the groups must be sociocentric, and membership must be mutually exclusive.

What, then, about concentric structures? I suggest that concentric structures can and often do coexist with diametric structures. However, they will never be forms of dual organization. Dualistic structures, yes. Dual organization, never, because the units are separate but not *equal*. I suspect that such structures will frequently be egocentric, of the sort "my group versus others."

The fact that such systems can and do coexist with diametric structures should not require us to abandon the notion of dual organization. The problem with Lévi-Strauss's analysis is that he tries to analyze these contrasting structures as parts of a single system. Each can and should be analyzed as an autonomous or at least a semi-autonomous system, with its own constituent roles, spheres of activity, and so on.

Concentric structures can be usefully analyzed as triadic structures. However, such an analysis is only justified when and if there is some on-the-ground social entity that can best be understood in such terms.

Finally, I am reluctant to join Maybury-Lewis in seeing dual organization as having its roots in the propensity of the human mind to think in antitheses. I suspect that dual organization has its roots, not in the *notion* of reciprocity, but in the real world, in the symmetrical reciprocal relationships in the social life of a society, perhaps in something as fundamental as two men exchanging sisters in marriage.

Chapter 13

PANOAN KINSHIP TERMINOLOGY AND SOCIAL ORGANIZATION

In this chapter I examine the problem of Panoan marriage section systems in terms of the internal logic of the systems rather than their relationship to problems of social organization in lowland South America. I will argue that some of the problems raised by Alf Hornborg (1988, 1991) and others regarding Dravidian/Kariera/two line/two section systems are a result of cultural bias in the models with which we work but are not problems from the perspective of the societies we study. Specifically, I refer here to the problems of the affinal status of mother and the "unilineal illusion" (Hornborg 1991).

As a base from which to begin an examination of Panoan kin terminology and social organization, let me summarize the defining features of the Cashinahua system, not only because I know it best, based on my own fieldwork, but because my data on the Cashinahua are more detailed and complete than the data I have on any of the other Panoans. Furthermore, the Cashinahua represent, I would argue, an example of the fullest logical development of what I will postulate as the proto-Panoan system.

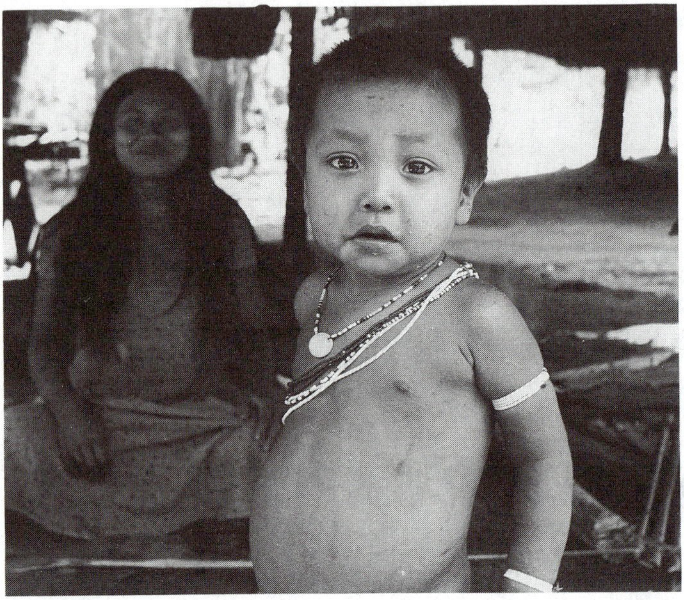

Kimu, a duabake *boy with his* inanibake *mother in 1957.*

Baxi, a inanibake *girl with her doll in 1957. She and her younger sister became the wives of Kimu.*

Kimu in 1993 with two of his daughters by Baxi, deceased, and her sister/co-wife.

Cashinahua Kin Terminology and Social Organization

The notion that all Cashinahua are kinsmen, *hunikuinbudan dasibi en nabuki*, is basic to an understanding of the kin terminological system. But not all *nabu* are *en nabukuin*, my real kin. *En nabukuin* is an egocentric, bilateral network of co-resident kin composed of ego's nuclear or polygynous family of procreation and ego's nuclear family of orientation, that is, ego's *nabibu*, plus the co-resident cross-sex siblings of ego's parents and their children.[1] At the core of each properly formed local community, *maekuin*, are two males who have exchanged sisters in marriage plus their offspring. One male must be a member of the *inubake* moiety; the other male must be a member of the *duabake* moiety. The sister of the *inubake* must be a member of the *inanibake* moiety while the sister of the *duabake* must be a member of the *banubake* moiety. An *inubake* male and his *inanibake* sister must be members of either *awabake* or *kanabake* marriage sections, while a *duabake* male and his *banubake* sister must be members of either the *yawabake* or *dunubake* marriage sections. An *awabake* marries a *yawabake* and a *kanabake* marries a *dunubake*.[2] A man is a member of his father's moiety and his FF's marriage section; a woman is a member of her FZ's moiety and of her MM's marriage section.

The cross-sex sibling relationship, *pui*, is the most basic and enduring social relationship in Cashinahua society, even more important in many respects than the mother-child, *ewa-bake*, relationship (see chapter 8). Children are expected to outlive their mothers, whereas *pui* are expected to be one's contemporaries throughout most of one's life. The *pui* relationship is characterized by affection, loyalty, and mutual support. The "unity of siblings" also is characteristic of the relationship between same-sex siblings, *betsa*, but this amity of *betsabu* is more likely to be attenuated by competition, disagreements, and petty squabbles than is acceptable between *puibu*.

Three additional terms are used to designate siblings, *huchi*, *chipi*, and *ichu* (older brother, older sister, and younger sibling). The *betsa* and *pui* relationships are defined as highly egalitarian; "we are all siblings." The relationship between elder and younger siblings, that is, between *huchi* or *chipi* and *ichu*, is hierarchal in character. There is the expectation that the elder brother will care for, economically support and assist, provide guidance and moral support for a younger sibling who in turn is expected to obey, cooperate with, and accept the leadership of the elder brother. Likewise, an elder sister is the source of warmth and affection; she often bears a heavy responsibility for the childcare of her younger siblings. In the face of conflicting demands or expectations, ego gives preference to the obligations due to *chipi* over those to all other kinsmen except possibly those of a mother to her child.

Sibling terms are extended to include all the members of ego's *xutabu*, that is, ego's marriage section, which also includes persons two generations older than ego, for example, FF and MM/FFZ, and persons younger than ego, as, SS and SD for male ego and DS and DD for female ego, also called *baba*. All of ego's *xutabu* are either *betsa*, same sex "sibling," or *pui*, opposite sex "sibling"; *xutabu* who are older are also *huchi* "elder brother" or *chipi*, "elder sister," and those younger are *ichu*, "younger sibling." However, MM is usually called *chichi* rather than *chipi*. In direct address, the vocative forms of *betsa* and *pui* are never used; instead, the vocative forms of the moiety names, *inun*, *duan*, *inanin*, *banun* are used.

All siblings, in the extended sense of that term, may be referred to as one's *xuta*, and be addressed as *xutan*. Use of the vocative moiety terms or *xutan*, rather than *huchin*, *chipin*, or *ichun* stresses the egalitarian nature of obligations between any interacting ego and alter rather than stressing the differential and hierarchal obligations that obtain between older and younger siblings.

Ego's father is *epa* and *epakuin* (vocative form *epan*, reciprocal for male alter is *epan*, for female alter is *achin*); all male members of father's marriage section are also *epa*, but not *epakuin*. FZ of a male is *achi* and *achikuin* (vocative form *achin*, reciprocal *epan*); all female members of father's marriage section are also *achi*, but not *achikuin*. FZ of a female is *yaya* (vocative form *yayan* is a self reciprocal) and *yayakuin*; her same sex marriage section mates are also *yaya*, but not *yayakuin*. Ego's mother is *ewa* and *ewakuin* (vocative form *ewan* is reciprocal for female alter, for male alter the reciprocal is *kukan*); all the female members of mother's marriage section are also *ewa*, but not *ewakuin*. Mother's brother is *kuka* and *kukakuin* (vocative form *kukan* is self-reciprocal for male alter, for female alter the reciprocal is *ewan*); all male members of mother's marriage section are also *kuka*, but not *kukakuin*.

A male ego calls his MBS and FZS *chai*, male cross-cousin or brother-in-law; a female ego calls her MBS and FZS *bene* or, if he is older, *chaita*, male cross-cousin or husband. The terms are extended to include all of alter's marriage section mates, including MF and for male ego DS, for female ego SS. DS and SS may also be called *baba*. A man addresses his *chai* as *chain* or by the appropriate vocative moiety term. A woman addresses her older cross-cousins as *chaitan*. She never uses the term *bene* in its vocative form to address a male cross-cousin; the appropriate vocative moiety term is used instead or she addresses him by his *ainin kena*, his "wife name," that is, the short name that is one of the set of names he receives from his FF or FFB.

A male ego refers to his FZD and MBD as *ain* or, if she is older, *xanu*. A female ego calls her FZD and MBD *tsabe*, or if she is older *xanu*. These terms are extended to include alter's marriage section mates. Both male and female egos use the term *xanu* for FM who is a member of the same marriage section as FZD and MBD. The vocative forms are *tsaben* and *xanun*. A man never uses the vocative form of *ain* but uses her *benen kena*, her "husband name," i.e., the short name which is one of the set of names she receives from her MM or MMZ.[3]

A man refers to his sons and daughters as *bake*; he addresses them as *epan* and *achin*, respectively. He may also refer to his sons as *beden*. A woman also refers to her sons and daughters as *bake*; she addresses them as *kukan* and *ewan*, respectively. The term *bake* is extended to include the sons and daughters of ego's same sex siblings and the same generation marriage section mates of both the sons and daughters.

A man refers to his ZS as *dais*, the same term a woman uses to refer to her BS. He addresses his ZS as *kukan*; she addresses her BS as *epan*. A man refers to his ZD as *babawan* (a contraction of *baban ewan*, grandchild's mother); a woman uses the same term to refer to her BD. A man addresses his ZD as *ewan*; a woman addresses her BD as *yayan*. For both male and female ego, DH is *dais* and SW is *babawan*.

Fundamental Features of Cashinahua Kin Terminology

I would like now to examine some of the defining features of the Cashinahua kinship terminological system, particularly as they relate to the moieties and marriage sections, two line terminology, unilineality, and unilocality.

For any ego there are eight core terms within the three medial generations. The + 1 generation consists of two sibling pairs, *epa-achi/yaya* and *kuka-ewa*, who between them provide ego either with siblings, *betsa* and *pui*, or with opposite sex cross-cousins/spouses, *ain* and *bene*, and same sex cross-cousins/spouse's siblings, *chai* and *tsabe*. These two sibling pairs in turn produce two sibling pairs on the – 1 generation level. Ego's cross-sex sibling, *pui*, provides cross cousins/spouses, *dais* and *babawan*, for ego's children, *bake*. These four sibling sets constitute the basis of the marriage section system; all other kin are included in the four sections by metaphorical extension.[4]

My informants consistently emphasized the unity of these sibling pairs. They argued that F and FZ together provide the primary kin of ego's generation. F provides ego with siblings; and *achi/yaya*, who is first and foremost FZ and only secondarily mother-in-law, provides her brother's children with cross cousins/spouses, *ain* and *bene*. My informants often reminded me that *achi/yaya* is always FZ, only sometimes, and then only after one has become an adult, does she become mother-in-law.

What then is the status of M and MB? Are they consanguines or affines? Although mother clearly provides male ego with siblings (the Cashinahua distinguish between full and half siblings), she does not provide him with a social identity. Males get their social identity, namely moiety membership, through their fathers and marriage section membership through their FF. Although females get their marriage section membership from their MM, and thus through their M, they get their moiety membership from their FZ. On the other hand, *kuka*, unlike *yaya*, contributes nothing to any ego's social identity. He is first and foremost MB, and secondarily father-in-law.

Ten terms remain to be fitted into the structure established by the four marriage sections. In ego's generation and the second ascending generation are *huchi*, older brother and FF; *chipi*, older sister and MMZ; *chichi*, MM; *chaita*, older FZS and MF of a female; *xanu*, older MBD. In the second descending generation, *baba* applies to all four types of grandchildren. However, for a male, his SS and SD are also classified as his *betsa* and *pui*, respectively, and as members of his marriage section, and his DS and DD are also classified as his FZ's children, *chai* and *ain*, respectively, and as members of the marriage section from which he selects his spouse(s). A woman also classifies her DD and DS with her *betsa* and *pui*, respectively, and her SS and SD with her FZ's children *bene* and *tsabe*, respectively, and as members of the marriage section from which she selects her spouse.

There are four terms for persons in the first descending generation: *bake*, son and daughter; *beden*, son of a male; *dais*, cross-sex sibling's son; and *babawan*, cross-sex sibling's daughter. Male informants often stressed that *beden*, son, and *bake*, daughter, are junior members of the marriage section of F and FZ, while *babawan* and *dais* are junior members of the marriage section of M and MB, reminding me that they are addressed by the vocative terms *epan*, *achin*, *ewan*, and *chain*, respectively.

On the second ascending generation the term *chichi*, which could be considered a variant of the term *chipi*, stands out in that, unlike the other four terms applied to persons at that generation level, it is never used to refer to older kin in ego's generation. Although the term may be used to refer to any female in the second ascending generation of ego's moiety and marriage section instead of *chipi*, most informants use the term only to refer to actual mother's mother. Her role is emphasized by the statement "*Chichidan en chipikuinki*," (*chichi* is my real older sister). Given uxorolocality, MM is usually the most significant senior woman, other than mother, in the life of a child. It is she who intervenes when mother is annoyed, who pampers, who cuddles and wipes away tears, who gives choice tidbits of food, especially when one is displaced by a newborn sibling.

The term *baba*, grandchild, is also a bit of an anomaly in that it violates the distinction between both moieties and marriage sections, but informants are quick to point out that not all grandchildren are the same. Both male and female ego classify the children of their sons as *betsa*, same-sex sibling, or as *pui*, opposite-sex sibling. They classify the children of their daughters as either same sex or opposite sex cross-cousin: DS is *chai* for a male and *bene* for a female; DD is *ain* for a male and *tsabe* for a female.

Cashinahua kin terminology is clearly a two-line system. The problems are, however, "How are the lines defined and what is the relationship between the two-line terminology and the moieties and marriage sections on one hand and to unilocal residence on the other?" I agree with Hornborg (1988) that unilineality is an illusion if, and only if, we define unilineality solely in terms of patrilateral transmission of membership in the sociocentric moieties and marriage sections.

Unilineality is implicit in Cashinahua kin terminology but it is a unilineality with reference to the sex of ego. Membership in the patrimoiety is transmitted from father to son for male ego. For female ego, membership in what is fundamentally a male concern, that is, the moieties, is transmitted through FZ. *Ego's membership in a marriage section is transmitted through the same sex parent and from that parent's same sex parent, that is, through F and from FF for male ego and through M and from MM for female ego.*

Although a review of my fieldnotes earlier led me to revise my analysis of the status of female moieties vis-à-vis the male moieties (see chapter 8), the significance of matrilineal transmission of marriage section membership for a female ego eluded me until I was working on this chapter. There are at least four reasons for my failure to understand what is clearly present in my fieldnotes: (1) I never had to view kin relations through the eyes of a female ego in my social interactions during fieldwork and found it difficult to do so when analyzing my field data. (2) I charted the distribution of all kin terms primarily in relation to the moieties; that is, ego's line was always patrilineally defined. (3) I worked with kinship terms from a male ego's perspective only (see figure 16), or I combined the terms for both male and female on a single chart (see figure 17) despite the fact that the distribution of terms from the perspective of a female ego never seemed right. (4) I never systematically compared the kin-type equations with reference to the factor of gender of ego (see figure 34). An examination of figures

Figure 34: Cashinahua Kin Terms by Alternating Generation and Sex of Ego.

MALE EGO			FEMALE EGO		
FF	**B**	**SS**	**FF**	**B**	**DS**
betsa	betsa	betsa	pui	pui	pui
huchi	huchi	baba	huchi	huchi	baba
	ichu	ichu		ichu	ichu
MM	**Z**	**DD**	**MM**	**Z**	**DD**
pui	pui	pui	betsa	betsa	betsa
chipi	chipi	ichu	chipi	chipi	ichu
chichi	ichu	baba	chichi	ichu	baba
MF	**MBS/FZS**	**DS**	**MF**	**MBS/FZS**	**DS**
chai	chai	chai	bene	bene	bene
		baba	chaita	chaita	baba
FM	**MBD/FZD**	**DD**	**FM**	**MBD/FZD**	**DD**
ain	ain	ain	tsabe	tsabe	tsabe
xanu	xanu	baba	xanu	xanu	baba
F	**S**		**F**	**S**	
epa	bake/beden		epa	bake	
M	**D**		**M**	**D**	
ewa	bake		ewa	bake	
MB	**ZS**		**MB**	**BS**	
kuka	dais		kuka	dais	
FZ	**ZD**		**FZ**	**BD**	
achi	babawan		yaya	babawan	

16, 17, and 34 highlights the problem. Note that Hornborg's charting of Cashinahua kin terms within a traditional Dravidian chart (see figure 35) also restricts itself to male ego.

Are the Cashinahua unilineal? If we focus on the moieties, they are patrilineal only if we interpret the female moiety sections to be subsections of the male moieties. If, however, our focus is on the marriage sections, we can say that the Cashinahua have a bilineal system of recruitment. When we focus on the localized kin groups that serve as the context of ego's day-to-day activities, the *nabukuin*, we are dealing with a bilateral kindred. The kin terminology reflects all three principles of recruitment.

Finally, there is the problem of whether or not mother is a consanguine or an affine. Hornborg (1991) has argued that "for any specific Ego, the kin-affine distinction is applicable only to alternate generations." I would suggest that for the Cashinahua, mother *is*

Figure 35: Cashinahua Kin Terms Arranged as a Dravidian System from Hornborg (1988:169).

GEN.	MALE		FEMALE			
+2	FF	*huchikuin*	FM	*xanukuin* *ainkuin*	MFZ	*xanukuin* *ainkuin*
	MF	*chaikuin*	MM	*chichikuin*	FFZ	*chichikuin*

KIN (Lineal kin, parallel collaterals, affines of affines) — *AFFINES* (In-laws, cross collaterals)

GEN.	KIN: MALE		KIN: FEMALE		AFFINES: MALE		AFFINES: FEMALE	
+1	F	*epakuin*	M	*ewakuin*	WF	*kukakuin*	WM	*achikuin*
	FB	*epakuin*	MZ	*ewakuin*	MB	*kukakuin*	FZ	*achikuin*
	MZH	*epakuin*	FBW	*ewakuin*	FZH	*kukakuin*	MBW	*achikuin*
0	B	e *huchikuin* *betsakuin* y *ichukuin*	Z	*chipikuin* *puikuin* *ichukuin*	WB	*chaikuin*	W	*ainkuin* *xanukuin*
					MBS	*chaikuin*	MBD	*ainkuin* e *xanukuin*
					FZS	*chaikuin*	FZD	*ainkuin* e *xanukuin*
					ZH	*chaikuin*		
−1	S	*bedenkuin* *bakekuin*	D	*bakekuin*	DH	*daiskuin*	SW	*babawankuin*
					ZS	*daiskuin*	ZD	*babawankuin*

GEN.	MALE		FEMALE	
−2	SS	*babakuin* *betsakuin*	SD	*babakuin* *puikuin*
	DS	*babakuin* *chaikuin*	DD	*babakuin* *ainkuin*

SOURCES: Kensinger 1984b:229.

DEVIATIONS FROM THE TWO-LINE PATTERN	CONCEIVABLE IDEOLOGICAL OR BEHAVIOURAL CORRELATES
FF=B, MF=MBS, FM=MFZ=FZD, B=SS, Z=SD, FZS=DS, MBD=DD	Alternating generations
FF≠ MF, FM=MFZ≠MM=FFZ, SS≠DS, SD≠DD	Lineal principles

a consanguine and that the kin-affine distinction is only relevant in ego's generation and that of ego's offspring. This is represented in figure 36.

Sexuality and affinity are an inherent part of the meaning of the relationship between cross cousins of the opposite sex. Informants

Figure 36: Cashinahua Kin Terms Organized as a Two-line System Showing Focal Kin Types Only.

MALE EGO					FEMALE EGO			
EGO'S LINE		OTHER LINE			EGO'S LINE		OTHER LINE	
MALE	FEMALE	MALE	FEMALE		MALE	FEMALE	MALE	FEMALE
FF huchi betsa	MM chichi chipi pui	MF chai	FM xanu ain	+2	FF huchi pui	MM chichi betsa	MF chaita bene	FM xanu tsabe
F epa	FZ achi	MB kuka	M ewa	+1	MB kuka	M ewa	F epa	FZ yaya
B huchi betsa	Z chipi pui	ZH/WB chai	W xanu ain	0	B huchi pui	Z chipi betsa	H chaita bene	BW/HZ xanu tsabe
S bake beden	D bake	DH dais	SW babawan	–1	S bake	D bake	DH dais	SW babawan
SS betsa baba	SD pui baba	DS chai baba	DD ain baba	–2	DS pui baba	DD betsa baba	SS bene baba	SD tsabe baba

consistently emphasized that opposite sex cross-cousins were the people whom one married and with whom one had premarital or extramarital sex. When questioned about it, they agreed that, although marriage and/or sex with the other members of the linked marriage section two generations removed was acceptable, it rarely happened because of age differences. Some informants viewed the possibility with distaste while others insisted that it was possible and advisable for a boy to be introduced to sex by his FM and a girl by her MF.

The kin-affine distinction is also relevant in the – 1 generation, I would argue, because the offspring of ego's cross-sex siblings are or will be the spouses and sexual partners of ego's children. Parents, particularly mothers, are concerned about marrying off their children even in Cashinahua society. Many female informants expressed concern about the unmarried status of their sons, about who would cook his meals, make his hammock,[5] and tend his garden. However, they rarely expressed similar concerns about their daughters who would in all likelihood be married before or shortly after puberty.

Toward a Proto-Panoan Kinship System

It is impossible for me to provide as detailed an analysis of the other Panoan groups as the summary of the Cashinahua just presented. Hornborg (1988:161–171) has nicely summarized the data available on the Amahuaca, Mayoruna (here listed as Matses), and Sharanahua. I add here data on Cashibo, Capanahua, Marubo, Matis, and Shipibo, and also additional data on the Matses. Tables 1 through 9 provide the kin terminologies available to me.

All the Panoan kin terminologies are two-line in character. Amahuaca, Cashibo, and Shipibo equate FF with MF and MM with FM in typical Dravidian fashion. Like the Cashinahua, the Capanahua, Marubo, Matis, and Sharanahua differentiate all four grandparents and equate them with the four kin categories of ego's generation. Matses has alternate terms for MF; one term equates MF with FF, the other does not. Despite this anomaly, the Matses appear to follow the Cashinahua pattern. In the generation of grandchildren the evidence is less clear because our data are less complete. In Amahuaca, *xota* or a form of it is used for FF and a man's SS and woman's DS, just as is the cognate xuta in Cashibo. In Marubo FF is equated with older B and B with SS for a male, DS for female; MM is equated with Z, and with SD for male, DD for female; MF is equated with FZS and with DS for male, SS for female; FM is equated with MBD/FZD. In Matses, identical or related terms equate ego's generation to the +2 generation. The Matis follow the Cashinahua pattern, except that the equations use alternate terms in ego's generation to make the links. Capanahua and Sharanahua are similar to Cashinahua in showing links/equations between ego's generation and the +2 generation.

In the +1 and -1 generations links or equations appear in some of the terminologies. See, for example, in Matis the equation of M and ZD for male and BD for female and the equation of FZ with D; the equation of MB and ZS for male and BS for female. These are, like in Cashinahua, equations consistent with patrilineality. On the other hand in Marubo, the equations by a female ego of F with ZS for male and BS and of MB with S and F with BS indicate matrilineality, congruent with the possibility of matrimoieties suggested by Julio Melatti (1977).

It would appear then that two patterns are reflected in the Panoan terminologies: traditional Dravidian two-line terminology (Shipibo and Cashibo), for which there is little or no evidence of moieties and/or marriage sections; and a Kariera-like two-line terminology

(Cashinahua, Capanahua, Marubo, Matis, Matses, and Sharanahua) for which there is clear or suggestive evidence for moieties and/or marriage sections. Gertrude Dole (1979) suggests that the Amahuaca once had moieties. Proto-Panoan social organization in all likelihood was based on persistent symmetrical marriage exchange, probably of the sister exchange sort. Whether or not the exchange was between moieties and marriage sections or between cognatic groups is less clear.

Finally, a brief comment on whether or not the Cashinahua pattern is Kariera. The only significant difference between Kariera and Cashinahua occurs in the kin equations dealing with kin in the second generation ascending and descending. For the Kariera, FF = SS and SD, MF = DS and DD for male ego; MM = DS and DD, FM = SS and SD for female ego. In Cashinahua, FF = SS, MM = SD, MF = DS, and FM = DD for male ego; FF = DS, MM = DD, MF = SS, and FM = SD for female ego. Both terminological systems suggest patrilineal transmission for males and matrilineal transmission for females. The Cashinahua maintain the distinctions between the B-Z pairs on each generational level while the Kariera use only the appropriate same-sex term from each pair. Is the difference significant? I am not sure, but my sense of loyalty to the Panoans makes me hope it is.

Table 1: Amahuaca Kin Terms by Alternating Generation Clusters

	FF	**B**	**SS,m/DS,f**
m.	ïpaxïndi xotaxïndi	wïtsa hochi ol. chambi yr.	wawa xota
f.	ïpaxïndi	pui hochi ol. chambi yr.	wawa
	MM	**Z**	**SD,m/DD,f**
m.	ï'axïndi chuaxïndi	pui chuka ol. chipi yr.	wawa
f.	ï'axïndi	wïtsa titi ol. chipi yr.	wawa
	MF	**MBS/FZS**	**DS,m/SS,f**
m.	hochixïndi ïpaxïndi	ïnra	wawa
f.	hochixïndi	wïndï	wawa
	FM	**MBD/FZD**	**DD,m/SD,f**
m.	ï'axïndi	a'in	wawa
f.	ï'axïndi	chaiya	wawa
	F	**S**	
m.	ïpa ïpatsa	wakï	
f.	ïpa ïpatsa	wakï rarï wïrï	
	M	**D**	
m & f	ï'a	a'inwakï	
	ï'atsa yaxui	wakï (xando)	
	MB	**ZS,m/BS,f**	
m.	kuka	pi'a	
f.	kuka	rarï	
	FZ	**ZD,m/BD,f**	
m.	achi	xotan'a	
f.	achi	achi	

Table 2: Capanahua Kin Terms by Alternating Generation Clusters

	FF	**B**	**SS,m/DS,f**
m.	xohta	bocha	
f.	xohta	poi ol. roha yr.	baba
	MM	**Z**	**SD,m/DD,f**
m.	chichi	choca	
f.	chichi	hohshi ol. shara yr.	
	MF	**MBS/FZS**	**DS,m/SS,f**
m.	chahi	chahi	
f.	chahita	bene bene huetsa HB bene ahte other than H	baba
	FM	**MBD/FZD**	**DD,m/SD,f**
m.	xano	haibu hawin hutsa hawin ati	baba
f.	xano also MMB	tsabe also BW	baba
	F	**S,m/BS,f**	
m.	papa papahuetsa coca	baque	
f.	papa papahuetsa coca MZH??	baque hihna BS huanoni BS/BDH	
	M	**D**	
m.	mama mamahuetsa	baque	
f.	mama mamahuetsa	baque hihni BD	
	MB	**ZS,m/BS,f**	
m.	coca	huanoni piasha	
f.	coca	huanoni	
	FZ	**ZD,m/BD,f**	
m.	achi		
f.	yaya	hihni also BSW	

Table 3: Cashibo Kin Terms by Alternating Generation Clusters

	FF	**S**	**SS,m/DS,f**
m.	xuta	xucën buchi ënchi	baba xuta
f.	bënta FFB	rarë bacë buchi/pui ol. ëchi yr.	baba xuta
	MM	**Z**	**SD,m/DD,f**
m.	chichi	chirabacë pui/enchi	baba
f.	chichi	xucën chuchu ol. ënchi yr.	baba
	MF	**MBS/FZS**	**DS,m/SS,f**
m.	xuta	chai chata	baba
f.	bënta	bënë H bënë itsi ZH bënta xuta yr.	baba chai
	FM	**MBD/FZD**	**DD,m/SD,f**
m.	chichi	aini ainitsi xanu	baba
f.	chichi	tsabë ñe xuta	baba
	F	**S**	
m.	papa papaitsi FB	bacëbëchicë nacë	
f.	papa xuta	bacë tuá	
	M	**M**	
m.	tita titaitsa MZ	bëchicë	
f.	tita titaitsa MZ	tuá	
	MB	**ZS,m/BS,f**	
m.	cucu	piaca	
f.	cucu	piaca/papa xuta	
	FZ	**ZD,m/BD,f**	
m.	nachi WM	piaca/aini/xanu	
f.	ñe [also BW] xuta [also HM/BD]	piaca	

Table 4: Cashinahua Kin Terms by Alternating Generation Clusters

	FF	**B**	**SS,m/DS,f**
m.	huchi/ betsa	betsa huchi ichu	baba betsa ichu
f.	huchi pui	huchi ichu pui	baba pui ichu
	MM	**Z**	**DD,m/SD,f**
m.	chichi chipi pui	pui chipi ichu	baba pui ichu
f.	chichi chipi betsa	betsa chipi ol. ichu	baba betsa ichu
	MF	**MBS/FZS**	**DS,m/SS,f**
m.	chai	chai	baba chai
f.	chaita bene	bene chaita ol.	baba bene
	FM	**MBD/FZD**	**DD,m/SD,f**
m.	xanu ain	ain xanu	baba ain
f.	xanu tsabe	tsabe	baba tsabe
	F	**S**	
m.	epa	beden bake	
f.	epa	bake	
	M	**D**	
m & f	ewa	bake	
	MB	**ZS,m/BS,f**	
m & f	kuka	dais	
f.	kuka	dais	
	FZ	**ZD,m/BD,f**	
m.	achi	babawan	
f.	yaya	babawan	

Table 5: Marubo Kin Terms by Alternating Generation Clusters

	FF	**B**	**SS,m/DS,f**
m.	ochtxo/ otxi	otxi ol. buchi/bicha taque=baque ebemera [half B through F]	srocó bicha
f.	ochtxo/otxi	otxi ol. bicha yr. onibaque ebemera srabo	baba onibaque [half Z through F]
	MM	**Z**	**SD,m/DD,f**
m.	txichtxo/ txitxo	txitxo ol. txira yr. taque	txitxo txira
f.	txichtxo	txitxo ol. txira yr. taque	srocó [associated with naming transmission] txira
	MF	**MBS/FZS**	**DS,m/SS,f**
m.	txaitxo	baba MBS txaitxo FZS	baba/txai
f.	txaitxo	bene H txai/baba baba	baba txai
	FM	**MBD/FZD**	**DD,m/SD,f**
m.	paîtxo	pano/aî	baba
f.	paîtxo/ [vr of pano]	tsabe pano/baba	baba
	F	**S**	
m.	papa epa FB epatxo ol.	baque yome epasrco	[-txo=older;-srco=younger]
f.	papa epa FB	baque yome coca ZS	
	M	**D**	
m.	ewa	baque/natxisrco BD	
f.	ewa/ewatxo	baque/ewasrco SD	
	MB	**ZS,m/BS,f**	
m.	coca ol. srabõtoa yr.	srabõtoa yr. coca ol.	
f.	coca/cocatxo	epasrco	
	FZ	**ZD,m/BD,f**	
m.	natxi/nachitxo	ewasrco	
f.	natxi	natxisrco	

Table 6: Matis Kin Terms by Alternating Generation Clusters

	FF	**B**	**SS,m/DS,f**
m & f	buchi	buchi ol. mashku yr.	baba mashku
	MM	**Z**	**SD,m/DD,f**
m.	chichi	chuchu ol. chibi yr.	baba
f.	chichi	chuchu ol. chibi yr.	baba chibi
	MF	**MBS/FZS**	**DS,m/SS,f**
m.	chayro	dawës kaniwa	kaniwa baba
f.	buntaro	buntaro ol. kaniwa yr.	kaniwa baba
	FM	**MBD/FZD**	**DD,m/SD,f**
m.	shanon	shanon ol. kaniwa yr.	kaniwa baba
f.	shanon	tsabwë	tsabwë baba
	F	**S**	
m.	bakwë	bakwë	
f.	amioka	bakwë yr. kuku ol.	
	M	**D**	
m.	tita	nachi ol. nachiana yr.	
f.	tita ol. nini yr.	tita ol. nini yr.	
	MB	**ZS,m/BS,f**	
m.	kuku ol. piak yr.	kuku ol. piak yr.	
f.	kuku ol. bakwë yr.	amioka	
	FZ	**ZD,m/BD,f**	
m.	nachi ol. nachiana yr.	tita piak	
f.	chaya babanë	chaya ol. babanë yr.	

Table 7: Matses Kin Terms by Alternating Generation Clusters

	FF	**B**	**SS,m/DS,f**
m.	buchido	buchi utsi/mascku tsidionquit dada (classificatory B)	baba
f.	buchido	utsi buchi ol. mascku yr. tsidionquit yr.	baba classificatory B
	MM	**Z**	**SD,m/DD,f**
m.	chichi	chuchu/hu chibi/uënembo	baba
f.	chichi	chuchu/chu chibi yr. utsi	baba
	MF	**MBS/FZS**	**SD,m/DD,f**
m.	buchido chaido	chai dawës/cania	baba
f.	buchido chaido	mëntado	baba
	FM	**MBD/FZD**	**DD,m/SD,f**
m.	shanu	shanu	baba
f.	shanu	tsabwë	baba
	F	**S**	
m.	papa/pa papautsi FB pabo "distant F"	mado	
f.	papa/pa namia	mado	
	M	**D**	
m.	tita/ta titaitsa MZ	champi	
f.	tita/ta tautsi MZ champi yMZ	champi	
	MB	**ZS,m/BS,f**	
m.	cucu/cu piac yMB matses	matses ol. piac yr.	[Romanoff gives piac only]
f.	cucu/cu mado yMB	namia	
	FZ	**ZD,m/BD,f**	
m.	nachi	tita	
f.	chaya	babanën	

Table 8: Sharanahua Kin Terms by Alternating Generation Clusters

	FF	**B**	**SS,m/DS,f**
m.	shota	ochi ursto	shota
f.	shota	ochi ol. ursto yr.	fafa
	MM	**Z**	**SD,m/DD,f**
m.	chichi	chipo ol. chiko yr.	shota
f.	chichi	chipi ol. chika yr.	fafa
	MF	**MBS/FZS**	**DS,m/SS,f**
m.	chata	chai	fafa
f.	chata	bimbiki	fafa
	FM	**MBD/FZD**	**DD,m/SD,f**
m.	shano	bimbiki	fafa
f.	shano	tsafu	fafa
	F	**S**	
m.	upa	faku	
f.	upa	faku	
	M	**D**	
m.	uwa	faku	
f.	uwa	faku	
	MB	**ZS,m/BS,f**	
m.	koka	pia	
f.	koka	rari	
	FZ	**ZD,m/BD,f**	
m.	achi	pia	
f.	yaya	rari	

Table 9: Shipibo Kin Terms by Alternating Generating Clusters

	FF	**B**	**SS,m/DS,f**
m.	papayosi	huëtsa	baba
f.	papayosi	poi	baba
	MM	**Z**	**SD,m/DD,f**
m.	titayos̈han	poi	baba
f.	titayos̈han	huëtsa	baba
	MF	**MBS/FZS**	**DS,m/SS,f**
m.	papayosi	huëtsa chai WB/ZH	baba
f.	papayosi	bënë H bënëitsa ZH huëtsa ??	baba
	FM	**MBD/FZD**	**DD,m/SD,f**
m.	titayos̈han	poi ?ahuin W ?ainhuëtsa BW	baba
f.	titayos̈han	tsabë huëtsa ??	baba
	F	**S**	
m.	papa epa FB/MZH	baque nosha BS	
f.	papa epa FB/MZH	baque cóco ZS [kokobaque Abelove]	
	M	**D**	
m.	tita huata MZ/FBW	bake nosha BD	
f.	tita huata	bake ?ini ZD [inibaque Abelove]	
	MB	**ZS,m/BS,f**	
m.	koka rayos WF	pia ZS rayos DH	
f.	koka baquënqui HF	cocobaquë [chio baque Abelove] baban?ëhua SW	
	FZ	**ZD,m/BD,f**	
m.	nachi rayos WM	pia ZD baban?ëhua SW	
f.	yaya baquenëhua HM	chiobaquë babanëhua SW	

Chapter 14

LEADERSHIP AND FACTIONALISM IN CASHINAHUA SOCIETY

Studies of leadership are generally written from the point of view of a loyal follower, a disgruntled ex-follower, an "objective" outsider, or a theory-conscious social scientist. The following account of leadership and factionalism in Cashinahua society attempts to convey the ways in which the Cashinahua view their own system; it is a compilation, abstracted and condensed, of some of the many statements received from a wide range of informants during eighty-four months of fieldwork between 1955 and 1968 in several villages on the Curanja River of southeastern Peru. I have avoided technical jargon except where the injection of Cashinahua concepts would require a detailed discussion beyond the scope of this chapter, for example, the kinship and marriage systems. Furthermore, I have tried to avoid interpreting informants' statements in terms of theories currently espoused by political anthropologists and political scientists.

Leadership among the Peruvian Cashinahua is evanescent, often most obvious in its absence. Informants frequently talked about the headman, *xanen ibu*, while seeming to be almost imperceptibly influenced by his presence in the village. The headman's leadership is subtle; he leads by soft persuasion and quiet example. Rarely does he raise his voice to harangue his kinsmen; rather, he strokes them lightly with words, never talking too much. His judgments are largely impartial and fair, more frequently pragmatic than idealistic. He is cool and confident, a good hunter, generous with his food but slow to give advice unless asked. His is not the ability to coerce, but to persuade or, perhaps more accurately, to lead his kinsmen gently to consensus. Yet, when matters of great importance for the well-being and tranquility of his village arise, he is firm and forceful, not beyond twisting a few arms and collecting a few IOUs. He uses the invisible reins of power ever so lightly, yet his absence from the village for more than a few days is noticeable; the village runs less smoothly.

His symbol of office is a basket of feathers from which are made the harpy eagle-wing feather back rack with its tails of black and brightly colored feathers, the train of harpy eagle-tail feathers, and the magnificent headdress of red macaw tail feathers and white plumes made of wispy leg feathers from the harpy eagle. These are worn during *chidin*, the headman's ceremony, a ritual for restoring unity to the village when dissent and factionalism threaten the social fabric.

His leadership is also given formal recognition by outsiders. Visitors arriving in the village generally go first to the hearth and hammocks of their closest kinsmen; however, they always stop by the headman's hearth before visiting any others or carrying out the business that occasioned their visit. Foreigners—that is, non-Cashinahua—either automatically go to the headman's hearth or are directed there.

This is, admittedly, a somewhat idealized version of Cashinahua leadership. However, in a village with an abundance of food, with no serious illness, and without any major factional disputes, the headman's behavior over a period of three or four months frequently approximates the above description.

Although a headman may have some influence outside his village because he is a man-with-knowledge, *huni unaya*, the village is his primary sphere of action. Ideally, each village is socially, economically, and politically autonomous. It consists of a single, large, palm-thatched house occupied by two senior males, who have exchanged sisters in marriage, and as many consanguines and affines as they can attract. Postmarital residence is normally matrilocal, but the two focal males need not be residing with their father-in-law if they have enough other kinsmen around them to assure economic self-sufficiency. If the population of a village is sufficiently large, say, about twenty adults, two houses may be constructed, each containing a single extended family, plus assorted hangers-on, and each headed by one of the focal males. In recent years, the residential pattern has changed by the dispersion into separate houses of the hangers-on and occasionally even matrilocally extended families. The focal males are not, however, heads of households. Rather, they are the leaders of the localized segment of their respective patrimoieties, and thus can expect the support of their sons, brothers, and other moiety mates, males who are dispersed within a single large house or residing in different houses. Although men may give orders to their wives, daughters, and sisters, they have little actual influence over the day-to-day activities of the women of their household. The village, and not the household, is the male's sphere of influence. In a sense, each village has two headmen. However, one generally has more influence, holds the symbol of office, and is called *xanen ibu*. Any man who exercises leadership is called *xanen ibu*. Varying degrees of headmanship are recognized, thus, *xanen ibu ewapa*, large headman, and *xanen ibu pishta*, little headman. However, the second focal male, even if he is rather ineffectual, is called *xanen ibu* and not *xanen ibu pishta*. This differential in leadership between the focal males does not produce political factionalism.

Factions may develop out of the political ambitions of individual males. However, they are more likely to arise as a result of intravillage disputes between consanguines rather than between affines, that is, conflicts within the local moiety segments, rather than across moiety lines. Since factions consist of at least two males who are potentially the focal males in a new autonomous village, disputes for headmanship are usually between the more influential members of the competing focal pairs.

In such a setting, a successful headman is one who is able to resolve these disputes or limit their impact on village life by manipulating both consanguineal and affinal ties in order to either socially isolate his opponent or restrict his opponent's sphere of influence. Some factional disputes escalate to a point where these methods are insufficient, and the village fissions.

The nature of Cashinahua leadership can best be seen in the context of actual factional disputes. Therefore, I turn now to an examination of two specific cases.

Case 1: An Aspirant to Leadership Who Fails

Dibi was a politically ambitious migrant to Xumuya. His long-range goal was to establish an autonomous village over which he would preside as chief, not in the traditional Cashinahua style, but in that of the Brazilians and Peruvians. He married the two widows of Ori, a man he had been cuckolding for many months prior to his death. These women were sisters of Dici, who was married to two of Dibi's sisters. His marriage thus set the stage for establishing a powerful faction based on two males from the opposing moieties linked by sister exchange. In addition, Dici was not politically ambitious; nor were any of Dici's brothers, whose support Dibi needed to realize his ambitions, since he had no other close kin in the village. As migrants to Xumuya, Dici and his brothers shared many of Dibi's frustrations. Because the dominant faction in the village, headed by Crow and Madi, controlled the best hunting areas as well as the best actual and potential garden sites, the migrants had to use less desirable areas, most of which were at some distance from the settlement. Thus, over a period of eight months, Dibi was able to gain considerable support by clashing frequently with Crow about a wide variety of topics. He often accused Crow of selfishness, a most serious accusation of a breach of the etiquette of leadership.

Dibi failed in his leadership bid for two reasons, only one of which illustrates the topic of this paper. First, his indiscrete amorous escapades[1] and his attempts to seduce most of the females of the village produced considerable friction and antagonism, resulting in his being expelled from the village. Second, he was unable to cope with his competitor's skilled manipulation of consanguineal and affinal ties, which undermined Dibi's leadership within his own faction.

Crow at first took no steps to oppose Dibi's faction-producing activities. The influx of migrants put a strain on the food resources of the village, and he hoped that Dibi and Dici would establish an independent village, even suggesting several possible sites and offering help in the initial clearing of new garden tracts. Dici was reluctant to move, however, because three of his brothers were without wives and had better chances of finding mates in Crow's village. In addition, other than his mother, there would be no older women to assist his young wives with the chores. Thus, when it appeared that the added population intended to stay for the foreseeable future, Crow began to exert his influence. Through conversations with his mother's brother, his mother, and his MBS, he arranged for his MB to take Dici's mother as a fourth wife.[2] This marriage opened the possibility for Dici and his brothers to use the hunting territory of their "father," thus linking these males to Crow's MB as well as to Crow's MBS, the co-leader of Crow's faction.

Crow then arranged for the marriage of his ZS to the daughter of Dibi's wife by a prior marriage. And finally, he arranged for his sister to marry Dici's brother Au, and when that marriage failed, he quickly arranged for her to marry Dici's brother Masi. When Masi's wife objected to his second wife and left him, Crow and his brother-in-law, Madi, together arranged for her to marry Madi's half-brother, Yapu, who was without a wife and had been planning to go to another village in search of a spouse. Figure 37 illustrates these manipulations. These new marriages led to a reshuffling of some hunting territories and garden sites or made new areas available to Dici and his brothers.

Figure 37: Major Figures in the Factional Dispute between Dibi and Crow.

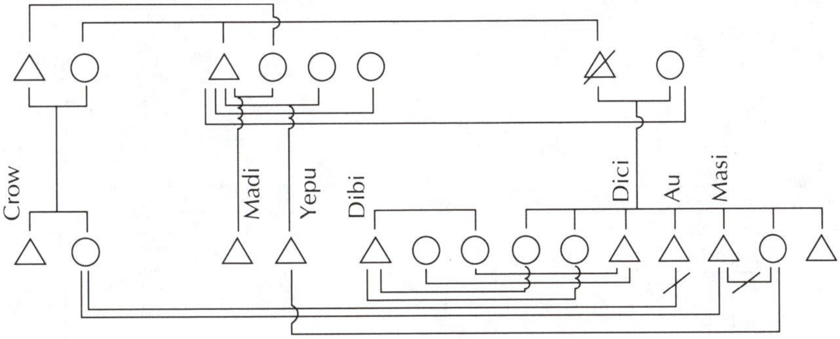

As a result, although he was unable to incorporate Dici and his brothers into his faction, Crow succeeded in severely weakening the ties between Dibi and Dici and thus reduced the intensity of the factional disputes.

Case 2: A Headman's Failure Leads to Village Fissioning

When I began my fieldwork in the village of Maneya, the focal males were Awa and Nowa; Awa was recognized as the headman. Shortly thereafter, the entire population of two other groups moved into the village, both groups having split away from the Maneya group some years earlier.[3] One group was a viable social entity under the leadership of Pipi; the other focal male was Tana. The second group consisted of two brothers, Toma and Shika, and their wives, who earlier had left Pipi's village in a dispute over women.

All groups recognized the headmanship of Awa. But Pipi, having been headman in his own village, almost immediately began to vie with Nowa for the leadership of the local segment of their moiety. The struggle continued for four years, both factions manipulating kin ties without much success. Awa arranged the marriage of his son to Shika's daughter, a move matched by Pipi's arranging the marriage of his FZS to Toma's daughter. Awa tried to gain the support of Dini and his brother Doro, his brother's sons, by showing them favors and through the friendship between them and his son Crow. Pipi retaliated by threatening to break up Dini's marriage to his half-sister, thus retaining the support of Dini and his brother (see figure 38).

Figure 38: Major Figures in the Factional Dispute between Awa and Pipi.

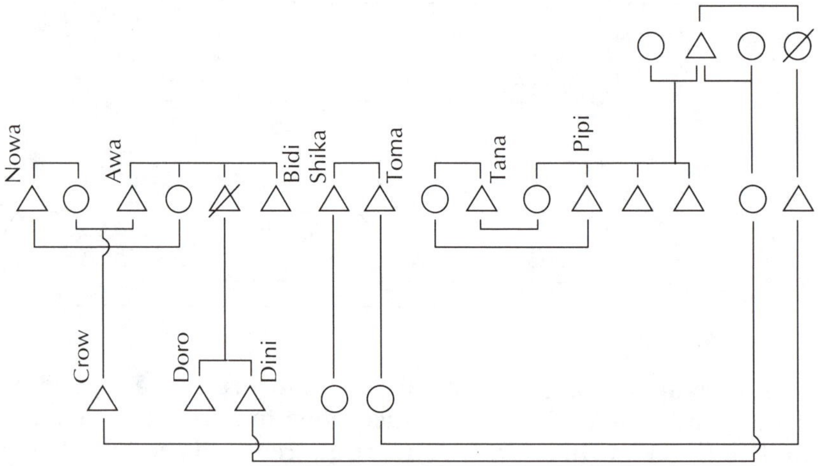

Awa was convinced that Pipi wanted to be headman and considered him arrogant and uncooperative. As tensions between them increased, so did the disputes between and within their factions, and Awa's statements of the village consensus regarding disputed matters showed increasing partiality toward members of his faction, resulting in further disagreements.

Shortly after several of Pipi's brothers migrated to Maneya from Brazil in the spring of 1959, a Peruvian trader arrived at the village port. Pipi met him and escorted him to his own house, bypassing Awa's house. That evening as the men gathered to eat, Awa recounted the hospitality he and his faction had given Pipi and his faction when they moved to Maneya. He argued that Pipi's behavior vis-à-vis the trader was an insult to his leadership and that perhaps it would be wise if Pipi and his faction made new gardens at a new site and moved there permanently when they began to produce. Pipi responded by charging Awa with selfishness and unfairness in dealing with disputes. After the corn harvest in January and February 1960, Pipi and his faction moved into their new village, returning to Maneya only to harvest manioc and plantains until those crops began to produce in the new gardens in sufficient quantity to support their dietary needs.

Awa's leadership was weakened by his battle with Pipi, and shortly thereafter he turned over leadership to his son, Crow, who along with Nowa's son, Madi, became the focal males in the village. This move angered Awa's brother, Bidi, who felt that the leadership should have gone to him. However, having no brother-in-law in the opposed moiety (he had married two of his classificatory sisters), he was unable to establish the focal male tie needed to establish leadership.

Discussion

The behavior described in these two cases rarely involved overt hostility and verbal conflict. The village presented to visitors a picture of peace and tranquility. On the other hand, the gossip indicated a virtual snake pit of intrigue. Reality lies somewhere in between; periods of relative calm were punctuated by the occasional eruption of disputes.

The headman, however, sees life as a constant struggle to allocate his resources, his energy, and his influence wisely among the multiplicity of often conflicting kinship demands. He knows that his leadership will last only so long as he successfully meets these obligations. For him, life is neither heaven nor hell; it is a chase of an elusive quarry, a hunt that demands all the skills he can muster.

Young girls dressed for kachanawa *in 1956.*

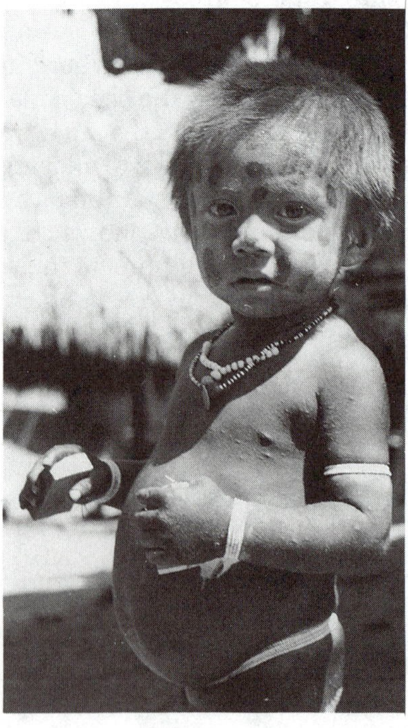

A well dressed young boy in 1956.

Chapter 15

INVISIBLE PEOPLE
OSTRACISM IN CASHINAHUA SOCIETY

In a society like that of the Cashinahua where no person, male or female, adult or child, has the right to force another person to obey a command should that person choose not to obey, where the resort to physical force is viewed as a greater offense than the one to which it is a response, how does one avoid chaos and anarchy? Why is it that for the most part people usually choose to behave in the manner expected of them by their peers and others? Is the notion of the orderly society based on any kind of reality, or is it simply an illusion created by social actors or by those who observe and analyze their behavior?

Robert Murphy (1971:38–39) has argued that "social anthropology is beset by a basic contradiction [that] arises from the fact that, although we search for order, social life is visibly chaotic." Whether or not order exists in human societies, all societies at least harbor the illusion that things are orderly, that everything is for the most part under control. Edmund Leach (1968:130) has argued that "the notion of order is a human notion and psychologically a most necessary one."

In his introductory textbook, Murphy (1986:145) wisely chose, as is often his wont, to reject "a prevalent belief in our society that social control, or the maintenance of public order, is wholly contingent upon the formal laws governing conduct and the legal sanctions taken against deviants." Instead, he discusses the "informal, noncodified means," including ostracism. "Ostracism, whether voluntary or imposed, is one of the worst penalties society can exact, for it inflicts a social death while the person is still alive" (147). He continues, "Social ostracism in small-town America has sent many people to seek refuge in the anonymity of the city, but in primitive societies there are no alternatives to life in tight little communities."

In this paper I want to discuss two cases of ostracism observed during my fieldwork with the Peruvian Cashinahua.[1] Although the same sanction was used, it was a response to two quite different offenses. I will also discuss why my informants agreed that the sanction worked in one case but failed in the other, although in both cases the disruptive behavior that triggered the sanction was terminated.

In Cashinahua society, ostracism consists of a person's being treated by his or her fellows as a nonperson, as if he or she were not present. No one speaks to persons being shunned; no one recognizes their presence or interacts in any way with them. Although they are totally isolated socially, no attempt is made to restrict their movements and activities, because to do so would acknowledge their presence.

Ostracism generally works because most Cashinahua consider it a fate just slightly less life threatening than death. Informants invariably became uncomfortable when talking about the subject. The decision to subject a person to shunning is made formally or informally by the whole community when and if a person's misbehavior is deemed to be either (a) sufficiently grave to jeopardize the health, welfare, or safety of the community or (b) excessively disruptive of social relationships. In the discussion that follows, Case 1 illustrates an offense that poses a threat to the physical well-being of members of the community; Case 2 illustrates an offense viewed as so disruptive of social relationships as to threaten society itself.

Case 1: The Case of the Frustrated Lover: Kadi Chapu

Kadi Chapu returned to the village from his garden about 2:00 P.M. carrying a bushmaster he had killed a short distance from the village. He was bringing it for the visiting American zoologists to see. In the process of killing the snake he had broken its skin, thus freeing its spirit. The villagers excitedly *ede*'ed, *extu*'ed, *een*'ed. Mothers kept their children away from the snake; various of them chided Kadi for bringing it to the village, thus making a clear trail for the snake's spirit to follow. Several men commented that he would have to go on a month-long fast, characterized by rigorous food taboos, abstinence from sex, and culminating in a purification ritual. They discussed the personal inconvenience of such rituals but noted that the entire process would make him a better hunter by clearing his system of any accumulation of *yupa*, the substance that causes a man to miss the target when he shoots his arrow. To everyone's surprise, Kadi Chapu joined the men for the evening meal and ate everything, including the prohibited meat, manioc, and ripe plantain soup. Several men chided him for this misbehavior; his brother reminded him that such behavior could jeopardize the health and safety of the village, especially that of his infant nephew who was living in the same household. Kadi parried all the criticisms by saying he would begin the fast in the morning.

In my discussion with him that evening he told me he had no intention of going through the rituals because doing so would interfere with a torrid romance in which he was involved. He did not mind the fasting, but he would not go through the purification ritual at the end of the month because it demanded total sexual abstinence for the entire preceding thirty days. He was, he said, having affairs with three different women, one of which was particularly exciting.

During the next several days various informants told me that although Kadi was observing the food taboos at public eating occasions, he was eating prohibited foods in secret. And worse, he had met and had sex with all three of his lovers—in fact, four times, with the favorite. Gossip was rampant, comments expressing disapproval of such behavior were made in his presence without being aimed at him directly, and on two occasions older women tried to shame him publicly for his unseemly behavior. Unrepentant, Kadi continued to pursue his amorous adventures and to eat prohibited foods.

Six days after Kadi killed the snake, his nephew became sick. People openly blamed the illness on Kadi's shameless behavior. That evening when he came to the men's gathering to eat, no one acknowledged his presence. They did not prevent him from eating, but they handed him nothing. As the meat dishes were finished, the man sitting to Kadi's right picked up a bowl of corn soup, took a drink, and passed it to the man on his right and so on around the circle to the man sitting on Kadi's left, who finished the contents of the bowl and put it on the ground empty. When Kadi spoke, no one responded. They looked past him and through him but gave no indications that they were aware of his presence.

During the next two days, Kadi went about his life as usual. He worked in his garden and went hunting. When he brought two wild pigs back to the village, everyone, including his lovers, ignored the pigs as they had been ignoring him. When he brought me the two rear quarters of one pig, I followed the lead of others and ignored him and the proffered gift.

By the following morning, Kadi was showing signs of desperation. He went from hearth to hearth, talking to everybody. People acted as if they neither saw nor heard him. He came to my house and begged me to talk with him; I continued working without acknowledging his presence. By noon he crawled into his hammock, assumed a fetal position and began to cry quietly.

Late in the afternoon he peeled some green plantains and roasted them in the coals of his brother's wife's fire and brought them with him to the men's circle for the evening meal, throughout which he quietly sat and munched on his dry fare, ignoring the prohibited meat and sweet gruels. By the next evening the community was convinced that he was indeed observing the required fast, and so the following morning they responded to his greetings. In my interviews with him in the succeeding days I became aware of the searing emotions that had led to his capitulation.

Kadi was a normal, healthy seventeen-year-old. He lived with his two sisters and their husband and children and with his older brother, his older brother's wife, and their children. When he was four years old, his father had been killed by a jaguar; his mother died two years later. He had grown up in the household of his married older brother and sisters.

He spoke of occasions during his childhood when his parents and siblings had responded to his misbehavior and temper tantrums by ignoring him. He recounted one particular experience when everyone was going poison fishing in a stream across the river from the village. He had been misbehaving for several days, and earlier in the day his mother started to ignore him. As people waded into the river to cross, nobody picked him up to carry him across the deepest part of the channel; and when he tried to swim, the current caught him and carried him downstream. Everybody ignored his cries for help. After struggling back to the riverbank, he returned alone to the empty village. At first he was in a rage and broke several large cooking pots, but when he heard spirits in one of the houses, his rage turned to terror. His cries for help went unanswered. He crawled up to a platform in the eves of the house where his kinsmen found him several hours later, rigid with fear and staring blankly at his surroundings.

He had recurrent dreams about this and similar experiences, always wakening from them bathed in perspiration. And during the shunning he had just experienced, he was afraid to fall asleep because these nightmares haunted his sleep. It was the nightmares, he said, more than the refusal of his lovers to have sex with him or to acknowledge his amorous advances or to accept his offer of meat, that finally led to his decision to follow the expectations of his fellows.

Case 2: The Case of the Red Hot Lover: Dinis[2]

About 9:00 P.M. the peace and quiet of the village was shattered by raised voices and then screaming from Usirin's house. His wife, Dasiu, fled the house sobbing, and ran across the plaza to the house of her classificatory father. For a short while the murmur of voices and sobbing could be heard before quiet returned to the village. My informant told me that Usirin had beaten his wife because she refused to have sex with him and angered him by saying that he was a lousy hunter and a lousy lover. Why should she give him sexual favors for nothing when a real hunter was glad to give her meat in exchange for sex? Such flaunting of an affair rightly angered Usirin, justifying the beating, according to my informant. The following morning Dasiu returned to her home after Usirin left to go hunting. Except for some quiet gossiping about the event, life in the village went on as before.

About a week later, the quiet of the village was broken again by yelling and screaming from Usirin's house. When Dasiu rushed out of the house, Usirin followed, striking her repeatedly with a tapir-hide whip. When she tripped and fell, he stood over her and continued the beating. At that point two of her classificatory brothers rushed from their house, threw Usirin to the ground, and kicked him. Dasiu ran to her classificatory father's house. After a few minutes her brothers and Usirin returned to their houses, but the murmur of conversations, some agitated, could be heard throughout the village. It continued for almost an hour.

The following morning Usirin went hunting, as did most of the men. Dasiu stayed in her father's house, where some of the women came to pick with palm thorns her blood blisters caused by the tapir-hide whip and to commiserate with each other about their problems with husbands and lovers.

Unlike after the previous beating, the atmosphere of the village was charged; the preceding evening's events were the major topic of conversation. Late that afternoon, after the men had returned from hunting and had bathed, they gathered as usual near the headman's house to eat. Each man brought bowls of manioc or plantains and meat; their wives brought them bowls of corn or ripe plantain gruel. Conversation was subdued and somewhat strained. When nothing but gruel remained to be consumed, Uxasa, one of Dasiu's brothers, berated Usirin for beating his wife. Although he had a right to beat her and she probably deserved it, he should not have pursued her when she fled and clearly should not have struck her with the whip after she fell.

Usirin responded that he had been angry, that she had taunted him with her affair with Dinis, about having made love with him in Usirin's own hammock that afternoon. Her brothers responded that she was having an affair because her lover provided her with game animals, and a woman has a right to do so if her husband does not provide sufficient meat. Usirin's brother, Dapida, joined the argument, saying that perhaps Usirin wasn't the best hunter, but that he was the best turtle tracker in the village. What other woman had more turtles tied under her house waiting to be butchered and eaten? In addition, her husband had provided her with large gardens so that she had an abundance of vegetables.

At this point everybody got into the discussion. Charges and countercharges were made. At various points women, eating in another circle nearby, added additional input into the rapidly heating argument. Just as it seemed that tempers would explode, the old headman cleared his throat, stretched, scratched his groin, and launched into the myth about the oversexed tapir (see chapter 20). The audience responded enthusiastically throughout the story, giggling, making ribald comments, grimacing, clutching their groins, moaning, and laughing.

When the headman finished the tale, Dasiu's classificatory father told another story about a deer married to an agouti who failed to provide for his wife, because the food he brought was food that deer, but not agouti, ate. Again comments from the audience formed a counterpoint to the storyteller. Four other traditional stories followed, each adding new nuances to this once removed discussion of the dispute. Throughout, the audience expressed their opinions of each story.

Finally, the old headman again cleared his throat, scratched his groin and said "Now, as the ancestors told us . . ." and launched into a new story. This was not one of the traditional, stories although it was in the form of these. It contained some of the cast of characters of the preceding six stories. People listened carefully to his speech, after which they commented freely. "It was a good story," "That's what I think," "*Habiaskaki*, that's the way it is," and so on. The group quickly disbanded, each family returning to their hearths and hammocks.

As I was informed the following day, the story contained a series of recommendations, but without ever naming any of the parties to the dispute. First, that Usirin should agree to the marriage of his young daughter to a suitor who had been seeking Usirin's approval of the match, thus bringing a successful young hunter and perhaps a more varied meat supply into the household. Second, that Dasiu owed her husband respect as a good provider and should she continue to have affairs she should carry them out with discretion, and without flaunting them in her husband's face, and that since she was eating food he provided, she should accept the conjugal obligations implied by that acceptance. Third, that Dinis should be ostracized until he mended his ways because his amorous behavior was causing so much disruption within the community.

Throughout the storytelling, Dinis had been silent. It was his indecorous behavior that provoked the dispute, and it was for him that the headman reserved the harshest judgment, ostracism, until he gave evidence that his amorous predation would cease or at least be carried on discreetly.

The following day no one spoke with Dinis. He went from house to house only to be ignored, even by his wife and former sexual partners. He came to my house, and despite the fact that I studiously ignored him, he talked at length. He didn't mind the shunning, he said. Why should he care if they would not talk to him? They envied his penis. If he left the village, they would miss the game animals he always brought back from the hunt. He could go to Pipi's village. They would welcome him there. No, he wasn't going to be chased away like a capybara from his gardens and hunting trails. His resolve lasted two days. He packed his possessions into his canoe and went downriver, *alone*.

Informants were in complete agreement that ostracism had failed; although it rid the village of a troublemaker, it cost them a successful hunter. Dinis was a shameless misfit who never learned how to behave, they argued. He was an orphan. His mother died when he was about two years old. An older sister cared for him for about two years until her husband died and her new husband did not want him around. He then lived with his aged, widowed, and husbandless maternal grandmother, who was loosely attached to the household of a distant kinsman where she did much of the drudgery in exchange for the food they ate and a place to hang her hammock. Their presence was tolerated by their housemates; neither was especially wanted. When his behavior became intolerable around the house, his grandmother would take him to the garden or forest, where he would play or work with her, free from the scowls and demands of their housemates. Occasionally they would hike downriver to another village where they would visit his classificatory mother's brother and other distant kinsmen. Dinis bullied his grandmother, who in turn doted on him. His grandmother cuddled and coddled him, protected him from disapproval of any sort. To put it bluntly, she spoiled him. Shortly after his initiation, when he was about age ten, his grandmother died, leaving him at the mercy of the housemates from whom she had protected him for six years. Shortly after her death, he fled to the village of his classificatory mother's brother, whose son, a boy about three years older than Dinis, befriended him and taught him to hunt and make gardens. These were good years; he had a friend. His behavior apparently was normal for a boy his age.

All this ended abruptly when Dinis' cross-cousin married and, burdened with the obligations of being a son-in-law, could no longer spend his time leisurely working and playing with Dinis. Furthermore, the new wife's mother disliked Dinis, and probably with some justification. From her point of view, he was boisterous, rude, and shameless, and she clearly seemed to consider him a threat to the tranquility of her household.

At thirteen, Dinis ran off to live with a Brazilian family, at whose place he worked for three years. These were hard years. Disobedience was harshly punished by kicks, slaps, and beatings. Why he stayed is unclear. I suspect that fear kept him from running back to his kinsmen. He spoke often about the threats made by his Brazilian "father" to hang him up by his thumbs, to sell him to downriver traders, or to castrate him. After a particularly severe beating for insolence, he fled back to a Cashinahua village where he was taken in and cared for by his cross-cousin. All of his kinsmen were outraged by the visible proof on his body of the severe beating he had received, so that when his Brazilian "father" came searching for him, they smuggled him out of the village, claimed that he had died from infected wounds, and threatened to report the "murder" to the priest on his next visit to the village. (Several axes and machetes bought their promises of silence.)

Dinis was delighted to be back with "his" people. He was a hard worker and a good hunter. He was charming, witty, disarming, handsome, and horny. Lovers were readily available in exchange for the game he brought back to the village. His sexual escapades would have been tolerated and perhaps even been considered amusing had they been carried out with discretion, but they were not.

Dinis' cross-cousin arranged for him to marry the cousin's prepubescent sister, in hopes that the marriage would curtail his sexual exploits. His efforts were in vain. Dinis continued his campaign to cuckold every male in the village regardless of age or relationship to him. He told me of this with glee and in considerable detail. When sanctions were imposed and his position in the village became untenable, he fled to another village, then another. Four years and two marriages later, he migrated to Peru with his wife and about twenty of her kin, and we are back to where we started the examination of his case.

Ostracism had failed because Dinis never learned how to behave. During the crucial years from three to ten he was sheltered from most disapproval by a grandmother who failed to train him or allow others to do so; he was never properly socialized. During his three years with the Brazilians he felt isolated and alienated; he had been treated as a servant or slave, slept under the house with the pigs and dogs, was never able to play with children his own age, and ate alone in the cookhouse. Thus, the threat of ostracism did not strike terror in him. He knew he could survive; he had done so for three alien years.

Discussion and Conclusions

In light of these two cases, what conclusions can we draw about the nature of social controls in egalitarian societies like the Cashinahua?

First, sanctions against antisocial or asocial behavior are effective to the degree that the individuals subjected to them have been socialized into feeling those sanctions as threatening their well-being. By *threaten*, I do not mean that they see the sanction against them as a warning of potential physical violence. Rather, they perceive the sanction as a warning of the loss of their social persona. The effectiveness of ostracism as a form of social control is predicated, as least in Cashinahua society, on childhood reactions to the practice of "looking through" a child as a means of gaining proper behavior. It is the psychic trauma of early childhood experiences, where recognition of one's existence is withheld, that motivates the adult to mend his ways. Dinis, because his grandmother protected him from such experiences, seemed immune to shunning.

Second, in the absence of a single authority or agency with coercive powers there must be (1) agreement among the members of the society that the violation poses a threat to the health, welfare, or safety of the community or one of its members, or threatens to rip the social fabric, and (2) a willingness of the members of the group to act in concert. A corollary of this point is that egalitarian societies appear to be concerned not with protecting the perpetrator of an offense from the consequences of his misdeeds but with protecting society. Thus, the socialization process is more concerned with the development of a social conscience than with building strong egos. Notice that although Dinis's grandmother's behavior, which screened him from social disapproval and thus helped to protect his ego from the trauma of shunning experienced by most Cashinahua children, may have been useful preparation for the three years he spent with the Brazilians, it ill prepared him for living in his own society.

Third, in a society where physical coercion is rejected as a means of social control, the socialization process must include mechanisms that make effective use of psychological pressures. The reference in Dinis's case to the emasculations of the horny tapir was not a threat of physical violence but a reminder that, just as the loss of the genitalia leads to a death of sexuality, the loss of personhood leads to social death. In Kadi Chapu's case, behavior that causes actual or potential physical harm to another is balanced by the withdrawal of recognition of one's social persona.

Finally, I suggest that social control, or at least the illusion thereof, can be sustained in egalitarian societies only so long as the ultimate sanctions are seen as leaving no desirable alternatives for the miscreant. For Kadi Chapu, the loss of his social persona threatened his self-identity. Dinis, on the other hand, was convinced that *he* did not need the approval of others, that he could go elsewhere and be himself, to another Cashinahua village or if need be a Peruvian or Brazilian town. I last saw Dinis in the jail of a small Peruvian border town. He had been caught in bed with the comandante's wife.[3]

Chapter 16

FOOD TABOOS AS MARKERS OF AGE CATEGORIES IN CASHINAHUA

Eric Ross (1978:16) in his paper, "Food Taboos, Diet, and Hunting Strategy: The Adaptation to Animals in Amazon Cultural Ecology," concluded that "emic inedibility also represents an accurate probabilistic statement of etic hunting realities."[1] Let me attempt to restate this indigestible, if not inedible, quote. What I think Ross is saying is this: Native prohibitions against the hunting and the consumption of certain animal species corresponds to a high degree with an outside observer's scientific assessment of the prospects for successful hunting of these species.

I agree with Ross that there is a good chance that there can be a high degree of agreement between the native's and the scientist's assessments that a particular hunting strategy will or will not produce an adequate long-term game supply. The native may be aware that he cannot depend on the hunting of certain species as the mainstay of his meat supply since he has available to him many of the data that serve as the scientist's basis for reaching the same conclusion. However, the line of reasoning used to reach that conclusion may or may not coincide with that of the scientist; the hunter, that is, may not be aware of the carrying capacity of an ecological zone for tapirs, but he is aware that tapirs generally produce only a single offspring at lengthy intervals in contrast to the more frequent multiple births of certain rodents, and he therefore knows that he is more likely to encounter rodents than tapirs.

I also agree that a taboo may, and often does, function to prevent the decimation of a species which, given its breeding characteristics and/or an ecological niche incapable of supporting large populations, would have low survival chances were it to be intensively hunted. However, I suggest that these facts in themselves do not provide "an intelligible or cogent explanation of the emergence and/or perpetuation of dietary taboos on major animals or their temporal or spatial content or occurrence" (Ross 1978:1).

My argument here is that (1) taboo systems are ideological systems and that the reasons for their perpetuation, and perhaps their emergence, are at least partly ideological; (2) that the viability of the taboo systems is to a large extent the result of the degree to which the taboo system is integrated with other aspects of the ideological system; (3) that taboo systems, and probably all aspects of ideological systems, may result in behavior that can be both adaptive and maladaptive; (4) that the degree to which societies enforce taboo systems is frequently related to prevailing economic circumstances, namely food shortages; and (5) that belief systems that consistently produce maladaptive behavior significantly reduce the survival chances of both the societies and their belief systems. Discovering the ecological factors that justify limiting the exploitation of certain species and demonstrating the beneficial ecological effects of these prohibitions on the species concerned does not explain how these prohibitions emerged or why they persist. Nor, on the other hand, does an understanding of the ideological systems provide all the answers. I suspect that the degree to which taboo systems will be explained as being the result of ecological or ideological factors will depend to a large extent on the ideological commitment of the ethnographer.

I have no theory to explain the origins of Cashinahua food taboos, and at this time, I do not wish to hazard even a guess. Instead I will (1) describe briefly the Cashinahua system of food taboos and the cosmological system within which it operates; (2) examine the way in which some of these taboos are used as defining features or as markers of Cashinahua age categories; and (3) draw some conclusions about the implications of these data for our understanding of the system of food taboos and its persistence.

Taxonomies of Food, General and Specific Taboos

All Cashinahua informants, including children as young as four years of age, are able to enumerate a wide range of dietary prohibitions, which are both general and specific in character. Unlike Ross (1978:1, note 2; see also Basso 1973:16), I will deal with both general and specific taboos since they share certain explanatory features within Cashinahua cosmology. General taboos are always spoken of in terms of food items that "we never eat" (*nun pismaki*) as opposed to those things "we habitually eat" (*nun pimiski*). These designations correspond but are not identical to the Cashinahua classification of food into three dyadic pairs of categories: *piti kuin*$_1$ versus *piti kuinman*$_1$, "ideally and jurally real versus unreal food," or, *piti kuin*$_1$ versus *piti bemakia*$_2$, "individually and existentially real versus unreal food," and *piti kayabi*$_3$ versus *piti bemakia*$_3$, "pragmatically real versus unreal food" (see chapter 7).

For example, the Cashinahua classify all meat as either *yuinaka kuin*$_1$ or *yuinaka kuinman*$_1$. *Yuinaka kuin*$_1$ includes tapir, deer, peccaries, monkeys, birds, rodents, armadillos, alligators, and the like. *Yuinaka kuinman*$_1$ includes felines (including weasels, badgers, and wild dogs, all of which the Cashinahua classify as *inu*), vultures, birds of prey, bats, snakes, marsupials, sloths, anteaters, capybara, rabbits, and so on. Generally, when informants say that "we habitually eat" or "we never eat" an animal species, they are speaking of this ideological classification. However, they may also be using the *yuinaka kayabi*$_3$ versus *bemakia*$_3$ classification which reclassifies some species defined as *kuinman*$_1$ (inedible) as *kayabi*$_3$ (edible) in light of ecological circumstances, namely the scarcity of meat that is classified as *kuin*$_1$. This generally is the case when a village is old and the preferred game supply has been depleted by years of hunting to the point that a dependable supply of the *kuin*$_1$ animals is unavailable. *Kayabi*$_3$ also is used to define those species which are *kuinman*$_1$ but may be eaten by all persons belonging to certain age categories. (I will discuss the notions of edibility versus inedibility as defined by age categories below.) The animals that can be reclassified in this way include marsupials, sloths, anteaters, capybara, and rabbits.

Individual Cashinahua informants may choose to classify animals as *kuin*$_2$ or *bemakia*$_2$ for highly idiosyncratic reasons, including a personal dislike of the taste or texture of the meat, hunger, a perverse desire to flout accepted norms, or a personal encounter

A successful hunter carrying two peccaries, animals that are yuinaka kuin.

with an animal during supernatural experiences while in a trance, under the influence of a hallucinogen, or in a dream. Some animals can never be classified as *bemakia*$_2$ and thus are never prohibited as food; others can never be classified as *kuin*$_2$ and thus can never be eaten. (These restrictions correspond to the classification of these animals as *yuinaka pehaida* and *yuinaka chakahaida*, respectively.)

Specific taboos are always spoken of in terms of items that a specific ego "is not able to eat" (*pitidumaki*) at a specific time and under specific circumstances. They involve the prohibition against food items that are classified as *piti kuin*$_1$ and/or *piti kayabi*$_3$. Thus, persons who are involved in a ritual fast are prohibited from eating all meat, all sweet foods, and all condiments, foods that under normal circumstances would be defined as edible. In addition, persons belonging to certain age categories may not eat certain otherwise edible foods at specific times during their membership in an age category. For example, an adult male may not eat strong meat like tapir, deer, or peccary for several weeks after the birth of a child; nor may he eat spider monkey of the same sex as the child during its infancy, nor may he eat stingray while the child is a toddler. Thus, specific taboos operate for limited periods of time and within clearly defined contexts for particular individuals or class of individuals. It should be noted that although a man may be prohibited from eating certain animals, he is not prohibited from hunting these animals. Likewise, a woman may harvest and cook foods that she cannot eat.

Cashinahua Explanations of the Taboos

Cashinahua informants offer three kinds of explanations for not eating certain foods: traditional, gustatory, and cosmological.

When asked why they did/would not eat an item of food, many informants would respond that it was because their parents or ancestors did not eat it. However unsatisfactory such a response may be to the ethnographer, it cannot and should not be ignored as at least a partial explanation for the persistence of a dietary restriction. Whether or not we wish to acknowledge the fact, we frequently act as we do because that is how we learned to behave as children and not as the result of making a conscious choice based on reason.

My informants often said that they did/would not eat certain foods because they had a bad taste. This reason has no real explanatory value with reference to the category of foods that they never eat (*nun pismaki*) since few, if any, informants have ever tasted these items, foods that are classified *piti bemakia*$_3$. However, certain animals within the categories *piti kuin*$_1$ and *piti kayabi*$_3$, which are never the object of general taboos and rarely of specific taboos, are never eaten during certain seasons even by persons not obligated by specific taboos to refrain from eating them, because, in fact, they have a bad taste due to their seasonal consumption of fruits.

Cosmological explanations are much more complex and are of greater importance for understanding both the general and specific systems of dietary prohibitions. I turn now to a brief examination of Cashinahua cosmology before discussing its relationship with the taboos.

The Cashinahua cosmos contains three basic categories: people, spirit beings, and nature. People and spirit beings live with and within nature and "own" it, or, to be more precise, they have rights of usufruct. The principal, but not exclusive, domain of spirit beings is the deep forest. The intermediate area is a transitional zone frequented by both spirit beings and males in search of food. Females, unless accompanied by males, rarely enter the transitional zone; such intrusions are said to endanger the safety and health of both the intruder and her community because this encroachment on the spirit's territory by human females throws female spirits into a jealous rage while driving male spirits into a sexual frenzy. On the other hand, human males can and regularly do move in and out of the transitional zone and occasionally into the deep forest with relative impunity.

Hunters are always concerned about maintaining harmonious relationships with the spirit beings. To do so requires that they (1) avoid waste of the shared resources of nature and (2) use proper hunting techniques and etiquette. In addition, men attempt to establish cordial relationships with spirit beings encountered during hallucinogenic experiences and dreams. The spirit familiars and spirit pets gained in this way protect and assist the hunter. Women are also interested in preserving good relationships with spirit beings. However, since the primary locus of interaction between people and spirits is in the transitional zone of the forest—the area of spirits and human males—the discussion that follows will be written primarily from a male perspective.

Cashinahua hunters should not shoot more game than the community can reasonably eat; nor should they shoot more than they can carry unless they call for and get assistance from others. All animals that are killed, except snakes, should be carried back to the village for consumption or, if the animal shot is classed as totally prohibited, for disposal. A hunter reluctantly leaves a spider monkey that died after being shot but failed to fall and so hangs in an inaccessible location suspended by its prehensile tail.

Wounded animals that escape are tracked for hours, and the search is abandoned only when sunset approaches and the hunter must leave the forest before night sets in. He generally returns the following morning to continue his search.

Hunters are careful to follow proper techniques. For example, they should use only the force necessary to capture an animal and should dispatch it quickly; if the animal's spirit has difficulty escaping the body, it is likely to be angry and probably vindictive. They should kill a snake without breaking its skin to prevent the escape of its spirit. They should shoot harpy eagles in flight.

And finally, Cashinahua hunters observe proper hunting etiquette. Here we turn our attention to the relationship between people and spirit beings and animals. People have exclusive use of a limited number of species, which are never the object of general or specific taboos and thus may always be eaten, with one exception to be discussed below. Spirits never interact with, touch, or eat the spirits of these species. On the other hand, spirits have exclusive ownership of certain species, which are always the object of general taboos and may never be eaten by people; they may, however, be killed by hunters under certain circumstances. For example, a hunter may kill a jaguar or snake in self-protection. Should he do so, he must undergo a ritual fast and purification in order to placate the spirits and to protect himself and the community from their revenge.

The contrast here is between animals the Cashinahua classify as *yuinaka pehaida*, and thus $kuin_1$, $kayabi_3$, and $kuin_2$, but never $bemakia_2$, and *yuinaka chakahaida* and thus $kuinman_1$, $bemakia_3$, and $bemakia_2$, but never $kuin_2$.

All other animals are the object of specific prohibitions, adherence to which either maintains or restores harmonious relations with the spirit beings. A Cashinahua who follows a specific taboo normally may expect little interference from, and often the assistance of, spirit beings. Many of these specific restrictions apply only during certain periods during the life cycle, and it is to these I now turn. For the purpose of brevity, I will not discuss in this chapter the dietary restrictions associated with curing of illness or rituals unless they are directly and primarily associated with a stage in the life cycle.

Taboos and the Life Cycle

Beginning with birth, each Cashinahua potentially develops through four life stages: childhood, youth, adulthood, and old age (see figure 39).

Figure 39: Life Stages in Cashinahua.

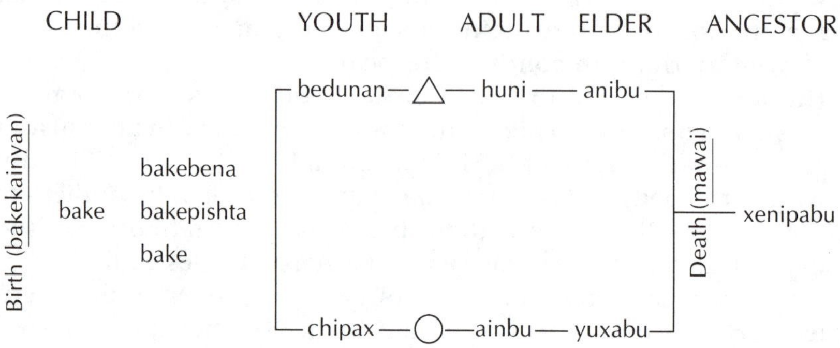

Childhood, *baketian*, lasts from the moment after birth, *bake kainyan*, when the baby is picked up, bathed, and put to the breast, through initiation between the ages of nine and twelve. During that time the child passed through three substages: *bake bena* (from birth to crawling), *bake pishta* (from crawling to walking), and finally *bake* (from semi-independence from the mother to the initiation rites). Informants disagree about when *bake pishta* ends and *bake* begins. A few argue that it ends with weaning, at a point between two and four years. Most say that it ends when the child begins to spend significant amounts of time with peers and older children, between four and five.

The diet of a *bake bena* consists of mother's milk but may be supplemented by small quantities of maize, plantain, and manioc gruels; meat is prohibited. A *bake pishta* continues to consume mother's milk, but its diet rapidly expands to include first foods, including meats, which are *piti pehaida*, then *piti kuin*$_1$, and finally *piti kayabi*$_3$, but may not eat foods classified as *chaka*$_4$ and *bemakia*$_3$. From this point onward throughout the rest of the life cycle, statements regarding the foods that may be eaten should be read with the understanding that some of these foods also may be prohibited temporarily in connection with treatment for a personal illness or participation in a public or private ritual. A *bake* can eat anything but those few animals classified *piti chakahaida*. Initiation rituals involve a month-long prohibition on eating all meats, condiments, and "sweet" foods.

The initiated male youth, *bedunan*, is generally free to eat whatever he wants. He may temporarily choose to refrain from eating the animal species he is currently learning to hunt; this is particularly true of larger animals.

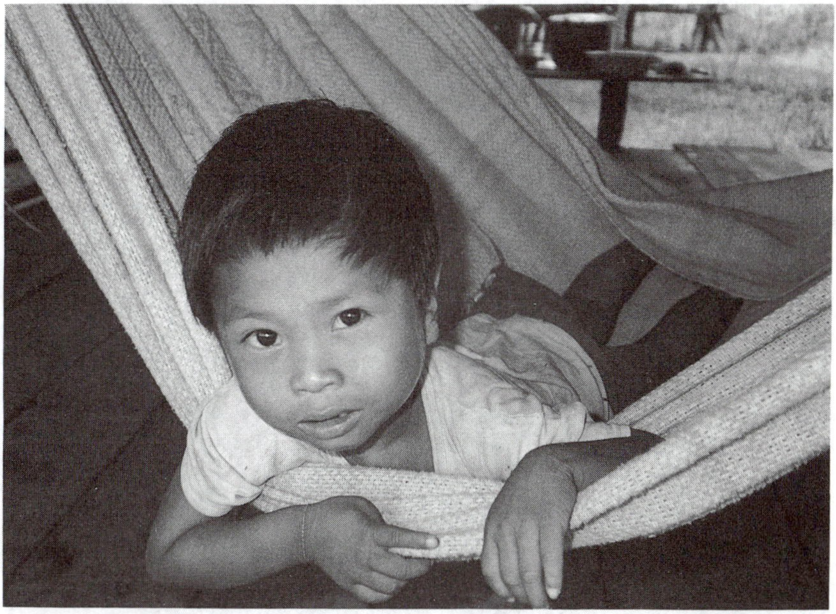

A young boy, bake, *viewing the activities of the village from his hammock.*

The initiated female youth, *chipax*, is also free to eat whatever she wishes, except during her first menses, when she may not eat condiments, and may eat only meats classified as *yuinaka pehaida*. During later menses she may also eat *yuinaka pe*. She often refrains from eating specific species while learning particular crafts, refraining, for example, from eating stingray while learning how to spin.

The minor restrictions continue from initiation until entry into adulthood. Informants disagree on the time when the transition from youth to adulthood is made. Some say that it occurs with marriage. Most argue that since first marriages are usually fragile, adulthood begins with the conception or birth of a couple's first child.

Adulthood encompasses the most productive years of a Cashinahua's life; it is also the period during which the person is subject to the largest number of dietary prohibitions. A male becomes a full adult, *huni*, when he assumes the full responsibilities of husband and father, including the responsibility for adhering to the specific dietary restrictions that relate to his role as provider and protector of his children. Likewise, a female becomes a full

A young girl with her father prior to her introduction during the initiation rituals which transform her from bake *to* chipax.

adult, *ainbu*, when she assumes the full responsibilities of wife and mother, including the responsibilities for adhering to the specific dietary restrictions that relate to her roles as provider and protector of her children. Many of these taboos are in effect only for specific periods during the early years of each child.

For example, a *huni* may eat only meat classified *yuinaka pehaida* during the first month of his child's life, gradually adding to his diet those meats that are *pe* and *kuin*$_1$, with certain clearly defined exceptions, such as those mentioned above. These restrictions apply throughout the time his child is *bake bena* and *bake pishta*, that is, during the period of greatest vulnerability in the life cycle, and thus are forms of preventative medicine. He may also refrain from eating certain foods when the child is ill; these restraints are forms of curative medicine. Should he violate proper hunting techniques or etiquette, he also will observe dietary restrictions and at times go through a month-long fast and purification to protect the health and safety of his child. Such taboos are forms of protective medicine. Food taboos that serve simultaneously as preventative, curative, and protective medicine are most consistently obeyed.

Because a man's activities frequently take place in the forest, where contacts with and offenses against spirit beings are more likely to occur, the father of a *bake bena* or *bake pishta* is subject to a greater number of food prohibitions during these periods in the lives of his children than at any other time in the life cycle. He also avoids hunting in the deep forest, the primary domain of spirit beings.

The Cashinahua are quite explicit about one of the major functions these taboos serve in addition to the medical ones discussed above, namely, the establishment of the child's identity. The man who observes the taboos identifies with the child as pater, *epa* $kuin_1$, and thus establishes the child's social group membership, a fact of no small significance in a society with a patrilineal rule of descent. Numerous informants said to me when speaking of their father, "he is my real father (*epa* $kuin_1$); he didn't eat X (a specific species) when I was a *bake bena*."

Likewise, an adult woman, *ainbu*, observes a series of specific food taboos during the time her child is *bake bena* and *bake pishta*, which are also preventative, curative, and protective. Because most of her activities take place within the confines of "people" territory, she is less likely to encounter and offend spirit beings than is the child's father. However, during her menses she must be careful to observe food prohibitions scrupulously and to prevent the child from coming in contact with menstrual blood, which is defined by the Cashinahua as contaminating and capable of weakening a child touched by it.

The observation of food taboos establishes the child's mother as mater; birth has already established her as genitrix and thus real mother, *ewa* $kuin_1$.

The point at which a man changes from adult male, *huni*, to old man, *anibu*, and a woman changes from adult female, *ainbu*, to

A man, huni, *with his young daughter,* bake pishta, *in 1957.*

"Now I am an old man, anibu. *I have many grandchildren."*

old woman, *yuxabu*, is unclear. It is more clear for a female than a male, however. A woman who has gone through menopause and has no children who are *bake bena* or *bake pishta* is a *yuxabu*. She may eat anything she wishes to eat except meats classified *yuinaka chakahaida*. A man potentially becomes an *anibu* when he no longer has children who are *bake bena* or *bake pishta* and is free to eat what he wishes, except *yuinaka chakahaida*, so long as he does not continue to hunt game actively. As he gets older and his hunting is confined to the transitional zone, he observes few food taboos. Both an *anibu* and a *yuxabu* may optionally observe food taboos during crucial periods in the early years of their grandchildren, particularly of their namesakes, *xutabu*.

It should be noted that in addition to defining, in part, who is one's real father and mother, *epa* $kuin_1$ and *ewa* $kuin_1$, observance of food taboos on behalf of a young child by adults other than the parents is an indicator of those persons who are part of the child's network of close, *kuin*, kinsmen, namely MM, MF, FM, FF, MB, and FZ, and who have obligations toward and responsibilities for the child's welfare.

Thus, specific food taboos become one of the defining features or markers of the various stages in the life cycle of an individual. Informants frequently identify a person's membership in an age category by noting the observance of a food taboo or lack thereof.

Summary and Conclusions

Cashinahua food taboos are dietary rules which in part define appropriate and inappropriate behavior on a permanent or temporary basis. These taboos relate to and in part define the taxonomic status of flora and fauna; that is, whether species of plants and animals are real food. The four overlapping taxonomic devices used by the Cashinahua provide both the flexibility needed in order to allow them to respond to short-term food shortages and the potential for long-term changes should conditions change irreversibly. The traditions learned by a growing child act as inhibiting factors in situations of change, as do taste preferences, which are also learned either as part of traditional knowledge or personal experience.

Cashinahua taboos result in behavior that contributes to the maintenance or restoration of harmonious relations between people and spirit beings. Although revengeful or capricious actions by spirits are not the only cause of illness, food taboos contribute to the protection from, and the prevention and curing of, illness caused by either spirit beings or elements of nature.

And finally, dietary prohibitions are part of the defining features of the various stages in the life cycle of the Cashinahua. They also define in part the relationship between and obligations toward individuals and classes of individuals within the social system.

Therefore, we can argue that Cashinahua food taboos contribute to both the ordering of their universe (the conceptual/ideological system) and to the maintenance of order (the regulation of behavior among and between people, spirit beings, and nature). Such an argument does not necessarily explain why a system of dietary prohibitions exists, but it does contribute to our understanding of why such a system may persist even in the face of ideological or ecological pressures for change.

Chapter 17

LIVING WITH SPIRIT BEINGS

TRIBAL RELIGION IN AMAZONIA

Early in my fieldwork, I became aware of Cashinahua spirit beliefs. I spent much of my time participating in men's work, often hunting. During these hunts my companion would pause occasionally to indicate the presence of spirits, *yushin*, or to point out herbs used to treat illness. When we returned to the village, I asked him to tell me about our day's events. Frequently included in these reports were discussions about indicators he had seen of the presence and activities of spirits.

The Cashinahua believe that there are two aspects to the world. The first is the visible, tangible, material part we experience in our daily lives. This aspect is paralleled by the invisible side of the world which, under normal circumstances, we can neither see nor touch but which we can see and experience in our dreams or hallucinations. Just as the visible world is the domain of human beings and all other living things, the invisible world is the domain of the spirits.

The Cashinahua cosmos contains three basic categories—people, nature, and spirits—each of which consists of a physical and a spiritual component. People have both a physical body and no less than five spirits. Nature has a physical element that people see, touch, eat, and so on, and a spiritual element seen and used by the spirit beings. Spirit beings are primarily spiritual, but they may gain physical substance by entering into natural items and people or by transforming themselves magically into physical beings.

The Cashinahua have a detailed knowledge of their physical environment. Knowledge of faunal behavior is needed to make them successful hunters. Many of them know the names, growth habits and uses of much of the flora. Herbalists, called *huni batadauya*, have large pharmacopoeia of plants they use to fight disease. The Cashinahua also are attuned to the annual climatic cycle. For the most part nature is seen as orderly and predictable. But it can be quirky and even chaotic, like a thunderstorm out of season, or an eclipse. These unpredictable events are explained in myths either as quirks of nature or, at times, as the responses of spirits to human misbehavior. Because humans and spirits share a common world, albeit different aspects of it, it is incumbent on them to share the resources of nature. Desecration or waste of nature may be punished by disaster or illness. One can never be sure, so it is better to be safe than sorry.

When I began my studies of the Cashinahua as a missionary intent on providing them with a translation of the Bible and saving their souls, I expected to find them living in fear and superstition, fearful of the spirits and practicing all kinds of weird rituals to placate the spirits. My expectations were not realized.

The Cashinahua neither fear nor worship the spirits; they accept them as part of the environment, like trees, animals, and people. Like people, spirits can be unpredictable and capricious. They can be pleasant and cooperative or malicious and spiteful, depending on their moods. Their moods run the gamut of human emotions—joy, pleasure, happiness, frustration, despair, anger, and so on. But because they are invisible to most humans, it is impossible to sense their moods and anticipate their actions.

For example, the spirits of fertility are attracted by the sound of laughter, singing, and feasting characteristic of the fertility rituals and come to join the party, bringing with them fertility for women and gardens. If the party is a bust, either because there was not enough food—particularly meat—or because there was a lot of tension between the human participants, the spirits leave, taking their fertility with them. As a result, women do not conceive and the gardens produce poorly.

The Cashinahua believe that every human being has at least five souls or spirits:

bedu yushin, the eye spirit, is the spirit that lives in one's eye. When you look a person in the eye, you can see his/her eye spirit.

This spirit leaves the body when one becomes unconscious or when one gets drunk on manioc beer or fermented honey or gets high on the hallucinogenic beverage *nishipae*. The spirit's activities are the hallucinations one experiences. Death occurs when the *bedu yushin* permanently leaves the body and makes its journey to the sky, where it joins the spirits of the ancestors and becomes *nai yushin*, a sky spirit.

yuda bake yushin[1], one's "body child" spirit. Each living person is encased in this spirit. When you look at a person, you see this casing. *Yuda bake yushin* also refers to one's shadow or reflection in water or a mirror. This spirit leaves one's body when one becomes unconscious or dies. This explains the visible change in the body's pallor with unconsciousness and death. Therefore, one is careful never to step on another's shadow or to interfere with another's reflection in a stream or pond of water, lest one causes harm to that person. At death the *yuda bake yushin* retraces in reverse the life of the individual until it reaches its birthplace, where it is transformed into a *ni yushin*, a forest spirit.

nama yushin, dream spirit, leaves a person's body through the nose or mouth when one goes to sleep. Its activities are what one experiences in dreams. Therefore, one must be careful never to wake another person suddenly, lest they be awakened before the dream spirit has had a chance to return to the body. A person who does waken suddenly or feels disoriented upon awakening should stay in or return to his/her hammock and go back to sleep or at least rest quietly in order to give the dream spirit a chance to return. At death the dream spirit drifts away from the village to take up residence in the tops of tall trees.

Each human has two additional minor spirits, *pui yushin*, spirit of feces, and *isun yushin*, spirit of urine. When a person defecates or urinates, one looses a portion of one's spirit. Therefore, care must be taken to defecate or urinate where a foe cannot get access to one's feces or urine, lest they practice sorcery against one, causing illness or death. The same caution applies to all bodily exuviae, including nasal mucus, hair, saliva, vomit, fingernails, toenails, perspiration, scabs, and so on. Because of the intimate connection between these substances and a person, they carry with them part of one's spirits when separated from the body. At death, the spirits of defecation and urination leave the body, falling to the ground, where they are dissipated by the next rain.

The Cashinahua were always curious about who I was, about my background, my family. Someone would ask, "*Epa min hayamen*?" "Do you have father?" "Yes." "*Hatimen*?" "How many?" "Only one." "Do you have mother?" "Yes." "How many?" "Only one." They seemed distressed by my answers. "Do you have brother?" "Yes." "How many?" "Only one." "And sister?" "Yes, only one." By this point in the discussion they were concerned and confused. "Do you have father-in-law?" "No." "Do you have mother-in-law?" "No." Now they were most distressed. How could anyone be so poor in kin? (See chapter 13 for discussion of Cashinahua kinship reckoning.) I wanted to convey to them that although I had only one brother, he was my twin. But I had no words to do so until one day when a woman returned from the garden with a stem of bananas. Several of the bananas were doubles; they were fused or partly fused down their length. I asked what they were called. They said, "*tsupibu*." I then asked one of my language teachers if, when a women gives birth to two babies one right after the other, you would call the babies *tsupibu*. He assured me that is what they would call them.

The next time they questioned me about my family, following the same routine described earlier, I gave them the added information *en tsupibuki*. They laughed hysterically. My teacher took me to the bank of the river where they dump the garbage and pointed to the body of a pet parakeet that had died some days earlier and was now crawling with maggots. *Pitsu tsupibuki*. "The parakeet is wormy," he said. It turns out that there are two forms of *en tsupibuki*. If the pitches of the last two syllables are low followed by high, it means "I am a twin." If the pitches are both low, it means "I am wormy." It is not clear which I said, because they would never have expected me to say that I was a twin, since no adult Cashinahua would ever be able to make such a statement. Twins are caused, they say, by a woman's becoming pregnant by a spirit. Twins, therefore, are called *yushin bake*, "spirit children," and are destroyed when they are born. When they finally understood that I was telling them that I am a twin, they immediately withdrew from me and avoided me for several days until the headman decided that I really could not be a spirit child because I was so dumb and incompetent in the forest. No spirit's child could ever be such. Needless to say, I became most interested in understanding more about the nature of spirits.

The Cashinahua interact with spirits on a daily basis, either consciously or unconsciously, just as they interact with nature and with one another. And they do so without thinking or worrying about the spirits. They know that if they behave in ways that are found acceptable to their fellow citizens, they are unlikely to offend the spirits. During dreaming and hallucinations, their souls interact with spirits, and here they are on more dangerous ground because their eye spirit or dream spirit has gone into the invisible side, to the realm of the spirits. Unless they are shamans, *huni muka dauya*, "man with bitter medicine," who have spirit familiars and protectors, it is always possible that their spirits could either be kidnapped by the spirits or be charmed and seduced into becoming a spirit's spouse or lover. Such a person falls into a deep coma or dies because his spirit cannot return to his mortal body.

Shamans serve as intermediaries between human society and the spirit world. They are men, or occasionally women, who show a capability to become a shaman because of excessive, vivid dreaming. A man who would become a shaman must actively pursue the spirits through dreaming or frequently drinking the hallucinogenic brew. He must abstain from sex throughout his quest because the smell of women's vaginal secretions enrage certain spirits. He loses interest in matters of everyday life. When he goes to the forest to hunt, he is not successful because the animals talk to him as friends, and he is unable to shoot them. His appearance becomes slovenly and he loses weight; food loses its appeal to him. After several months, he becomes intoxicated through taking tobacco snuff or drinking the hallucinogenic beverage and falls into a deep trance, during which one or more spirits takes up residence in his body, becoming his protector and guide. Following the trance he usually regains strength and returns to a state of normal health and activity. He may go through the whole sequence several times in order to accumulate additional spirit helpers. He then is able to diagnose the cause of illness in persons who have not responded to the herbal medicine provided by the herbalist, the *huni bata dauya*, "the man with sweet medicine" (see chapter 18).

Illness may have two sources. Most illness is thought to be natural; it happens just like birth, aging, and death. It is just part of normal human existence. Such illnesses respond to the treatment by the herbalist. Where they fail to respond to herbal medicine, people suspect that spirits are causing the illness, either because they have offended the spirits or because the spirits are acting as agents of a sorcerer. These are the cases in which the shaman is called upon to go into a trance and discover the source of the illness. He may recommend herbal medicine or may try to remove the cause through sucking or massage, or he may call on his spirit familiars to remove the offending spirit. Sometimes the patient recovers. Failure does not threaten the belief in either the herbalist's or the shaman's medicine. After all, death, too, is a natural thing. Plants and animals die, so must humans. That is the way it always has been and that is the way it always will be.

Cashinahua religion, then, can be said to be a system of beliefs about living with spirits. These spirits are the by-product of human attempts to come to terms with living in a physical world over which one has little control but which places limits on one's choices and activities.

Chapter 18

CASHINAHUA MEDICINE AND MEDICINE MEN

Medicine, *dau*, is an important domain in both the thought and behavior of the Cashinahua. This paper summarizes my data on this domain, focusing primarily on the medical specialists.[1]

The Cashinahua distinguish two major categories of medicine, *dau bata*, "sweet medicine," and *dau muka*, "bitter medicine." Each type is distinguished from the other by the manner in which a practitioner becomes a full-fledged specialist, his methods and materials, as well as the social values attached to his role.

Dau bata is associated with the role *huni dauya*, literally "man medicine-with," often also called, *huni bata dauya*, "the man with sweet medicine." It consists of herbal remedies that either grow wild in the jungle or, less frequently, are grown in the gardens. Glands and glandular excretions of some animals are also classed as *dau bata*. Most faunal medicines are used as charms, and all such medicines are connected to rituals. Also included in this category are the ornaments worn for rituals and festive occasions (see chapter 23). Although this subclass of medicine is known and made by all post-initiate members of the society, the *huni dauya* is the recognized authority on this medicine.

Muka dau, "bitter medicine," is an ill-defined spiritual quality possessed by the *huni mukaya*, literally "man bitter-with," which is obtained from the spirits during the process of becoming a specialist. Some informants claim that there are different varieties of *muka*, depending on the spirits from which it is obtained, and that each variety is used for a different kind of treatment. Most informants argue that *muka* is *muka*, but when pressed about it, quickly say that they do not know much, if anything, about the subject.

The *Huni Dauya*

The *huni dauya* is essentially an herbalist. He is qualified to treat two types of disease: (1) those that the patient "has," *haya*, including fungi, swellings, sores, dysentery, boils; and (2) those that the patient "feels," *tenei*, or "is," such as pain, nausea, laziness, sleeplessness, failure in hunting, anger, selfishness, and feelings of personal inadequacy. In general, both types of disease are thought to be of natural origin (very few informants ever told me that these diseases were due to supernatural causes even though speculation about supernatural causes is very frequent when illness occurs).

Each symptom is thought to be a separate illness and is given a separate name that describes either the appearance of the ailment, the physical sensation it produces, its location, or the natural causative agent. What Western medicine considers a single disease exhibiting various symptoms is thought by the Cashinahua to be not a single disease but several diseases occurring simultaneously. For example, the fever, chills, dizziness, and nausea that accompany malaria are four different diseases, each of which must be treated separately because each may occur in combination with other symptoms at other times. Thus, nausea, whenever it occurs, requires the use of the same medicines no matter what other symptoms are present.

For each disease (symptom) a single medicine or class of medicines is used as treatment. Each is named, the name reflecting the nature of the disease for which it is a cure, or some particular physical or therapeutic characteristic of the herb itself. Some herbs are disease specific, but most are used for more general treatment.

All Cashinahua adults know (or, as they say, "have") some medicine, much as most Americans know simple first aid. This does not make them herbalists, who are recognized as particularly knowledgeable specialists who are consulted in cases where "first aid" fails to produce a cure.

In general any man or woman may become an herbalist, if he/she demonstrates sufficient interest, ability, and willingness to work for a long period of time under an older specialist, and manifests a sincere desire to be helpful to the society in general. Since I was unable to obtain data about female specialists, the present descriptions refer only to males, although my informants told me that the same rules apply for females. Medical knowledge is generally passed on from father to son or father-in-law to son-in-law, mother to daughter or mother-in-law to daughter-in-law. The herbalist-to-be apprentices himself to an older herbalist who takes him into the forest and teaches him the skills while gathering the herbs needed for treatment of a disease. He first learns the names, appearance, and location of all medicinal materials and the diseases against which they are effective. He is then taught how to diagnose diseases. Finally, he begins to practice his skills under the watchful eye of his mentor.

Unless the medicine being prescribed is considered dangerous and too powerful if not taken as required, the herbalist rarely treats the patient personally. When his services are requested, he goes to the jungle, gathers the appropriate herbs and, upon returning to the village, presents them to the person making the request with instructions for their use. The person requesting the medicine or the patient then gives/takes the treatment in the prescribed fashion.

According to the Cashinahua, medicine always works. But where cures do not follow treatment, the following excuses are given: the medicine was improperly given or taken, the diagnosis was incorrect, or the disease has a supernatural cause and will not respond to normal treatment. The herbalist is not held responsible for the failure to produce a cure or for deaths that may follow treatment. However, if his patients consistently die or fail to improve, his reputation as a curer is weakened or destroyed, and he will be consulted with less frequency.

Herbalists are highly valued by the Cashinahua, each community desiring to have a successful, well-trained one residing in the village. In 1968 only two men, who resided in different villages, were recognized as first-class herbalists. Members of the other five villages consulted these men when their own less skilled herbalists were unable to produce cures. To my knowledge neither of these two men had apprentices when I left the field. [When I returned to Peru in 1993, there were herbalists, widely recognized for their skills, living in most of the villages, several of whom had learned their trade from these men.]

The *Huni Mukaya*

The *huni mukaya*, the man with bitter medicine, functions as shaman, diviner, sorcerer, and prophet. In the capacity of shaman and diviner he is consulted openly, particularly with reference to sicknesses that fail to respond to the treatment of an herbalist or that exhibit unusual symptoms not generally treated by an herbalist. Such illnesses are thought to be of supernatural origin. Upon request he takes snuff made from locally grown tobacco and goes into a trance-like state. He then runs his hands over the body of the patient who is lying before him in a hammock or on the floor. When aware of the cause of the problem, he either recommends treatment or, if a foreign object is present in the body because of sorcery, he removes it by sucking on the part of the body nearest to its location. Treatment prescribed by the shaman frequently includes herbs, which must be obtained through the herbalist and taken along with the obligatory fasting that always follows (and may precede) any treatment by the *huni mukaya*.

In his capacity as sorcerer the *huni mukaya* may be requested by a member of his local community to practice witchcraft against a personal enemy, generally a person residing in another village or a member of a neighboring tribe. (If the person who is the object of sorcery is a local resident, he will not be a member of the social core of the local group; that is, he will not be a member of the *huni mukaya's* extended family or the extended family to which it is linked in a marriage alliance.) Such requests are made in utmost secrecy.

In his capacity as prophet, the *huni mukaya*, at the request of the headman of the village, attempts to learn from his spirit familiars either what is happening in other places or what will happen at a later date that will affect the members of the village. Such a request is frequently made in order to obtain additional information following an *ayahuasca* session. (Any adult male may take the hallucinogen *ayahuasca*, which is taken in order to learn about events removed in time and/or space)(Der Marderosian et al. 1970; and see chapter 23). The information gained from these sessions is often incomplete and since the *huni mukaya* is able to communicate with the spirit world without the use of *ayahuasca*, he is requested to get additional details.

Informants are unclear about the manner in which *muka* is used. Most informants, however, are agreed that a person who has muka has power to influence the supernaturals to do his bidding. Unlike the herbalist, who learns his trade from a successful and accomplished practitioner, the shaman learns his art from the spirit beings who give him *muka*.

Any person, male or female, with a propensity for dreaming may become a shaman. A person desiring to become a shaman "pursues dreams"; that is, he takes whatever steps are necessary to maximize the number of dreams he will have in any night. My informants were very indefinite about how such steps were taken, emphasizing, rather, the results of excessive dreaming. The person in pursuit of spirits and *muka* becomes listless, somewhat withdrawn from the other members of his society, loses his appetite, expresses disinterest in sexual matters (both verbally and physically), and becomes unsuccessful at hunting. This last, according to the informants, is due to the fact that when the person goes hunting, the animals try to talk to him and treat him as a friend; therefore, he is unable to shoot them. He wanders about the village and into the jungle as if in a daze, and after an indefinite period of time he is "seized" by the spirits and falls to the ground unconscious or in a trance-like state. This is the point at which he receives *muka* from the spirits. After regaining consciousness or recovering from the trance-like state, he requests from the herbalist spirit medicine with which he bathes his body in order to avoid further seizures. Some shamans become unconscious or go into an involuntary trance-like state after the initial experience and are said to obtain additional *muka* with each new occurrence. The shaman does not lose any of his *muka* either through using it for a client or through failure to practice his art. He may lose some or all of his *muka*, however, while dreaming, when spirits with whom he is not familiar or spirits working at the behest of another shaman steal it from him. Persons who dream a lot but do not wish to become shamans request medicines from the herbalist to calm their dream-spirit and to prevent it from becoming friendly with other spirits.

The degree of success and thus power of the shaman is directly related to the number and variety of spirit beings with whom he is familiar. Lack of success by the shaman is credited either to his not having sufficient *muka* or to the overpowering strength of spirit forces hostile to the shaman.

The Cashinahua are very ambivalent about shamans and shamanism. A *huni mukaya* who practices his art for the benefit of his community is highly valued. However, his presence in the community constitutes a continual threat to the other members of the group, in that wherever and whenever a shaman is present, the number of spirits, both friendly and hostile, is considerably increased. In addition, deaths that are diagnosed as being caused by sorcery may be avenged by the kinsmen of the deceased, who may kill either the shaman or any of his close kinsmen.

At present I know of no powerful shamans practicing among the Cashinahua. Several informants claimed that one man had a little *muka*. When I asked him about it, he hesitantly admitted that at one time he had some but claimed that he had lost it; at least, he does not at present seem to be practicing the art. The last powerful male shaman died about 1950 or 1951, and a woman known as "a little shaman" died in 1964. During the summer of 1966, none of the Cashinahua were actively trying to become a shaman; rather, two men were taking medicine to avoid becoming one. Both insisted that the process was dangerous and inconvenient; it interfered with or negatively affected their skill as hunters.

Conclusion

Although both systems of medicine have been affected by the increased contact with outsiders during the last three decades, the *huni dauya* has been more fortunate than the *huni mukaya*. Although neither system proved adequate in the face of the influx of new diseases resulting from contact, the medicine of the *huni dauya* continues to produce cures for many diseases. In addition, his/her pharmacopoeia has been expanded by the addition of Western medicines obtained from traders and missionaries. On the other hand, given the general ambivalence of the Cashinahua toward *muka dau* and the absolute failure of the last powerful *huni mukaya* to deal with disease brought into the village by traders (he died in an epidemic he failed to halt), there has been a serious decline of interest in the role. All informants agreed, however, that the absence of any *huni mukaya* seriously jeopardizes the health of the tribe, since only a *huni mukaya* has the power to deal with the spirits with relative safety.

Chapter 19

BANISTERIOPSIS USAGE AMONG THE CASHINAHUA

We drank *nixi pae*. Before starting to chant, we talked a bit. The brew began to move me and I drank some more. Soon I began to shake all over. The earth shook. The wind blew and the trees swayed. . . . The *nixi pae* people began to appear. They had bows and arrows and wanted to shoot me. I was afraid but they told me their arrows would not kill me, only make me more drunk. . . . Snakes, large brightly colored snakes were crawling on the ground. They began to crawl all over me. One large female snake tried to swallow me, but since I was chanting she couldn't succeed. . . . I heard armadillo tail trumpets and then many frogs and toads singing. The world was transformed. Everything became bright. I moved very fast. Not my body but my eye spirit . . . I saw lots of gardens full of manioc and plantains. The storage sheds were full of corn. The peanut racks were full. . . . I came down the trail to a village. There was much noise, the sound of people laughing. They were dancing *kacha*, the fertility dance. Everybody was laughing. Many women were pregnant. I was happy. I knew we would be well and have plenty to eat.

This excerpt from the report of one informant illustrates the basic aspects of *Banisteriopsis* usage among the Caṣhinahua. *Nixi pae*, the vine drunkenness, also known as *ayahuasca* by the local Peruvians (and the term I will use from this point on), is prepared from the stalks of several lianas of the genus *Banisteriopsis* and the leaves of a shrub identified as a member of the genus *Psychotria*. Chemical analysis indicates that the active hallucinogenic agents of *Banisteriopsis* are harmine and harmaline; that of the *Psychotria* is dimethyltryptamine (DMT) (Der Marderosian et al., 1970).

Banisteriopsis is considered by the Cashinahua to be the basic ingredient of *ayahuasca*. Although *Psychotria* is clearly viewed as an additive, it is an important ingredient, without which the hallucinations are said to be less vivid and of shorter duration.

Any initiated Cashinahua male may drink *ayahuasca*. Usage varies widely: some men never drink it, others imbibe every time a brew is prepared. *Ayahuasca* bouts rarely occur more frequently than every other week, and then only after dark, generally beginning about eight in the evening and lasting until two or three in the morning. General consensus about the need or advisability of drinking seems to determine the timing of *ayahuasca* parties.

Although all the men know how to prepare the beverage, it normally falls to one or two men from each village to make the preparations. The host goes to the jungle and without any ritual or ceremony selects and cuts one to two meters of *Banisteriopsis* and three to five branches of *Psychotria*. On returning to his house, he cuts the vine into six-to eight-inch segments that he pounds lightly with a rock and places in a clay cooking pot with two-to four-gallon capacity. The leaves and buds of the *Psychotria* are stripped from the branches and added to the pot, which is then filled with water. A fire is lit around the base of the pot and allowed to burn until the water nearly reaches a boil. The brew is steeped for about an hour, after which it is ladled off to cool in smaller pots.

As the hour for the affair approaches, the host places some stools and logs near the hearth. Each man, when he arrives, goes to the pots and dips out about one pint of the liquid. He sings or chants several phrases over the brew, asking it to show him many things, and then gulps it down. He then joins the others and talks or chants quietly while waiting for the effects of the drug to begin. After fifteen minutes he may drink another pint, particularly if he wishes to hallucinate freely, or as the Cashinahua say, "to have a good trip." [*Nixinpaewen en bai pe wai* "Vine drunkenness-with I trip make good." The term translated "trip" (*bai*) has the idea of a sightseeing excursion with house calls for visiting.]

Once the drug "begins to shake them," chanting begins in earnest. Each man sings independently. Chants often involve conversations with the spirits of *ayahuasca*; at other times they merely consist of the rhythmic repetition of the monosyllabic 'e 'e 'e 'e 'e 'e. Those who do not know the chants sit next to someone who does, swaying their bodies in time with the rhythm.

Although each man operates on his own, the group is very important, as it provides him a contact with the real world, without which the terrors of the spirit world through which he is traveling could be overwhelming. Frequently a group of men will line up on a log, each one wrapping his arms and legs around the man ahead of him. Only the men who are "strong," those who have had many years of experience with *ayahuasca*, will not maintain physical contact with at least one other person. *Ayahuasca* is never taken by a person alone.

The volume of the chanting rises and falls, punctuated by shrieks of terror, retching, and vomiting. No attempt is made to coordinate either the rhythm or pitch of the chants. Each man devotes his attention to what he is experiencing and his own search for knowledge.

In spite of the individual nature of the hallucinatory experience there is a high degree of similarity in the content and frequency of occurrence of particular hallucinations from individual to individual during any one night of drinking. Certain themes also recur every time they drink *ayahuasca*. The most frequent of these are (1) brightly colored, large snakes; (2) jaguars and ocelots; (3) spirits, both of *ayahuasca* and others; (4) large trees, often falling trees; (5) lakes, frequently filled with anacondas and alligators; (6) Cashinahua villages and those of other Indians; (7) traders and their goods; and (8) gardens. All informants speak of the sense of motion and rapid change, or as they say, transformation. Particular hallucinations wax and wane, interspersed by others in a very fluid manner. There is a sense of darkness interrupted often by flashing bright colors or brightness when the horizon seems to collapse. Time and space perceptions are distorted.

Hallucinations generally involve scenes that are a part of the Cashinahua's daily experience. However, informants have described hallucinations about places far removed, both geographically and from their own experience. Several informants who have never been to or seen pictures of Pucallpa, the large town at the Ucayali River terminus of the Peruvian Central Highway, have described their visits under the influence of *ayahuasca* to the town with sufficient detail for me to be able to recognize specific shops and sights. On the day following one *ayahuasca* party, six of nine men informed me of seeing the death of my *chai*, "my mother's father." This occurred two days before I was informed by radio of his death.

However, the most persistent comment about *ayahuasca* from all informants is, "It is a fearsome thing, I was very much afraid." Few informants have ever admitted that they find it a pleasant experience.

If they find it so unpleasant, so fearful, why do they persist in using the drug? The answer lies in the relevance of the hallucinations for personal action. The Cashinahua drink *ayahuasca* in order to learn about things, persons, and events removed from them by time and/or space that could affect either the society as a whole or its individual members.

Hallucinations are viewed as the experiences of an individual's eye spirit or dream spirit; they are portents of things to come or reminders of the past. Thus, after a night of drinking, the men discuss some of their experiences, particularly those which seem to have relevance for the society, such as visions of an abundance of food, or hunger and famine, health or sickness, and death. Although in most cases little can be done to alter events foreseen in visions, some precautions can be taken. For example, when famine is seen, gardens can be enlarged. Or, when a foreigner is seen coming, bringing sickness with him, they may decide to leave the village for an extended hunting trip. Such decisions will affect a man, his wife and his children, and on occasion his extended family. Rarely however, would decisions based on information gained through *ayahuasca* affect an entire village, and never the whole society.

Ayahuasca is used on occasion to obtain information about the cause of an illness that has not responded to traditional treatments (see chapter 18). In case of sickness, a person usually tries to cure him-or herself. When cure does not follow, an herbalist is consulted. After hearing the symptoms, he prescribes sweet medicine. Several such consultations are often required. If, after repeated tries, sweet medicine fails, a shaman is consulted. He reviews the history of the case and then consults his spirit familiars about the cause of the illness, normally an intrusive object of spirit that he then removes from the patient with a small quantity of *muka dau*, "bitter medicine" which resides in the shaman's body, and which must then be removed from the patient by the herbalist's sweet medicine. It is only when these procedures fail to produce the desired cure that the shaman resorts to *ayahuasca*. A special drinking session is called, during which the shaman consults with spirits outside his normal sphere of influence, who inform him of the cause of the illness, or a new chant that should be used along with sucking or massage, or the kind of sweet medicine to request from the herbalist, or that the illness is incurable.

In conclusion, the Cashinahua use *Banisteriopsis* as a means of gaining information not available through the normal channels of communication, which, in addition to other information, form the basis for personal action. The shaman's usage of *ayahuasca* is merely a specific case of a more general social phenomenon in a situation where his normal methods fail.

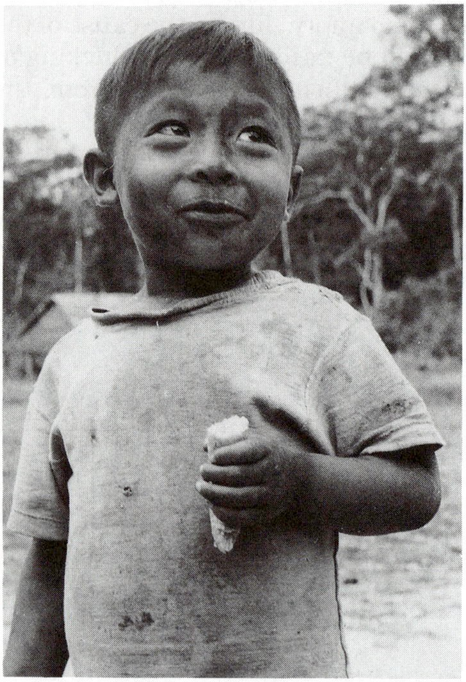

Roberto in 1963. In 1993 he was the pastor of the church in Balta.

A man with his face painted with a design identifying him as a member of the duabake *moiety. The designs on his chest are tattoos.*

Chapter 20

"YOU KILLED MY BABY!" DISPENSING MEDICINE IN THE FIELD

In the case of most anthropologists, the decision about whether to provide medical care to the group one is studying is a personal one. In my case, however, my position at the time mandated that I provide such care. I am sure, nevertheless, that had I had to make a conscious choice at that time, I would surely have decided to do just as I did. During my eighty-four months of fieldwork between 1955 and 1968 I treated the Peruvian Cashinahua for numerous medical conditions, dispensing a wide array of medicines. I began my work with the Cashinahua as a member of a missionary organization that considered providing medical care one of my duties and provided me with basic training in first aid and tropical medicine, with a medical handbook, and with a selection of medicines; the mission's medical doctor was available for consultation via two-way radio. I shared with my mission colleagues a conviction that Western medicine was superior to that available through native practitioners, the so-called "witch doctors."

My first patient was the headman, who had a large suppurating sore on the heel of his badly swollen foot and leg. My audience *ooh*'ed and *aah*'ed as the hydrogen peroxide boiled and bubbled around the lesion as they did several days later when I removed from his heel a core of wood, the swollen remnants of a twig that had penetrated his heel several weeks earlier while he was clearing brush in his garden. While he recuperated, he became my captive informant. While my success in treating the headman helped my rapport, it also caused animosity from the headman's brother-in-law, the village witch doctor/herbalist, who had been treating the headman without success. I suspect that my distrust of him was greater than his of me; after all, I thought he was the Devil's agent.

My success led to demands for medical treatment for scratches and scrapes as well as for headaches, malaria, intestinal parasites, eye infections, dysentery, and so on. Although several hours each day were devoted to medical care, I was learning the language while providing a service.

The first crisis came when I vaccinated the Cashinahua against smallpox. Despite my warnings against scratching, most of them scratched their vaccinations, which then spread down their arms, causing swelling, infection, and fever. The witch doctor and others accused me of trying to kill them. Through more than a week of round-the-clock care, I learned much about their concepts of illness and related food taboos. I was disturbed when I found that the witch doctor was following me on my rounds, treating each of my patients following my ministrations while also checking on my methods. They all survived—and so did I.

I was surprised one day when a group of women came to request "baby-making medicine" such as I had given Xuni. I informed them that I did not have such medicine. They argued that Xuni and her husband had worked for three years to make her first baby, and now she was pregnant again although she and her husband had not been "working at making a baby." They insisted that the medicine I had given her had clearly caused the pregnancy. I had in fact treated her some months earlier, giving her tranquilizers and antidepressants for hysteria and depression after she had suffocated her infant son by rolling on him in her sleep. The witch doctor came to my rescue by claiming that it was his medicine that had caused the pregnancy.

Demands for my medical services were an almost daily event. Listening to medical complaints and treating them consumed only a few minutes on a good day, but during epidemics I spent nearly the entire day attending to them, cutting into my time for research. Nevertheless, as a missionary I was doing my duty, and I was learning the language and culture. Furthermore, I was there for the long haul and was not worried about having to finish my studies before having to return to graduate school. Besides, it felt good to be needed.

Although he continued to resent me as a competitor, even the witch doctor and his family used my services. But my relationship with him changed drastically when I got a fungus on my feet that became increasingly debilitating, despite treatment with several fungicides in my medical kit. He came to my hammock and examined my feet, telling me that he had medicine that cured "rotten foot." My missionary colleague objected that accepting treatment from the witch doctor would be to dabble with the Devil's medicine, but I was unable to walk without great pain and agreed to his treating me. He went to the forest and gathered four bundles of leaves, which he blanched in hot water. He then mashed them into a pulp between the palms of his hands and while squeezing the mass in one hand, he coated my feet with the bilious green foam that ran down his thumb. After an initial burning sensation, the itching and pain in my feet subsided. Further treatments followed during that day and the next. I was able to walk without discomfort in two days, and within a week my feet were completely healed. It may have been the Devil's medicine, but it worked!

Living with the Cashinahua and gaining some understanding of their worldview already had challenged many of the assumptions and stereotypes I carried with me into the field, so the witch doctor's successful treatment of my foot was both deeply appreciated *and* profoundly disturbing. When I returned to the field after a year of graduate study in anthropology, a year that gave sharper definition to my doubts and alternative perspectives, I changed my approach to treating the Cashinahua by enlisting the witch doctor's advice and help in treating patients. Although I was still convinced of the superiority of Western medicine, I could no longer be comfortable viewing him or his medicine as satanic. We often worked together, discussing patients' symptoms, medical histories, and possible courses of treatment. I was expected to treat the "symptoms" while he addressed his treatment to the "cause(s)," particularly where his diagnosis included supernatural agencies.

After additional graduate study, I returned to the field for six months specifically to study with him. He was an "herbalist," *huni bata dauya*, the "man with sweet medicine," as opposed to the *huni muka dauya*, the "man with bitter medicine," the shaman (see chapter 18). He instructed me in the types of illness, how to recognize them, and how to treat them. He shared with me his vast knowledge of medicinal plants and how to prepare and administer them. His treatment of many rashes and fungal infections seemed to work better than the medicines in my kit.

My medical treatment was not always successful; some patients died. Fortunately, the Cashinahua never blamed me for those deaths although, as they told me later, there were times when they had decided to kill me if people died, particularly after the smallpox vaccinations. Only once was I threatened with death. During a visit, Xiku asked me to treat his five-year-old daughter for intestinal parasites. I agreed, on the condition that they stay in the village for the five days needed for her treatment, in line with my normal practice of always personally giving patients their medication when it was to be taken. He insisted that he had to return to his village and begged me to provide the medicine and assured me that he would give it to her according to my instructions. After much begging and cajoling by him and despite considerable reservation, I agreed to his request and carefully gave him the instructions for administering the drugs, chewable tablets especially for children. I reminded him that it was powerful medicine and had to be given exactly according to my instructions, which he correctly repeated for me several times. Mid-morning two days later Xiku's son-in-law came rushing into my house yelling, "Run into the forest." Xiku was on his way upriver in his canoe to shoot me because I had killed his daughter.

My instinct was to run, but I stayed and went to the river's edge to greet Xiku when he arrived. As his canoe neared the shore, I waded into the river, pushed aside his shotgun, put my arms around his shoulders and began the death chant. He got out of the canoe; we squatted on the sandbar and wailed. His son-in-law took his shotgun, and I escorted him to my house and offered him food. As he ate I talked, outlining what I assumed had happened. His daughter liked the first tablet; it was *batapa*, "very sweet," and she wanted another, then another until she had consumed all of the tablets I had given him within a matter of several minutes. "*Habiaskaki*," he said, "That's the way it was." I was overwhelmed with guilt, a guilt that was not helped by the herbalist's reminder that a real *huni bata dauya* always directly administers powerful or dangerous medicine to his patient.

I returned to Xiku's village with him and joined in wailing over his daughter's lifeless body. As we wailed, long strings of mucus hung from our noses. We carefully used these to coat her body. At one point during the wailing, Xiku turned to me and said, "You killed my baby." Sensing the guilt I knew he felt, I replied, "Yes, I killed your daughter." No need to remind him of the instructions not followed and the unheeded warnings of the medicine's potency. I helped to dig her grave, and we buried her.

As I reflect on the thousands of cases of medical care I provided for the Cashinahua, I have no regrets other than regrets that I was not always able to save their lives. In many cases I was able to ease their pain and cure their ailments. Very few Cashinahua died while I lived in their villages. But I was not flying blind. I had been given some training, and I was usually able to consult with a physician by radio when cases failed to respond normally to treatment or when I could not diagnose the problem.

If I were to start work with another group, would I provide medical care? Only if no other medical care were available, especially if I had no way of consulting with a physician. Providing medical care can consume vast quantities of time, and there are risks. A patient sometimes dies and, whether or not the treatment contributes to that death, one can be charged with killing the patient, especially in situations where linguistic and cultural differences are great and communicative competence is low.

Providing medical services in the field can contribute to establishing rapport. The success of my medical treatment of the Cashinahua helped them overcome their fear of me as an outsider just four years after they had been devastated by an epidemic following the visit of a Brazilian anthropologist. It is also a way of giving to the community rather than simply taking from it. As the herbalist taught me his system of medicine, I shared with him my knowledge, and when I left the field, I gave him a large supply of medicines, after consultation with the mission's physician, medicines he felt would complement his own pharmacopoeia.

Women on left are preparing cotton for spinning while the one on the right is spinning it.

Women working with cotton while man and boys look on. Note that the women are sitting on palm leaf mats while the man is sitting on a wooden stool. Women only sit on stools during the initiation rites. Men do not sit on palm leaf mats.

Chapter 21

DISPOSING OF THE DEAD

"There were so many bodies," the headman Awadetsati responded, rubbing his hand over his eyes as if trying to wipe away the memory. "All my people were sick, many were dying. Nobody had the strength to dispose of the bodies. Some of the dying crawled from the village so the stench of their decaying bodies would not disturb the ill." With these words, he got up from his hammock and ended our conversation.

This reference to the epidemic of 1951 during which four-fifths of the adult population died in less than a month was his answer to my query about when and why the Cashinahua stopped consuming the bodies of their dead. Our discussion was based on a text I had read to him, a text about Cashinahua mortuary practices recorded by João Capistrano de Abreu (1941:140–141) shortly after the turn of the century.[1]

Awadetsati's response is only part of the story, however. Funerary endocannibalism probably never was universally practiced by the Cashinahua even before the early 1900s, when a Brazilian policeman interfered, ordering them to bury a body they had already started to cook (Montag ms:5). The Peruvian Cashinahua continued to practice funerary endocannibalism until the 1951 epidemic. I do not have information on whether this incident marked the end of the practice among the Brazilian Cashinahua.

According to my informants, infants, children, and adolescents were never eaten. Adult women were occasionally eaten, usually only senior women who had many children or were the wives of powerful men. Most, but not all, mature adult males were eaten. In order to understand who was eaten and why, we must examine Cashinahua beliefs about the nature of death and the afterlife.

Death and the Afterlife

Death occurs when the eye spirit, *bedu yushin*, leaves the body and does not return. Temporary absence of the eye spirit results in unconsciousness or delirium, indicators of approaching death.

In addition to the eye spirit, also often called the real spirit, *yushin kuin*, four other spirits also leave the body at death, each spirit with its separate destiny. There is a difference of opinion among informants about exactly how many spirits each person possesses. All agree on the five discussed here; many add other spirits to the inventory, most of which involve character traits. Thus, some people are said to have a spirit of selfishness, envy, malice, and the like or, on the other hand, generosity, beneficence, benevolence, and so on.

The spirits of urine and feces dissipate quickly, washing away with the next rain to become part of the nearest stream and the soil, respectively. The Cashinahua show little concern about these spirits of the dead; mothers prevent their infants from crawling on the ground near the site of death until after the rain has washed the spirits away.

The dream spirit drifts away from the deceased into the gabled roof of the house, where it sits watching the mourners until the body has been disposed of. It then goes to the forest to linger among the orchids and bromiliads of the tall trees. A viscous substance called *yushin dexu*, spirit snot, hanging from twigs and leaves of bushes at the base of a large tree is interpreted as indication of a dream spirit's presence in a particular tree. Fellow hunters often commented when encountering this substance, "*Hawen nabu manui*," (it misses its kin).

The dream spirits of dead kin are encountered in the trees by the dream spirits of the living when they dream. These contacts are generally benign; dreams about the dead cause the dreamer to feel sad. If one's relationship with the deceased was less than harmonious, contact with the deceased's dream spirit may cause nightmares. However, the dream spirit of the dead is not a matter of great concern to the living since, with time and dimming of memory, encounters become less frequent.

Unlike these three spirits about which the Cashinahua show little concern, the eye spirit and the body spirit of the deceased are of major concern and the focus of their mortuary practices.

The Eye Spirit, *Bedu Yushin*

The eye spirit is the brightness in a person's eye. Through the eye one gains eye knowledge, that is, knowledge of the supernatural (see chapter 22), particularly during serious illness with delirium and during unconsciousness and hallucinations when one's eye spirit leaves the eye temporarily. Some informants insist that eye knowledge can also be gained through dreaming, when one's dream spirits interact with a wide array of spirit beings. It is only with the eye spirit that one can truly and fully see persons and objects in both their physical and spiritual substance. The trajectory of the eye spirit at death is determined by gender, age, and experience.

Infants, uninitiated children, and most women have little or no eye knowledge, so at death their eye spirits are ushered by the spirits of kin along the rainbow, *inka bai*, to the celestial village of the ancestors, where they are received as beloved consanguines. The eye spirits of older women, particularly if they have gained eye knowledge through being chant leaders or having taken the hallucinogenic beverage ayahuasca, must be assisted by chants by the living during the mourning period.

An initiated male's eye spirit requires greater assistance because it is associated with greater eye knowledge, particularly that acquired through hallucinatory experiences. During its travels downriver to the base of the earth and along the *inka bai*, it faces the dangers of being waylaid, attacked, and eaten by hostile spirits. The dangers are proportional to the eye knowledge possessed by the deceased. Thus, the eye spirit of a wise old man faces a perilous journey en route to the celestial village where, in contrast to his female counterpart, he is greeted as an affine, that is, with a degree of suspicion and reserve.

The Body Spirit, *Yuda Bake Yushin*

Yuda bake yushin, the body child spirit (hereafter simply the body spirit), encases a person like an outer skin. It is a person's aura, an indicator of the state of a person's vitality and health, a person's sheer physical presence. It also refers to a person's reflection in water or in a mirror, as well as a person's shadow. It is associated with body knowledge, or, knowledge of the physical world, physical skills, and so forth. The strength of one's body spirit is related to the quantity and quality of one's body knowledge. Thus, older men and women tend to have the most powerful body spirits. At death, the body spirit leaves the body, lingering in the vicinity until coaxed by the mortuary rituals to retrace the deceased's voyage through life until it finally returns to the place of birth, where it is transformed into a forest spirit, *ni yushin*.

Mortuary Rituals and the Body and Eye Spirits

The object of the mortuary rituals is to speed the body and eye spirits of the deceased on their way, by an expression of grief and sadness. These spirits are not the object of either fear or veneration. Like all spirits, however, they can be capricious and playful or spiteful and malicious; and although their activities can be beneficial or detrimental, they have the potential to be disruptive of the routines of daily life.

Mourning begins before death occurs.[2] When the dying person lapses into unconsciousness or is unresponsive, female kin begin to keen "*ėn en ėn en ėn en*." Close male kin may gather. At death a close male kinsman crawls into the deceased's hammock and holds the body in his arms during a short cycle of mourning, while other kin call to the deceased not to leave them. The body in its hammock is then lowered to the floor or the ground. The women form a line facing the body and dance a step forward and backward, wailing in a rhythmic chant, while waving their forearms up and down with palms up. Men form a line with their right hand on the left shoulder of the man in front of them, then chant and dance in a shuffle step around the body.

I never noticed any tears, but mucus ran copiously from their noses, forming long strings, which they carefully removed with their fingers and placed on the body until it was coated from shoulders to feet. Informants differed in their explanation of the practice. Most said that it was to bathe the dead in a physical expression of their grief; my most knowledgeable informants said that it was to remove the body spirit and prevent it from reattaching itself to the deceased.

The dancing and chanting continue for a time varying from a few hours to all night, depending on the time of death and the social position of the deceased. Wakes for older people tend to last much longer than for initiated adolescents and adults without married children. The wake ends when young affines wrap the body in its hammock in preparation for burial. It may then be wrapped in palm-leaf mats or placed in a section of an old canoe and carried out of the village by male affines for burial, along with personal possessions, in a meter-deep grave. The preferred site is in the abandoned village in which the deceased had last lived; an abandoned garden in the direction of this site is an acceptable alternative.

Prior to 1951, the bodies of senior males and some senior females were, after a period of wailing, tied into a fetal position, placed in a large pot, which was filled with water and then covered with another pot, and cooked. After placing the cooked body of a man on a palm-leaf mat and that of a woman in a woven basket, portions of flesh were torn off the carcass and eaten with boiled plantains. Later the bones were dried by baking and ground into a fine powder that was mixed into gruel, *mabex*, or stew, *beten*, and consumed.

Reports on Cashinahua mortuary practices show considerable variability, but all include ritual wailing and chants. Deshayes and Keifenheim (1982:240) report that when the former headman Awadetsati died in 1979, "men snatched up machetes and axes and within minutes the walls of his house were torn down." McCallum (1991) reports on dressing the body in its best clothes. She also notes that Christian prayers have been added to the rituals and that some Cashinahua identify the source and destination of the eye spirit as *Inka*, now equated with the Christian God.

Despite the variability in Cashinahua funerary practices and the accretions of Protestant and Catholic ideas to their cosmology, their worldview and the function of the rituals seem to remain unchanged. Mortuary rituals are designed to separate both the dead from the living and the living from the dead.

While the mourning rituals express grief and respect toward the eye and body spirits of the deceased, their primary goal is to separate these most powerful spirits from the vicinity of the village. The chants encourage the eye spirit to travel to the celestial village of the ancestor's spirits and the body spirit to begin its journey back to the place of its birth.

The mourning rituals are intense but rather brief, lasting less than twenty-four hours. Once the body has been taken from the village for burial, public mourning ceases. Women occasionally can be heard keening for several months when they think they are alone.

The deceased is not openly discussed; circumlocutions are used rather than a name when references to the dead are deemed necessary, but the person's name is not deleted from the vocabulary. As one informant told me, "When I hear somebody call my son's name, it makes me sad. I think of his namesake, my deceased father."

Following the death of a powerful man, they may hold *chidin*, the headman's ritual, that is normally held either in recognition of a new headman or, more frequently, when tensions have disrupted the normal flow of social interaction. The chants of the ritual refer to the cultural patterns learned by the ancestors from *Inka*, patterns that emphasize their ties with the ancestors and their identity as real men, *huni kuin*. The ritual also reaffirms their cultural values of egalitarianism in the context of social and economic reciprocity and the need to settle their differences amicably. *Chidin* reintegrates the social body after a part has been torn away by death.

Once the mortuary rituals are completed, the Cashinahua get on with the business of living. They do not live their lives to please or appease the spirits of the dead; the spirits are gone. Rather, they invest their energy in the mundane activities of the present, in producing and raising the namesakes of their dead.

Chapter 22

THE BODY KNOWS

CASHINAHUA PERSPECTIVES ON KNOWLEDGE

It was only a brief comment from a father to his young son, but it launched me on one of the most illuminating and exciting lines of inquiry during my seven years of fieldwork with the Cashinahua of eastern Peru. The men were sitting on low wooden stools or turtle shells around an assortment of bowls that only a little earlier had been filled with the normal daily menu of wild game, manioc, plantains, and gruel. Their discussion of the day's hunt was interspersed with the usual raunchy banter between brothers-in-law.

Awadetsati, the headman, cleared his voice, scratched his crotch and said, "In the days of the ancestors, there was a tapir."[1]

His audience chuckled in anticipation of the impending tale. The women, sitting on palm-leaf mats around the remains of their meal in another circle a short distance from the men, giggled and hushed the children.

"He was a horny creature who announced his carnal interests to anything that moved. He even propositioned a leaf that blew across his path."

"*Ede*," said Masa, "just like Siu," referring to his young brother-in-law, who retorted with a choice obscenity, much to the amusement of the audience.

"One day as he blundered through the forest, tapir encountered a *xawe*, a large land turtle. 'My,' he said to her, 'you are a gorgeous

Awadetsati, the storyteller.

creature. Let's fuck.' That's just what he said to her. She looked him over from the end of his long nose to his rump. 'You're a big one. And what a luscious penis! Sure,' she said, 'let's do it.' 'I've never screwed a creature like you,' he said. 'Where do I stick my penis?'"

Amidst considerable laughter and giggles, various members of the audience suggested possible alternatives.

"'Here,' she said, pointing to her mouth. Well, he shoved it in and started humping. '*Hun, hun, hun.*' When he was at the height of his passion, *CHUN*! Her jaws clamped shut."

"*Adai, adai*!" shouted the males as they clamped their hands over their genitals. The women *ii*'ed and giggled, their hands over their mouths.

"Turtle walked away, chewing. She had her supper. But Tapir crawled into the bushes and died. That's the way it happened long ago in the days of the ancestors."

Amidst comments from the audience, Bidu, the man sitting next to me on his turtle shell, leaned forward and said to his young son, cradled between his legs, "My son, that's what happens when all your knowledge is in your balls."

It was a funny line and I laughed, but Bidu's comment haunted me for weeks, even months. Where else can knowledge reside? How is knowledge acquired? What, for the Cashinahua, constitutes knowledge?

Tapir, all my informants agreed, had little knowledge, *una*, and all of it was in his balls. In contrast, a wise man, *huni unaya*, has knowledge throughout his whole body. "*Hawen yuda dasibi unaia*, his whole body knows," they say. When I asked them where specifically a wise man had knowledge, they listed his skin, his hands, his ears, his genitals, his liver, and his eyes. "Does his brain have knowledge?" I asked. "*Hamaki* (it doesn't)," they responded.

What do the Cashinahua mean when they say that the skin, the hands, the ears, the genitals, the liver, and the eyes have knowledge?

Una is that which one's body learns from experience. All knowledge associated with physical labor is located in the hands because they are the part of the body most directly involved in work. For example, when a man chops down a tree to clear a garden in the forest, he learns something about the nature of the tree and of his tool, about the force needed to make the cuts and where to place them so the tree falls in the desired direction, and about whether or not it falls cleanly to the ground relative to the surrounding brush and trees, and more. This knowledge, say the Cashinahua, resides in his hands because they held the axe that cut the tree and caused it to fall; thus, they are the conduit by which the knowledge entered the body.

Knowledge learned by and associated with the men's hands, *meken una*, involves hunting, fishing, making gardens, tools, bows and arrows, feather headdresses, and other objects. Women's hands know planting and harvesting gardens, cooking, weaving, making mats, baskets, pottery, and other objects. The Cashinahua say that knowledge learned by and localized in the hands are those physical skills in which the hands play a primary part, even if other parts of the body play an important role.

Let me give an example. Successful hunting requires considerable knowledge, not all of which involves use of the hands. It requires knowledge of the behavioral characteristics of the animals hunted based on observation. This knowledge, the Cashinahua say, is "skin knowledge," *bichi una*, as is all knowledge of the natural world. When I questioned why it was not "eye knowledge," since it was knowledge that came from observation, they told me that it was knowledge about the jungle's body spirit, *yudabake yushin*.

All living things, including people, animals, vegetation, and all other animate and inanimate aspects of nature, are said to have "body spirits." Thus when one sees a person or thing, one can be said to see its body spirit. Further, one learns about things like sun, wind, water, and rain through the sensations they produce on the surface of the body. It is in this sense that knowledge of the natural world is "skin knowledge," *bichi una*, that is, knowledge gained through and located in the skin.

To see the true nature of people and the things that make up the natural world, however, one also must understand the *bedu yushin*, the eye spirit, sometimes also called the real spirit, *yushin kuin*. The eye spirit dwells in a person's eye, leaving the body during unconsciousness and hallucinogenic experiences to travel in the world of spirits. The knowledge gained in these travels is called *bedu una*, eye knowledge. It is only with the eye spirit that one can truly and fully see persons or objects in both their physical and spiritual substance, that is, their bodies and body spirits. Without the eye spirit, a person can only know the surface of things, that is, their skin, and thus can only have skin knowledge.

We return now to our hunter. In addition to his familiarity with animal behavior, skin knowledge, which allows him to locate an animal, he needs to know how to approach it. Again skin knowledge. But once in position to shoot, he draws on hand knowledge, *meken una*, for the hand-eye coordination needed to make the shot and for judging just how far to pull the arrow back and when to release it in order to make a kill. The skills required to make his bow and arrows are also hand knowledge.

Women's skills are also kinds of hand knowledge. Take, for example, spinning and weaving. Cashinahua women spin cotton to make thread for their hammocks, skirts, and other fabric objects. When a woman can transform raw cotton into thread of standard thickness without lumps or weak spots, people say that her hands know. Much hand knowledge is needed for her to produce a piece of fabric of the right texture and denseness and with straight edges. However, when she weaves designs into the cloth she uses patterns learned through the activities of her eye spirit and/or her dream spirit and thus depends on eye knowledge.

A woman with much hand knowledge spins cotton into thread of standard thickness without lumps or weak spots.

Social knowledge is gained through and resides in the ears and therefore is called *pabinki una*, ear knowledge. The connection with the ear comes from the centrality of language in social discourse. Although speech, *hancha*, comes from the mouth, knowledge comes from hearing. The Cashinahua use two expressions to

A woman weaves a skirt.

distinguish between two kinds of hearing: *ninka babui*, soft hearing, and *ninka kushi*, hard hearing. Soft hearing involves listening and absorbing facts about social matters, that is, social awareness. Hard hearing requires digging beneath the surface to consider motivations and consequences, and the like. It results from both listening, *ninka*, and thinking, *shina*. The statement *en mia ninkai* can mean either that I hear what you are saying or I understand what you are saying. Although both kinds of hearing involve knowledge, it is principally the second kind of hearing, hard hearing, that is involved when they say a person knows a lot or has much ear knowledge.

Social misfits and persons who flaunt social conventions are said to be "*patapa*," deaf or "*pabinki kushi*," to have hard ears. They also may be described as having ears without holes, "*hatun pabinki shuiuma*," their ears are without holes. They are people without ear knowledge.

During my fieldwork in the 1950s and 60s, I never was able to find out a specific locus where thinking takes place. Several informants said that it occurred within the ears, *pabinki medan*; others located it in the heart or the liver. Most, however, insisted that thinking takes place within the body, *yuda medan*, without specifying any particular part. Still other informants found my questions incomprehensible or silly. Although I pressed to see whether thinking took place between the ears, that is, in the brain, my informants consistently rejected the brain, *mapu*, as the locus of thought. I will return to this a bit later.

The genitals are the locus and source of knowledge of mortality and immortality, of the life force. The reasoning here is complex. First, children, the product of the genitals and genital activity, give one immortality by enduring beyond one's lifetime. The sexual act is brief and fleeting, but through it one reproduces one's self. Male informants often spoke of never feeling more alive than at the moment preceding ejaculation, followed, however, by death, that is, muscle relaxation and the loss of tumescence. The men often said of a satisfactory orgasm that they died or that the woman's vagina killed them. Cashinahua women never discussed the sex act in these terms, perhaps because they rarely experience orgasm. Genital knowledge of mortality is also rooted in biological realities associated with aging. Men speak with reluctance about their decreasing ability to achieve erection in old age; women speak about the cessation of menses and the loss of fertility.

The last kind of knowledge is *taka una*, liver knowledge, the knowledge of emotions. It is in one's liver that one feels joy and sorrow, fear and hope, distrust and pleasure. They say of a person who is generous, pleasant, and happy that he or she has a sweet liver, *taka batapa* and that his or her liver knows a lot, *hawen taka una haida*. A stingy person with a nasty disposition who always is gloomy and pessimistic is one with a bitter liver, *taka muka*, and that his or her liver only knows a little, *hawen taka una pishta*. The amount of liver knowledge a person has and the state of the liver, sweet or bitter, expresses itself both in behavior and in demeanor, that is, on the surface of the body. A person with a happy disposition is said to have a sweet face, *besu batapa*, while a grumpy person is said to have a bitter face, *besu muka*. One informant described his mother in the following terms: *Hawen taka una haida hayaki. Hawen besu batapa haida. Hawen yuda dasibi batapaki*, meaning "Her liver has a lot of knowledge. Her face is very sweet. Her whole body is very sweet."

Because of my own cultural bias, I continued to ask my Cashinahua informants about whether some part of the body, namely the brain, served as a sort of central processing center or data bank of knowledge. They patiently and persistently rejected any separation of mind and body, insisting that different kinds of knowledge are gained through and reside in different parts of the body. The whole body thinks and knows.

However, when I returned to the field in 1993 after an absence of twenty-five years, I discovered that some of the Cashinahua now recognize two new loci of knowledge, namely the brain and the heart. Brain knowledge, *mapu una*, results from reading, writing, and schooling. Heart knowledge, *huinti una*, comes from the introduction of Christianity.

Brain knowledge is gained through formal schooling and literacy. A Cashinahua teacher, trained by the Summer Institute of Linguistics missionaries, started the first bilingual school in the early 1970s.[2] As a result, many of the Cashinahua are now literate to some degree. It is primarily those individuals with secondary-school education who identify the knowledge gained through literacy and formal education as brain knowledge, thus differentiating it from traditional kinds of knowledge.

A clue to the difference between brain knowledge and the traditional kinds of knowledge is provided by the way many informants use two words for "to know": *tapin* and *una*. *Tapin* is a kind of scholastic knowing that results from formal teaching, *tapinmai*. *Una* is knowing that is primarily gained through direct personal experience or through instruction and demonstration, *yusin*. Between 1955 and 1968 I rarely heard the word *tapin*, and then it was used primarily to mimic the speakers of related Panoan languages, who use the word *tapin* for "to know" rather than *una*. Currently the Cashinahua tend to use *tapin* only when talking about knowledge in the brain or heart while retaining the use of *una* for knowledge resident in other parts of the body.

Some Cashinahua, particularly those who have attended secondary school and who therefore have been taught some basic science by mestizo teachers, now say that when a person thinks the brain functions as a kind of nexus, connecting, coordinating and drawing on knowledge located in the ears, eyes, hands, skin, genitals, heart, and liver. One man told me that the brain is where it all comes together. Most, however, continue to say that thinking occurs within the body, "*nukun yuda medan nun shinamiski*" (we always think within our bodies) or "*nukun yuda yamakidi nun shinamiski*" (we always think throughout all parts of our body).

Heart knowledge, *huinti una*, is knowledge of matters associated with Christianity. Considering the heart as the locus of such knowledge is a result of missionary teaching about having one's heart washed by the blood of Christ, of giving one's heart to Jesus, and of the Holy Spirit dwelling in the believer's heart. One gains heart knowledge through the teaching of the missionaries and native pastors, by reading the scriptures, and from the conversion experience.[3]

Most Cashinahua, whether they were believers or not, consistently used the term *tapin* (to know about) when talking about heart knowledge gained through the teaching of the missionaries or native pastors and through their personal reading of the Bible. Some, but not all, of those who say they are believers use the word *una* when discussing their conversion experience and their knowledge of God the father, "*epa Dius*," of God's son, "*Diusun bake*," and our older brother Jesus, "*nukun huchin Jisus*," and of the Holy Spirit, "*Yuxin Pepa*," that is, good spirit. One believer informed me that only *una* knowledge gained through the conversion experience, prayer, and Bible study can truly be heart knowledge. Knowledge of the sort for which the word *tapin* is used, he insisted, produces head knowledge, not heart knowledge. Genuine heart knowledge allows the believer, and only the real believer, to say "*En unai*," I know!

A few of my informants reject both head and heart knowledge as genuine kinds of knowledge, *una kuin*, referring to them as *una bemakia*, in other words, knowledge that is outside the mainstream or that is alien. None of my informants cited possession of brain or heart knowledge as a requirement for being known as a wise person, a *unaya*.

What, finally, are the characteristics of a wise person in Cashinahua? They are people who have a lot of knowledge, *una haida haiyaki*. Their hands know; they are skilled workers. Their skin knows; they have an extensive and intimate knowledge of their physical surroundings. Through the activities of their eye spirits they have knowledge of the spirit world. Knowledge of their mortality and immortality resides in their genitals. Their liver provides them with a full range of emotions. A truly knowledgeable person is one whose whole body knows.

But the Cashinahua insist that the wise person is not simply one who has a lot of knowledge. This knowledge must be expressed in behavior. Wise persons are generous both with their knowledge and its by-products. They are helpful but reserved; they never force their knowledge on others. They are confident but humble; they know that their knowledge is incomplete, that there is always more to learn. They are socially sensitive, knowing when to engage and when to disengage. They are even tempered, patient, temperate in all things. And finally, they are attentive to the present, but know that it too shall pass.

For the Cashinahua, knowledge is derived from activity and in turn generates activity. It is in action, not in contemplation, that knowledge is both gained and given expression.

Although Western scholars tend to think about knowledge in terms of the Cartesian separation of mind and body, we recognize and talk about certain activities and knowledge as if they are at least to some degree separate from the cognitive and semantic operations of mind. For example, take the political ad that told us, "In your heart you know he's right," or consider how we speak of the manual dexterity of a skilled craftsperson or musician or the physical skills of a gifted athlete or dancer as if their specialized knowledge is deeply embedded in the very fibers of their being. Despite these exceptions, we tend to alienate mind from body and see the body as a mere instrument of the mind. We celebrate knowledge for knowledge's sake, divorced from action.

For the Cashinahua, knowledge is gained through bodily experience and expresses itself in bodily activity. A wise person is not only one whose whole body knows based on past experience, but one whose knowledge continues to increase as knowledge is put into action. Knowledge is alive. It lives and grows in a body that acts, thinks, and feels.

Chapter 23

FEATHERS MAKE US BEAUTIFUL

Public rituals are festive occasions for the Peruvian Cashinahua and, as befits such occasions, they adorn themselves with festive attire, the most colorful and striking of which are feather headdresses.[1] Feathers are used as either a primary ingredient or added adornments on most headdresses. This chapter examines the reasons the Cashinahua give for using feathers,[2] namely availability, beauty, and utility.

Why Do the Cashinahua Use Feathers?

Although the Cashinahua use feathers for such practical purposes as fletching two types of arrows and making fire fans, the most frequent use of them is for making objects to adorn the body, such as headdresses, or ear and nose ornaments, and for decorating artifacts used in rituals.

For the most part, the Cashinahua found my questions about why they used feathers silly. After all, any fool can see that feathers are beautiful and enhance the beauty of their wearer. But, the Cashinahua indulged me and with great patience answered my silly questions. Their answers roughly fall into three categories: feathers are available, they are beautiful, and they are useful.

Feathers Are Available

Men frequently told me that the reason they used feathers is because they hunt. They hunt and kill a wide range of bird species, both large and small, as part of the food quest. Some species, such as currasow, guans, and doves, are highly valued as food, but the Cashinahua will kill most birds, no matter how small, for meat. They also kill carrion eaters (the vultures) and raptors (the harpy eagle and the hawks) for their feathers but never eat them since their flesh is considered to be dirty and smelly. After shooting and killing a bird, a hunter plucks the feathers or, in the case of small birds like the tanagers, skins them. He then carefully stores the feathers and dried bird skins for later use.

By using some of the feathers of the birds they eat and most of the feathers of the raptors and carrion eaters, the Cashinahua minimize waste, an important consideration since they believe they share the resources of the forest with the spirits. Birds, animals, and all living things have a visible (physical) and an invisible (spiritual) component. Humans have the right to use the visible component of natural resources while spirits use the invisible. If people needlessly waste these resources, they place in jeopardy harmonious relationships with the spirits. The spirits, like humans, wear feather headdresses and other feather ornaments. If humans waste forest resources, the spirits might retaliate in a variety of ways, most particularly by leading the birds and animals deep into the forest, making hunting more difficult than it already is and greatly restricting the supply of meat. Men fear this fate not simply because it means hunger for meat but because it would threaten their sense of their adequacy as hunters and thus as men.

Feathers Are Beautiful

All informants said that they used feathers because they are beautiful. Birds are the most colorful and visually arresting part of the Cashinahua environment. Flowers, which may also be brightly colored, are for the most part hidden high in the forest canopy, visible only when their petals fall to the ground or if a tree is felled, something rarely done when trees are in bloom; the Cashinahua occasionally cut down trees for their fruit when the blooming season is long past. Thus, birds' feathers are the only constant naturally occurring source of color other than the greens and browns of the forest. Also, feathers are almost imperishable if cared for properly and thus a potentially permanent source of visual stimulation.

The Cashinahua say of feathers that they have good *dua*. *Dua* is a difficult word to translate. A freshly bathed and oiled baby that is chubby, cheerful, and asleep or nursing is said to have good *dua*. A nubile young girl with firm breasts in good health and with no skin blemishes also has good *dua*, as does a vigorous young adolescent male with firm muscles and a lively step. A perfectly and fully developed ear of corn also has good *dua*. The rays of the sun filtering through the clouds are its *dua*. A live macaw flying overhead has good *dua*, but when it has been shot it has bad *dua*; it has lost its life. But, when the macaw has been plucked, its feathers have good *dua*. A well-made feather headdress also has good *dua*. Those qualities that result in someone or something being said to have good *dua* are beauty, radiance, luster, sheen, and vitality.

What specifically are the characteristics of feathers that have good *dua*? To answer this question it is necessary to examine the Cashinahua classification of feathers because the criteria for determining whether a feather has good *dua* depend on the kind of feather it is.

The Cashinahua recognize three major classes of feathers: *pei*, the wing flight feathers; *hina*, tail feathers; *dani*, body feathers (including the coverts of the wings and leg feathers; the word also refers to human body hair). *Dani* may be further subdivided according to the part of the body from which they come but for our purposes the more general category will suffice. *Pei* have good *dua* if their edges are not frayed, their tips are not broken or worn, and if their coloration is normal and vibrant. *Hina* with good *dua* are straight with minimal fraying along their entire length, no breakage of the tip, and with no fading of their color. Both *pei* and *hina* are supposed to be *kuxi*, strong, that is, they are supposed to look durable. *Pei* are expected to be relatively rigid throughout their length as are the *hina* of most birds; the *hina* of the macaws should be somewhat flexible for the distal quarter of their length. *Dani*, in contrast, should give a sense of lightness, filminess, and airiness. Because they are small relative to either *pei* or *hina*, there is less concern about the perfection of their edges, so long as they have not lost their luster. In general, feathers from birds that are nesting or have recently hatched a brood or from birds that are about to molt or are molting have bad *dua*, while the fully grown feathers from birds that have recently molted always have good *dua*.

Feathers Are Useful

Although the Cashinahua use feathers for ornamenting a diversity of objects, they use them primarily for making or ornamenting five major classes of headdresses: *pei maiti*, wing feather headdress; *dani maiti*, body feather headdress; *xawan hina maiti*, red-macaw tail feather headdress; *paka maiti*, bamboo headdress; and *yushin maiti*, spirit headdress. In the first three classes, the type of feather used is the defining characteristic. In the last two classes, feathers are used only as decoration.

Wing feather headdresses are characterized by a three-quarter fan of wing feathers, *pei*, constructed on an open ring of vine, either rigidly tied (*kedex*) between two strips of vine or tied onto a length of cotton string. If they are tied rigidly between strips of vine, the strips with the attached feathers are formed into a ring and are attached above a decorative vine ring to which are attached one or more tiers of *dani*, preferably black and usually the covert feathers from the wings or the feathers from the legs of the birds. The decorative ring is attached to the primary ring so that it covers the base of the wing feathers. If the *pei* are tied on a string, the string with the feathers is attached at several points to the decorative ring. An optional strip of vine larger than that of the primary ring is usually attached at the back of the headdress where the component strip or strips are fastened together to form the ring. It holds the *pei* erect, but not rigid. One or more tail feathers, *hina*, of macaws or occasionally of a harpy eagle or a hawk may be rigidly attached at the same place, producing an erect tail, *hina biden*. Alternatively, one or more composite tails (made by tying *dani* on a string) and/or bird skins may be attached to the back of the ring and allowed to dangle down the back of the wearer's neck, *hina pania*. There is an intentional pun involved in this phraseology. *Hina biden* also means "erect penis" as opposed to *hina pania*, "limp or dangling penis/tail." On those occasions when the women perform the fertility rituals, *kachanawa*, and wear headdresses with tail ornaments, men will frequently taunt their mothers-in-law by saying, "*Achin, min hina biden hayaki*" (Mother-in-law, you have an erect tail/penis). To which she is likely to respond, "*Mina pania-ki*" (Yours is limp). Such an exchange between mother-in-law and son-in-law could only happen within a ritual context.

In addition to their use in headdresses, *pei* of macaws, currasows, harpy eagles, vultures, and certain hawks are also used to fletch arrows. Harpy eagle wing feathers also are used in the construction of the large backrack that is worn as part of the lead dancer's costume in *chidin*, the headman's dance.

Hina, tail feathers, are used primarily as ornamentation, except in the *xawan hina maiti*, the red-macaw tail feather headdress, where red-macaw feathers are the primary element. Depending on how many are available, between twenty and one hundred *xawan hina* are attached more or less perpendicularly around a ring of thick vine that is covered with a strip of woven cotton fabric or is tightly wrapped with heavy cotton string. They may be either unadorned or adorned at their base with two or more tail feathers from small birds or with one inch of the tip of a currasow tail feather. Two oriole tail feathers or a single one-inch tip of a currasow tail feather may be glued to the tip of the macaw tail feather with a mixture of beeswax and chicle. The weight of this addition causes the feather to bob up and down as the wearer dances. In addition, five to twenty white plumes, made of a corn husk around which harpy eagle or king vulture leg or body feathers are tied, may be attached to the headdress base. *Xawan hina maiti* may also be ornamented by strings of clam or snail shells, baby tapir hooves, and turtle toenails. This is by far the most spectacular headdress made by the Cashinahua, and only one is made at a time for use as part of the costume of the lead dancer for *chidin*, the headman's dance.

The headman initiates the *chidin* ritual when tensions between men threaten the tranquility of community life. The men all contribute feathers from their personal supplies and jointly make the headdress, back rack, and feather train worn by the chant leader. Any adult male who knows the chant may put on the costume and lead the ritual. As he chants, he bends forward slightly with arms and hands extended slightly from the sides of his body and dances backward in a slow shuffle step. He is guided by two men who hold his extended hands as he moves back and forth in the village plaza or within one of the houses. *Chidin*, which emphasizes male unity, is usually followed by the fertility rituals during which male-female antagonisms are acted out.

Macaw tail feathers are also used as *hina biden*, rigid tail, ornament for four kinds of headdresses—*pei maiti*, *dani maiti*, *paka maiti*, and *yushin maiti*. They are also used for men's ear and nose ornaments and to decorate masks and spears for ritual use. A tiered train made of harpy eagle tail feathers, supplemented with currasow tail feathers as needed, is worn around the neck and hangs down the chest nearly to the ground as part of the lead dancer's costume for *chidin*.

An initiate wearing a nawan tete dani maiti *for his initiation in 1965.*

In 1993, he is a teacher in the primary school in Santa Rey and the father of eight children.

Dani, body hair/feather, is the defining component of three species-specific types of body feather headdress: *nea dani maiti*, trumpeter bird body feather headdress; *nawan tete dani maiti*, harpy eagle body feather headdress; and *isa dani maiti*, porcupine quill headdress. The unmodified term *dani maiti* generally refers to *nea dani maiti*, the most frequently made and used of the three types. It consists of one to four flattened strips of vine to which trumpeter bird body feathers in bunches of up to six black feathers are tied at approximately 0.5 to 1 centimeter intervals; by slightly overlapping and varying the length of the feathers, added body is given to the headdress. The ends of the feathered strips are overlapped and tied so that approximately two-thirds to three-quarters of the ring is covered with feathers thrusting forward. Tiny red, yellow, and/or green leg, underwing, and neck feathers, mainly from macaws and parrots, may be glued to the distal ends of the black feathers using beeswax-chicle adhesive. The effect is one of lightness and airiness, and when the wearer moves, the feathers appear to shimmer. Some men use the black body feathers of the currasow and various other bird species in place of those of the trumpeter bird, *nea*. In this case the name of the headdress is changed to reflect the type of feathers used.

Harpy eagle body feather headdresses are made in the same manner as the rigid headdresses made with wing feathers. Harpy eagle feathers are highly valued both because of their scarcity, which is due to the great difficulties involved in their acquisition, and because of the beauty of the fluffy white breast feathers. Therefore, *nawan tete dani maiti* are the most highly prized and admired of all headdresses. As is the case with trumpeter body feather headdresses, the body feathers of herons and other birds with long filmy breast feathers may be substituted for harpy eagle body feathers, with a consequent change of name reflecting the kind of body feather used.

Isa dani maiti is made of the porcupine quills (hair). The base of the quills are tied between vine strips using a technique similar to that used in the rigid *pei maiti* and the harpy eagle breast feather headdress. However, the porcupine quill headdress is never trimmed with *dani* but rather is trimmed by four to six strands of black, white, blue, red, and/or purple string that wraps each quill in a simple loop stitch, keeping the quills properly spaced and rigid. Tails of body feathers, feather pelts, and snail shells may be attached to the back of the headdress and allowed to dangle down the nape of the wearer's neck and back. Baubles made of short pieces of arrow cane decorated with small red and/or yellow feathers

Body paint and the feather headdress enhance this couple's dua.

or of short strings of Job's tears and other items may be tied at various intervals to the vine strips so that they hang in front of the wearer's forehead.

Dani from a wide variety of birds is used as a decorative element on a varied array of both ritual and nonritual objects in addition to other types of headdresses. Long tails, made by tying *dani* from a variety of birds to lengths of cotton string, are attached to the harpy eagle wing feather backrack as part of the costume of the lead dancer in *chidin*.

Paka maiti are made of lengths of bamboo from which the tough outer bark has been shaved, leaving only a thin inner shell which, when slit lengthwise and held in the heat of the cookfire, can be opened into a thin, flat sheet. The ends of the sheet are overlapped to form a cylinder and sewn together using cotton thread. *Paka maiti*, which are always worn with the seam at the back of the head, may be decorated by inserting at the seam a single erect macaw tail feather, plain or weighted with the tip of a currasow tail feather, or by attaching a dangling tail or tails of *dani* feathers of assorted colors from a diversity of birds, and/or shells, and/or feather pelts. In some cases, designs may be painted on the surface, or *dani* may be glued onto the cylinder covering the entire outer surface.

Yushin maiti, spirit headdress, is made of a section of palm frond that has not yet opened and is therefore pale yellow rather than green. The leaf is unfurled and formed around and attached to a bamboo crown, *paka maiti*. Alternatively, the ends of the frond are overlapped and tied with vine to form a shaggy crown. A single, erect macaw feather, plain or weighted, may be inserted at the back of the crown.

Feathers are useful not only because they are beautiful and give beauty, both to the objects on which they are used and to the user or wearer of those objects, but also because they are kinds of medicine, *dau*. The Cashinahua classify as medicine any substance or object used to decorate the body and other objects. Thus, feathers used to decorate a headdress, rather than those that are structural are its *dau*, as are body paint, headdresses, necklaces, ear ornaments, and so on, when worn by people. They enhance the *dua* of persons and objects, giving them increased endurance, toughness, and stamina. *Dau* is always used in rituals to attract the attention of the spirits of fertility and may also be used in daily life, but not always for spiritual purposes. For example, if a man wishes to impress a potential lover, he may adorn himself with body paint, a headdress, or a lip plug, all forms of *dau*. He has a secular goal, the seduction of the female, but by using *dau*, he is trying to enlist the aid of the spirits in his amorous quest. *Dau* has supernatural qualities that enhance his *dua*, making him attractive to the spirits of fertility. The combination of his *dua* and the spirits, attracted both by the *dau* and his *dua*, are believed to make him sexually more attractive. In addition to enhancing a person's *dua*, feathers and feathered objects as *dau* provide protection against attacks by hostile spirits.

Feathers are also useful because they give visible representation to the normally invisible aspects of a person's *yuda bake yushin*, an aura that encases the body of each living person. Under normal circumstances, one's *dua* is all that others see of this aura. A person's shadow or reflection in water or in a mirror are other aspects of one's *yuda bake yushin*. But, while under the influence of the hallucinogenic beverage *nishi pae*, a man sees the *yuda bake yushin* as a black aura that encases the bodies of all human beings, out of which bright colors streak, radiate, and sparkle, particularly about the head. It is this vision that the Cashinahua attempt to replicate in the feather headdresses. Men who are adept at using *nishi pae* are said to have the clearest vision of this aura and, therefore, are the ones who usually make the headdresses with the best *dua*.

The headdresses considered by the Cashinahua to be the most aesthetically pleasing, that is, they have a lot of good *dua*—have four characteristic traits. First, they are well made; the elements used in their construction are of the best quality and they are carefully put together. Second, the elements are well balanced without being symmetrical. Third, they are not over wrought with too many elements or excessive decorative frills; simplicity without bareness is elegant. Fourth, they are unique: they are not exactly like any other headdress although all share common elements. The Cashinahua say that this uniqueness of vision comes from the hallucinogenic experiences of the maker.

Discussion and Conclusions

Although there is undoubtedly some significance in the choice of feathers used, the Cashinahua never referred to it when I asked them why they used feathers. And, although birds are present in mythology, ritual, and cosmology, their role is relatively minor and does not provide an adequate explanation for the extensive use of feathers in ritual attire. Nor do the Cashinahua say that they use feathers as a way of living in harmony with the spirits. Yet, their answers all point to this element. Feathers are used because they are available as a result of hunting, and not to use them could be seen by the spirits as wasting shared resources. The Cashinahua use feathers because feathers are beautiful and make them beautiful; they enhance *dua*, thus making their wearer attractive to the spirits of fertility, spirits whose assistance is needed to assure the fertility of the gardens and of women. Finally, they use feathers because they are good *dau*; as adornments to the human body they give endurance, toughness, and stamina as well as protection from spirit predation.

Bidishu wearing the macaw tail feather headdress during chidin, *the headman's dance in 1957.*

A young man wearing a bamboo headdress, paka maiti, *decorated with body feathers from a macaw.*

Ipu blows on an armadillo tail trumpet during a kachanawa *feast in 1962. He is wearing an undecorated bamboo headdress.*

Chapter 24

WHEN A TURD FLOATS BY

CASHINAHUA METAPHORS OF CONTACT

The mythology and cosmology of the Peruvian Cashinahua do not contain explicit references to either Peruvians or Brazilians. Throughout my fieldwork I often listened to them discuss, or talked with them about, the problems they had or were having with the traders for whom they worked rubber (*caucho*) and cedar. I was surprised at the frequency with which these discussions digressed, or so I thought at the time, to a recounting of, or a use of elements from, myths about Inka. I will argue in this chapter that the Cashinahua used the Inka myths both as models for understanding who the traders were and as models for interacting with them.

Inka and the Ancestors

Although the Inka myths constitute the largest body of texts about any mythic figure (approximately 25 percent of the corpus), it is unclear whether we are dealing with one or more figures: the major protagonist has several names and the texts refer to the Inkabu, the Inka people. Despite this problem, I will follow my informant's lead and deal with Inka in generic terms, that is, the characteristics of all the protagonists called Inka in the various stories will be treated as if they are characteristic of a single protagonist. As a result, Inka is a mass of contradictions and thus the object of considerable ambivalence both for the ancestors in the myths and those who tell and listen to the myths.

Inka has been described variously in the texts as human being and as spirit being. As human, Inka is classified as *huni betsa* "other man, outsider" versus *huni kuin* "real man, Cashinahua" and thus is like other groups with which the Cashinahua interact on occasion or know about, but not *nawa* "nonhuman being." Inka wears clothing consisting of a woven loin cloth and a sack-like garment that covers him from shoulders to knees. As a result, his sex was not immediately obvious as is the case with the Cashinahua male's belt under which he tucks his penis. He lives in a house in a village surrounded by kin, particularly children. He has a large garden, which several texts cite as exemplary in that it is clear and open, free of weeds and brush. He hunts animals for their flesh. He has a nasty habit, however, of killing and eating people, both kin and enemies; this contrasts with the Cashinahua tradition of funerary endocannibalism (see chapter 18). Except for his cannibalism, there is no indication in the texts that his lifestyle is in any major way different from that of other non-Cashinahua peoples, who for the most part are seen as not fully socialized but with the potential to be so. For example, when Inka takes a Cashinahua to wife, he does not reciprocate by giving a sister to his brother-in-law, and he responds in anger when his sister is stolen by his wife's brother. He does, however, act like a brother-in-law in that he is a trickster and a joker; his brother-in-law is the target of his shenanigans. As both a wife giver and a wife receiver, Inka and his brother-in-law are equals. Inka gave the Cashinahua vegetables and taught them how to make gardens. He also taught them how to make bows and arrows and how to hunt. However, he was not always a paragon of technical knowledge. One story describes him as a stupid klutz who was taught what he knows by a female bird.[2]

Thus, as a human, Inka was an *outsider* but a potential *affine*, the only mechanism for incorporating him into the society. As affine, he was appropriately a *trickster* and *joker*. Although not fully socialized in Cashinahua terms, he was a *family man*. As the source of gardens, vegetables, weapons and hunting techniques, he was an *agent for change*. And finally, he was the agent of death, a *cannibal*.

As a *spirit* being, Inka lived in the sky alone, except for a wife. Although he owned the sun, the darkness, and the cold, which he kept in bottles, and many other possessions, he was stingy and miserly. He was also the source of illness. His nature as spirit was quixotic, capricious, playful, mischievous, temperamental, and vengeful in turn. The suffering, pain, illness, sorrow, and anguish his acts caused were thus not necessarily intentional.

Traders and the Cashinahua

The Inka myths provided a convenient category for identifying the Peruvian/Brazilian traders when they appeared on the scene. There was some difference of opinion between informants about whether the traders were initially identified as *huni betsa* or as *nawa*, that is, as human beings, albeit not fully socialized, or as not fully human. But more on that later. The traders wore clothing that hid their sexual identity and, given their prudishness, their masculinity was a mystery until they attempted to seduce some of the Cashinahua women, usually without success. One trader took a Cashinahua woman with him when he left the village but when the woman's brother visited her, the trader did not behave as a proper brother-in-law should; he did not offer one of his sisters in exchange, nor did he share his possessions. Several of the traders were practical jokers and one, based on the descriptions given by informants, knew how to perform some magic tricks. All of the traders were married and had families, which they fed by making gardens and by hunting, although this was not apparent unless the Cashinahua visited the Peruvian village of Esperanza.

The traders were a major source of goods and new technology. They provided machetes, knives, axes, aluminum kettles, fishhooks, beads, cloth and mosquito nets, soap, shotguns and shells, and rum. They taught the Cashinahua how to make canoes, to work rubber, to skin animals so that the skins were commercially valuable, and to make manioc flour.

During or following every visit from a trader, sickness ensued, often of epidemic proportions. The Cashinahua interpreted these events in terms of Inka as spirit and concluded that the traders were not simply *huni betsa* but *nawa*. On several occasions a trader took one or more young boys away from the village, some of whom never returned, leading to the accusation that the trader was a cannibal: "he has eaten our children."

Discussion

Although the Inka myths allowed the Cashinahua to fit the traders into their own scheme of things and to partially pattern their interactions with the outsiders, the Cashinahua were only partially successful, for two reasons. First, the traders operated in terms of a totally different mode of exchange, namely, market and debt peonage, rather than the reciprocity that had characterized the exchanges between the ancestors and Inka. This was a continual source of confusion and no insignificant amount of anger to the Cashinahua. One informant angrily told me that one trader told him that he could not accept goods from or work for another trader, because "you belong to me." His sense of personal autonomy was affronted.

Second, the traders operated in terms of a hierarchal system and considered themselves to be morally, economically, and socially superior to the Cashinahua. They gave orders and expected to be obeyed, reacting angrily when their wishes went unheeded. This, of course, was incomprehensible to the Cashinahua, who, if they give an order, can only hope it will be obeyed. If compliance does not follow, they do not respond with anger and rarely resort to physical, verbal, or psychological coercion. To do so would reflect negatively on them and would be largely ineffectual. All of these factors were further complicated by the language barrier. Although the traders picked up a few words of Cashinahua, mostly nouns, and the Cashinahua learned some words and phrases in Spanish and Portuguese, communication between them was extremely limited.

As in the relationship between the ancestors and Inka, the Cashinahua feel considerable ambivalence about the traders. While traders are the source of highly valued goods and tools that have provided greater efficiency in Cashinahua subsistence activities, they have also been the source of sickness and death. More importantly, they are the cause of confusion, discord, and despair. They have exposed the Cashinahua to a world for which their previous experience and myths provide them inadequate guides for defining the situation and deciding the course of future action.

While in the field in 1968, I listened to many heated discussions between one group, which advocated flight upstream in hopes of avoiding further contact with outsiders, and another group arguing for moving downstream, closer to Esperanza and to the goods available there. The old headman argued that neither course of action was totally satisfactory. To move downstream would invite further predation, illness, and death, a high price for the goods they would get. But, he argued, the Cashinahua had become accustomed to some of the trader's goods, and when their axes and machetes wore out, they would want new ones and therefore would have to deal with the traders. Furthermore, the foreigners are out there, and the Cashinahua know that and are affected by their presence, even if they are not dealing with them face-to-face.[3] "When a man is bathing in the river and a turd floats by, he doesn't have to see who shat in the river to know that somebody is there. He is contaminated nonetheless."

A woman weaving in 1962. (See page 196 for a 1994 photo of her son, the boy standing with his hand on her shoulder.)

Dini in 1956 with his young daughter. Body painting indicates that he is a member of the inubake *moiety.*

Dini in 1994 with his son, daughter-in-law, and albino grandson. (See previous page for a picture of his wife, now deceased.)

Chapter 25

TWENTY-FIVE YEARS LATER

CONTINUITY AND CHANGE

On March 20, 1993, I returned to the Cashinahua village of Balta on the Curanja River of southeastern Peru after an absence of twenty-five years. Thirty-eight years had passed since my first contact with them. In the intervening years, the Cashinahua have changed and so have I.

Although this chapter focuses on the changes and continuities of the last twenty-five years, it of necessity must take into account what I learned during the eighty-four months I lived with them between 1955 and 1968. And although I use that thirteen-year period in the life of Cashinahua society as a baseline for the present study, I am not assuming that what I observed during those years represented traditional Cashinahua culture. Societies and cultures, like people, change through time. Practices and perspectives are modified in response to external circumstances, experience, and reflection.

The purpose of my recent fieldwork was to study how the Cashinahua have been able to remain at peace among themselves and with others during the past fifty years in view of the diverse pressures for change that increasing contact with outsiders and provocations for aggressive reaction have brought to bear on their society. I was particularly interested in how the Cashinahua were coping with effects of (1) their desire for access to goods, (2) demographic changes, (3) bilingual education and literacy, (4) Bible translation and evangelization, and (5) contacts with governmental and nongovernmental agencies.

Desire for Access to Goods

It was their desire for axes and machetes that motivated the Cashinahua of the Curanja River to end their twenty-year isolation from the outside world in the late 1940s. They traveled downriver to a Marinahua village where they came in contact with a Peruvian *patron*, who over the next decade provided them with (in order of importance) tools, beads, mosquito nets, clothing, aluminum pots, and enamel dishes. When I arrived in Maneya in 1955, all of the Cashinahua were deeply in debt and frustrated because the *patron* was so selfish. He in turn was equally frustrated because the Cashinahua were "lazy," collecting wild rubber, *caucho*, only when it did not interfere with their subsistence activities, hunting and slash-and-burn horticulture, and with their ritual cycle.

My acceptance by the Cashinahua was in no small part facilitated by the goods and medicines I provided for them in exchange for work, food, and crafts. By 1963 they were aware of an alternative to debt peonage, and with my help many of them were free of debt and had obtained the goods they so highly desired by exchanging products they produced for goods available through the *patrones* and the merchants in Esperanza.

Between 1969 and 1983, access to goods was greatly expanded through the efforts of Summer Institute of Linguistics missionary Richard Montag, who served as a broker for selling in Pucallpa craft and agricultural products. They also sold animal skins (particularly jaguar, ocelot, and alligator skins) and other goods to Peruvian traders, and my informants referred to this period as a kind of golden age. But this outlet closed. The sale and purchase of animal skins was curtailed by an international ban aimed at protecting endangered species. With Montag's departure, there was no one to arrange for the shipment and sale of Cashinahua hammocks and feather headdresses. The Cashinahua now have to rely on the Esperanza market for the goods they so highly desire.

In the late 1970s Montag established and bankrolled a store in the Cashinahua village of Balta, appointing his major translation assistant to run it. By 1993 it was abandoned, and the manager had moved downriver with several brothers and brothers-in-law to establish a new village. The business had failed because those who purchased goods on credit never paid their bills and accused the manager of selfishness and un-Cashinahua behavior, of being a *patron*. Furthermore, he was viewed by his brother-in-law, the headman, as a competitor for leadership, creating tensions in their relationship in addition to those resulting from the headman's debt to the store.

I was impressed by the quantity and quality of goods the Cashinahua possessed in 1993. Most have large wardrobes of clothes compared to the one or two dresses and one or two shirts and pairs of pants that were the lot of women and men in 1968. It was a bit disconcerting to see T-shirts emblazoned with the latest in American television icons, the Marlboro man, and campaign slogans for the 1993 mayoralty campaign in Esperanza. Men, women, and children now wear underwear or lingerie. Most possess a pair of shoes, boots, or flip-flops, which they wear on occasion. Aluminum kettles and enamel and plastic dishes have totally replaced traditional ceramic pots and bowls. Cosmetics, toothbrushes and paste, perfumes, and soaps are in widespread use. Shotguns have almost completely replaced bows and arrows.

The Cashinahua desire for Peruvian and Brazilian goods is immense, but the means for satisfying that desire are extremely limited. Esperanza has a population of about eight hundred, including three hundred military personnel. It is an economic backwater. Its only industry is a lumber mill whose market is limited by local needs. All goods come into the town either by boat from Brazil or by plane from Pucallpa. The only goods produced by the Cashinahua for which there is a market are foods, specifically farina, plantains, and meat. Prices for the goods the Cashinahua buy are set by the merchants as are the prices paid for the goods the Cashinahua sell; prices for the former are high and for the latter are low. This is a source of considerable frustration for the Cashinahua, who no longer are merely desirous of goods but dependent on many of them for their well-being.

Perhaps the most striking example of this pattern is shotgun shells. Sixteen-gauge shotgun shells cost $1.85 (US) per shell; .22 rifle shells are virtually unavailable. Therefore, Cashinahua hunters are reluctant to expend a shell on smaller animals, limiting their use to tapir, deer, peccary, spider and howler monkeys, and an occasional wild turkey (*paujil*). As a result, hunters frequently return from a hunt empty-handed, something that rarely happened when they were using guns and bows and arrows or bows and arrows exclusively. Meat, which has always been seen as the most

A woman making a bowl in 1957. By 1993, all ceramic products had been replaced by enamel or plastic dishes and aluminum pots.

A woman prepares to fire her bowls and pots.

important part of the diet, is now scarce. At least one-third of the days I was in the field, there was no meat in the village. Men, women, and children complained of being *pinsi*, hungry for meat. On several occasions after they had no meat for a week, several families resorted to killing and eating a chicken, and on one occasion a domestic pig. These are normally saved to sell to the Peruvians. The meat shortage is further exacerbated by the fact that meat is the most salable of Cashinahua products.

In light of the debate in the literature about whether there is an adequacy of meat in Amazonia, I should note that the shortage of meat the Cashinahua are experiencing is a result of a change in hunting patterns, not in the availability of game animals. Even in Balta, where game was depleted during the years when the population was above six hundred and became a contributing factor in the fissioning of the village, game is again readily available. Hunters frequently discussed passing up animals that previously had provided a significant portion of their catch because they were too small to warrant the use of ammunition. It is also interesting to note that the scarcity of meat has not resulted in a reclassification of the edibility of certain large animals, specifically the capybara, the giant anteater, and felines.

The Cashinahua are fully aware of the problems created by their desire for goods and discuss the advantages and disadvantages of moving closer to Esperanza in order to facilitate greater commerce. Most of the Cashinahua villages now have herds of pigs, cattle, and sheep as well as flocks of chickens, but transporting these animals two or more days by canoe is difficult, if not impossible. Butchering animals requires salt-drying the meat, which adds to their expenses and lowers the price. They have discussed increasing their production of cash crops such as beans and rice, but their experience is that there is a small market for these items, and the financial returns are minimal. For example, a 50-kilogram basket of rice is not sufficient to pay for a box of twenty-five shotgun shells.

The Cashinahua have an insatiable desire for goods that are only available through contact with the outside world, and their means for obtaining these goods are very limited. The result is a high level of frustration and in some cases despair. During a discussion with one informant in which he laid out for me an analysis of their economic situation worthy of a Ph.D. economist, he wondered whether having his most recent child, a five-month-old daughter, and perhaps even the previous two of his five children had been a wise idea, for as he concluded, "There is no future for them." This from the pastor and spiritual leader in Balta. Although his pessimism and despair seem to be based on a clear-eyed assessment of the economic climate, I suspect that he also has been influenced by the apocalyptic teaching of the Swiss missionaries; his sermons are filled with references to "the end times," Armageddon, and the second coming of Christ to rescue believers from this vale of tears. However, other informants shared his pessimism if not his despair.

Demographic Changes

There were fewer than one hundred Peruvian Cashinahua when I arrived on the Curanja River in 1955, four years after an epidemic had killed four-fifths of the adult population. They had only recently returned from the Brazilian Embira River, where they had fled after the epidemic. Life in Brazil was not to their liking, so many returned in September 1954 and planted new gardens. Another group returned in 1960. By 1968 there were about 450 Cashinahua living in five villages in Peru. The increase was partly due to the migrations but also occurred because of a drop in the infant mortality rate in response to the medical aid I provided for them. When Cecilia McCallum visited them in 1984–85, there were 833 people living in nine villages ranging in size of from 17 to 283 people, Balta being the largest.

By 1993 the Peruvian Cashinahua numbered 1,064, living in thirteen villages on the lower Curanja and upper Purus rivers ranging from 12 to 264 people; Balta is still the largest village. Only five of the 13 villages exceed sixty-five to seventy people, the threshold at which the traditional mechanisms of social control often become ineffectual, resulting in tensions and factionalism. Canto Gallo, Conta, and Piquiniqui on the Purus River have 116, 184, and 88 inhabitants, respectively; Balta and Santa Rey on the Curanja River have 264 and 146. However, only Balta seems to be seriously factionalized, but my time in the other villages was too limited to get a clear sense of their internal politics.

One of the first impressions I got when I arrived in Balta was of the incredible number of infants and children. Two-thirds of the population has been born since I left the field in 1968. Of greater significance is the change in number of live births per woman. Between 1955 and 1968 few women had more than four children, and they were the subject of gossip. If a woman had babies more frequently that every three to four years, the older women would lecture about her obligations to the infants she already had and would verbally harass her husband about being a sex fiend. In 1993 many women had six or more children, spaced about every other year; one had ten and was pregnant with her eleventh. The Cashinahua see this increase in children as a guarantee of their survival as a society. However, several women asked me to find out what kind of medicine Susan Montag took while in the field to prevent pregnancy.

The greater number of children per mother and decreased interval between births has resulted in a modification of gender roles. Men who previously paid little attention to their children until they were four or five years old now find themselves providing significant childcare to infants who have recently been replaced at their mother's breast by a new sibling. I even observed several fathers caring for infants while their mothers were busy. Several of my older informants commented about these changes, indicating that they thought it was an unfortunate but inevitable result of the increased birth rate. These were the same men, however, who doted on their infant grandchildren and bragged about how many grandchildren they have.

This increase in the number of children has had economic repercussions. Children have to be fed and clothed, and fathers with more than four children have to work harder than those with fewer in order to properly care for them. Several grandfathers commented to me on how much harder their sons have to work than they did at the same age because they have so many children. Mothers with more than four children seem harried and overburdened. Unlike their mothers, they do not have school-aged daughters to assist in caring for younger siblings for a good part of the day; they are in school from 8:00 A.M. until 1:30 P.M. five days a week.

Balta is unique. It is the only Cashinahua village to experience rapid expansion and disintegration, from 70 persons when it was founded in 1960 to more than 600 in the late 1970s to its present 264. The growth was associated with the establishment of a bilingual school and a public health clinic in the mid-1970s, when most of the Peruvian Cashinahua flocked to Balta to avail themselves of these services. Depletion of the game resources and increasing political factionalism resulted in groups returning to their old villages or establishing new villages. Traditional mechanisms for maintaining order and resolving disputes were not adequate for the increased population, and a new style of leadership, in which the headman had greater power and authority, was rejected.

Bilingual Education

The first bilingual school opened in Balta in 1973 with Mario Bardales Tuesta as teacher. By 1993 there were thirteen primary schools with twenty-five Cashinahua teachers, many of whom were taught to read and write by Bardales. There are secondary schools in Balta and Conta; the Balta secondary school has an enrollment of sixty-four students in five grades and a teaching staff consisting of five Peruvians and one Cashinahua, the Conta secondary school has forty-seven students with four Peruvian teachers who commute daily from Esperanza.

The schools have been extremely successful despite minimal resources. Most of the population between fourteen and forty years of age are now literate to some degree in Cashinahua and to a lesser degree in Spanish. Letter writing has become a fad. When I returned to Pucallpa from the Curanja, I was carrying thirteen or fourteen letters for Montag and fifteen letters for three Cashinahua students at the Misión Suisa's Bible School.

Teachers are hampered in their efforts by a shortage of books and supplies. Each class room contains between three and six grade levels. Teaching centers around a blackboard. Few students have notebooks and pencils; books and paper are scarce. As a result, teachers cannot give reading or writing assignments for one grade level to work on while they instruct another. Students must sit in silence and wait their turn to be taught at the blackboard. I watched in amazement as a teacher switched from algebra with one group to basic literacy in another to Peruvian history with a third, and so on. Instruction in the lower grades is in Cashinahua; in the upper grades it is in both Cashinahua and Spanish, depending on the subject.

The Cashinahua are proud of their ability to read and write. However, their ability to read is a source of frustration because, other than fourteen school books and the New Testament translation in Cashinahua, they have nothing to read.

I had an interesting conversation with one of my informants as he leafed through my laptop computer manual. "How many books do you own?" he asked. "At least twenty thousand," I replied. The number was beyond his comprehension. "And, I get about five new books each month." He paused before responding, "God's words are good to read, but that's all I have to read. I would be happy to get one new book each year." I suggested that he should write some, at which he laughed. However, before I left the tribe at the end of

Mario Bardales Tuesta in 1956.

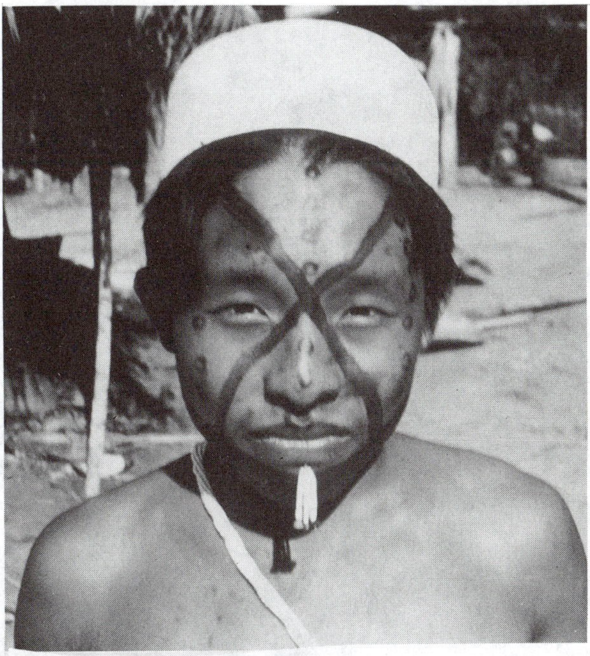

Professor Mario Bardales Tuesta, Director of Primary Education in Balta, in 1993.

The first graduating class from the secondary school in Balta.

May, he and three other men were keeping journals. We also agreed that when I return, we will prepare transcriptions of tape recordings I made of myths between 1955 and 1968 with some of my older informants, now deceased, and arrange to have them printed and bound. "Then," he said, "we will have a Cashinahua library and will be able to read our ancestors' words."

Many of the Cashinahua are satisfied to complete primary school. About twenty have completed secondary school. One male completed three years in a technical school in Pucallpa before returning to Conta, where he is frustrated because he cannot use his education. (There are no jobs requiring his skills available in Esperanza, and he is unwilling to leave his society to find a job appropriate to his education.) Eight men have been or currently are enrolled in the Bible School operated by the Misión Suisa del Peru in Pucallpa. Several young men expressed a desire to pursue their education beyond secondary school but have been frustrated in their efforts because they have neither the contacts to advise them about what schooling is available nor the financial means to pay for further study.

Despite their increasing ability to speak Spanish, the Cashinahua rarely do so in the village, limiting their use of Spanish to their interactions with Peruvians. Men are more likely to speak Spanish than women. Attempts on my part to use Spanish to discuss certain topics were rejected, even when Peruvians were present. Only a limited number of Spanish words have been incorporated into Cashinahua, usually technical terms.

Bible Translation and Evangelization

I was only able to observe the impact of missionary activities in three villages (Balta, Conta, and Santa Rey) but was informed that there are groups of believers in two other villages (Curanjillo and Canto Gallo). For the most part, the Cashinahua seem to be indifferent to Christianity. Only about 15 percent of the residents in the villages observed claim to be Christian. Church attendance averaged nine persons in the eight Sunday services I attended in Balta, five in one service in Santa Rey, and six in one service in Conta. In each case most of those attending were primary affinal or consanguineal kin of the pastor.

Only eight informants, all males, regularly used Christian religious terminology as part of their everyday speech or included comments about praying, God's will, and so on in our conversations. Only two men prayed in my presence in a context other than a church service. The headman prayed before two meals when I was his guest. His son, the pastor, asked me if he could pray at the end of our last conversation before I left Balta.

This almost immediately followed our discussion about the dilemma faced by a young believer whose application for the Misión Suisa Bible School had been rejected because he has two wives. "God's words," he informed me, "say that a pastor should only have one wife." I asked him for the chapter and verse of this injunction and told him about the polygyny of King David and King Solomon in the Old Testament and suggested that perhaps the injunction was of the missionaries and not of God. Remembering that I had once been a missionary, he asked, "You know God's words well, don't you?" he asked. "Yes, I know them well, but I don't buy them," I responded. "We will have to discuss this when you return in September," he said. He then said that our three-hour conversation had tired him out and perhaps it was time to go to bed.

Although only a small minority of Cashinahua are believers, they have had a greater impact on Balta than their numbers would suggest, largely because the headman is a believer. Several years ago he imposed a ban on alcoholic beverages in the village. Although he has succeeded in prohibiting Peruvians from bringing intoxicants into the village, his ban has not been 100 percent effective. Individuals occasionally purchase *aguardiente*, a cheap sugar cane rum, in Esperanza or make *masato*, a mildly intoxicating manioc beer. But the number and size of drinking parties has been greatly reduced, and drunken behavior is the object of scorn, not just by the believers but by the population generally. The headman in Conta, at the behest of the head teacher, a Christian, has banned the consumption of alcoholic beverages in the village; members of the community who wish to drink must go an hour downriver to Esperanza.

At the instigation of the Swiss missionaries who consider it to be the Devil's brew, the headman of Balta and his son, the pastor of the church, have inveighed against consumption of the hallucinogenic beverage *ayahuasca*. They have not been successful in gaining community support in their campaign to ban *ayahuasca* because the hallucinations that result from the drug are thought to provide information about events removed by time and/or space that are having or might have an impact on their lives. Several informants insisted that those who drink *ayahuasca*, unlike those who drink alcohol, do not become belligerent, bellicose, or aggressive, behaviors the Cashinahua find discomfiting.

Although my research in this area is still somewhat superficial, it appears that Bible translation and missionization has had relatively little impact on Cashinahua thought and behavior, even though several headmen and community leaders are believers. Trying to understand why this is the case will be a major goal of my research during my next fieldwork. I suspect that one of the reasons is that the Cashinahua believers are not aggressive "soul winners"; aggressiveness is not a Cashinahua virtue.

Contacts with Governmental and Nongovernmental Agencies

The influence of governmental agencies and officials has increased significantly since 1968 even though, with the exception of Conta, which is less than an hour by river from Esperanza, agents of the government rarely visit any of the Cashinahua villages. A medical team for the Ministry of Public Health that visited Balta for three hours in May 1993 to vaccinate women and children against measles were the first Peruvian officials in the village in eight months.

The Cashinahua teachers regularly have to report to the director of schools for the Purus-Curanja region, an official of the Ministry of Education, who has an office in Esperanza. His influence seems to be limited to the in-school activities of the teachers and students. He, or a representative of his office, annually visits each of the schools, albeit very briefly, to assess their compliance with government regulations.

Although he has never visited any of the Cashinahua villages but Conta, the mayor of Esperanza (who basically functions as the governor of the Purus district of the state of Ucayali) has established ties with the lieutenant governors in each of the Cashinahua villages. These lieutenant governors, often the village headmen, are appointed by the mayor and serve as liaisons between the Cashinahua and the mayor in his role as representative of both the state and national governments.

During my recent fieldwork I was only able to get data on the relationship between the headman of Balta and the mayor, but only from the headman's perspective; the mayor was not in Esperanza when I passed through town. Therefore, I am uncomfortable making any generalizations, and what follows should be viewed in these terms.

The headman was in Esperanza for discussions with the mayor when I arrived in Balta and did not return until nearly a month had passed, having been absent from the village for six weeks. He had returned to check on flood damage because the mayor was seeking flood disaster assistance from the federal government to deal with the flood damage that had occurred on the Purus River. The headman hoped to be able to cash in on this opportunity, talking about all the pasta, cookies, rice, and so forth that he could get from "his friend, the mayor." But only minor and limited damage to crops had occurred in the Curanja villages, dashing his hopes of extensive aid to enrich the village and enhance his prestige as a can-do leader.

It should be noted that Balta is badly divided, functioning for the most part as three villages. Considerable tension exists between the headman and the head teacher, tension far in excess of that which is normal between the two focal males in a village and between brothers-in-law. The headman seems to resent the fact that his co-focal male gets a government salary as teacher, but he as headman and government-appointed public health promoter does not. Everyone sees and knows about the goods and services the teacher brings to the community, and the headman seems to feel that he has to match or exceed his brother-in-law. The teacher is deferential to the headman, secure in his position within the community.

One week after he returned to the village, the headman called an "extraordinary meeting" of the community in which he announced a campaign, *campaña*, his term for the revitalization of the village. He provided few specifics, focusing instead on the need for cooperation and hard work. He informed everyone that "his friend, the mayor" wanted to help them. His son, the pastor, reviewed the economic scene, emphasized the need for innovative thinking about economic alternatives and urged everyone to get behind his father's leadership to solve their problems.

Since the departure of the Montags, the Misión Suisa del Peru has been the only nongovernmental agency working with the Peruvian Cashinahua. Two missionary women visit the Cashinahua villages for one month each year. Their efforts have largely been devoted to instructing and encouraging the believers. Pastors and would-be pastors are trained at the mission's Bible School in Pucallpa. Their impact appears to be slight.

Summary

Apart from the bells that call the children to school each day and believers to church on Sunday mornings, enhanced wardrobes, a plethora of Peruvian goods, and a larger but spatially dispersed population, Balta seems much as it was in 1968. The pace of life is slow and easy; people take time to relax and socialize, to play with their children and grandchildren. Balta seems peaceful and tranquil. But behind the facade tensions exist, animosities threaten to boil to the surface. They continue to use informal mechanisms of social control (like gossip, ridicule, avoidance, and shunning) and to abhor verbal or physical aggression. They are resisting all attempts by headmen to transform their offices into positions with real power and authority. They continue to value reciprocity in economic relations and to perceive market exchanges as exploitative. Men continue to proclaim their superiority over women, a superiority women neither acknowledge nor accept, but

The author with his "son, daughter-in-law, and grandchildren."

have quietly accepted added responsibilities for harvesting garden produce and in childcare. Despite increased contact with the outside world, they remain convinced of the superiority of their culture and of their equality as people with outsiders.

The changes that have occurred since 1968 seem to be more cosmetic than structural. The seeds for massive and disruptive culture change are present and may have sprouted; they have yet to develop to the point where they threaten to shade or crowd out their hosts.

NOTES

Chapter 1: An Experiment in Cross Cultural Communications

An earlier version of this chapter was first presented as a lecture at the Haffenreffer Museum, Brown University, and was published in modified forms in Kensinger 1973 and Kensinger et al. 1975.

[1] The *men* in this utterance does not mean "hand," but rather indicates a question.

Chapter 2: Subsistence Activities

An earlier version of this chapter originally appeared in Kenneth M. Kensinger et al., *The Cashinahua of Eastern Peru* (Bristol, RI: Haffenreffer Museum of Anthropology, 1975).

[1] The following statement and others of similar content were the most frequent responses to my questions about why men went hunting when there was abundant meat in the house: "I always go hunting when my wife nags or my children fuss. Nagging and crying make me uneasy. But if I go to visit my brother or sister, my wife says I'm visiting my lover and not spending time with my children. However, she always says 'that's good,' when I take my bow and arrows and go to the forest."

[2] Trapping is a recent addition (post-1963) to the hunting technology, having been introduced by Peruvian traders. It is used exclusively for capturing ocelots and jaguars, the skins of which are sold to the traders. Deadfall traps were introduced by several Louisiana State University zoologists.

[3] "*Nun hi deda bechi haida. Maeanu hawen kaunan nukun nabun ninkai. 'Yu, hunin daya haida,' hatun xinaminski.*" "We like tree-cutting very much. In the village our people hear it falling and think, 'Ah, a man is working very hard.'"

[4] Although there is almost a fire storm created by the blaze, I have never seen the fire spread into the surrounding jungle, even during the height of dry season.

[5] There is no good one-word term for translating into English the process called *mutsa*. It involves kneading, squeezing, stirring, blending, and so on, in order to saturate or thoroughly mix something with water.

Chapter 3: Hunting and Male Domination

An earlier version of this chapter was originally published in Susan Kent, ed., *Farmers as Hunters* (Cambridge: Cambridge University Press, 1989). Discussions with and criticisms from Tom Gregor, Lucien Hanks, Rhoda Halperin, Emi Ireland, Susan Kent, Patricia Lyon, Don Pollock, and Sally Sugarman helped to sharpen my argument.

[1] When discussing the meaning of *hunu*, male informants frequently argued that women are like *hunu bai*, "hidden gardens," while men are like *bai kuin*, "real gardens." See chapter 2 for a discussion of this.

[2] These terms mask the distinctions made by the Cashinahua but are used for clarity of exposition. The three classes of hunting are based on the contrasts established by three pairs of binary oppositions, namely between *tsaka* $kuin_1$ and *tsaka* $kuinman_1$, *tsaka* $kuin_2$ and *tsaka* $bemakia_2$, and *tsaka* $kayabi_3$ and *tsaka* $bemakia_3$. See chapter 7 for a discussion of these contrasts.

[3] Although Ross supports the protein deficiency argument, his data (Ross 1978, as cited in Chagnon 1983:87, table 2.1) show that the Jivaroan Achuara among whom he worked have a daily protein consumption of 84.4 grams per capita and of 116.2 grams per adult.

[4] Speth and Spielmann (1983) have argued that the problem may not be an adequacy or inadequacy of protein in the diet but the presence of adequate fat.

Chapter 4: Bawdy Rituals and Cashinahua Sexual Stereotypes

An earlier version of this chapter was first presented in the symposium "Gender Rituals and the Sexual Self," American Anthropological Association meetings, Chicago, November 21, 1987.

Chapter 5: Hardfaced Hussies and Flaccid Fellows

An earlier version of this chapter was first presented in the symposium "Shame on You!: Shaming and Social Control in Lowland South America," American Anthropological Association meetings, Washington, DC, November 1989.

Chapter 6: Why Bother? Cashinahua Views of Sexuality

An earlier version of this chapter was first presented in the symposium "Anthropology Rediscovers Sex," American Anthropological Association meetings, Phoenix, AZ, November 1988.

[1] This chapter is based on extensive conversations with both male and female informants as well as observations of male-female interactions. Male informants readily talked in great detail about sexual activity, real and imagined. Female informants were always ready to give me the latest gossip about ongoing or past affairs other than their own. Although marital fidelity is encouraged, especially by older men and women, infidelity is endemic, at least if one is to believe the rampant gossip. Both men and women are free to engage in pre- or extramarital sex so long as the affairs are carried out with discretion. Both marital and extramarital sex are a frequent topic of women's gossip and speculation and of the ribald joking between male cross-cousins; women, however, name names and males do not.

[2] It is my impression that the primary pleasure many women gain from both marital and extramarital sex derives from anticipating the rendezvous with her husband or lover and from being the object of his desire.

[3] In the 1960s both men and women began to wear western-style clothing, particularly when outsiders were in the village. By the 1990, such clothing was considered essential.

Chapter 7: Categories "Real" and "Unreal"

An earlier version of this chapter was originally published in Kensinger et al., 1975: 18–23.

[1] *Kuin* is being used here in the sense of polarity 1. Used in the sense of polarity 2, *huni kuin* can include other Panoan-speaking groups such as the Amahuaca, Marinahua, Sharanahua, Mastanahua, and others. However, only vocative kinship terminology is used with these groups and then only when they are interacting; that is, they may call a Sharanahua "cross-cousin" when speaking to him, but will never refer to him as such.

[2] But only if she is a classificatory cross-cousin. The marriage must not violate the rules of moiety exogamy, and village endogamy. In addition, she must not be a member of ego's alternating generation-namesake group or the alternating generation-namesake groups of his father and mother.

[3] This rule is inoperative during the fertility rites, *kacha nawa*, when a man frequently insults his mother-in-law, who is a member of the kin class *achi*, with impunity (see chapters 4 and 5).

Chapter 8: Cashinahua Siblingship

An earlier version of this chapter was first presented in a symposium at the 1983 American Anthropological Association and published in *The Sibling Relationship in Lowland South America, Working Papers on South American Indians* 7 (March 1985), pp. 20–24. Bennington, VT: Bennington College.

[1] English kin terms are abbreviated as follows: F = father, M = mother, S = son, D = daughter, B = brother, Z = sister, H = husband, and W = wife. Compound forms should be read as: FFZ = father's sister's daughter, MBW = mother's brother's wife, and so on.

Chapter 9: An Emic Model of Cashinahua Marriage

An earlier version of this chapter was originally published in Kenneth M. Kensinger, ed., Marriage Practices in Lowland South America, (Urbana: University of Illinois Press, 1985) pp. 221–251. This is a heavily revised version of a paper originally presented in New Orleans under the title "Fact and Fiction in Cashinahua Marriage." I have benefited from comments and suggestions from many of the participants in the symposium, especially Gertrude Dole, Jean Jackson, Patricia Lyon, and Judith Shapiro. Michael Brown, Gillian Feeley-Harnik, Rhoda Halperin, Martha Hardman de Bautista, Harriet Klein, Waud Kracke, Hal Oringer, David Price. The members of the South American Indian Caucus of Columbia University, Charles Wagley's South American Seminar at the University of Florida, and two of my classes at Bennington College also made helpful suggestions. What flaws remain are a result of my failure to follow their advice.

[1] The suffixes *-wan* and *-yan* are the phonologically conditioned forms of the morphemes *-wa* and *-ya*, which occur following a nasalized final syllable.

[2] For additional discussions of the differences between Pike's and Harris's definitions of etic and emic, see Burling (1969); Fisher and Werner (1978); Goodenough (1970: esp. 113–114, n. 15); Headland, et al. (1990); Kay (1970); Kensinger (1975b); and Merrifield (1968).

[3] Although polygyny is considered desirable by most Cashinahua, both male and female, only seventeen of sixty-four married males are polygynous; one man has four wives, one has three wives, and fifteen have two wives. The ideal polygynous marriage consists of a man's marrying two or more women who are actual sisters; nine of the polygynous males married in this way. Availability of wives is the primary limiting factor on polygyny. Almost as significant, however, is the attitude of a man's wife. Many wives object to the addition of a co-wife unless she is a full or half-sister. However, I know of two instances in which women exerted considerable pressure on their husbands, including refusal of sexual relations, until a new co-wife, not a sister, was brought into the household.

Male informants frequently said that they neither have nor want more than one wife because of the added economic responsibilities and the greatly increased workload that polygyny entails; they preferred to have extramarital affairs, which are easily arranged and carry with them no long-term responsibilities. Beside, his wife's approval of extramarital partners is not needed, as in the case with co-wives.

[4] The term *ainkuin* differs from *ainwankuin* in that it involves the application of polarity 1 to the kin term *ain* rather than to the marriage term *ainwan*. It designates a class of women who are actual first cross-cousins as opposed to women who are merely members of the kin class female cross-cousins, *ainbuaibu* (see Rule 1b). (Some informants were reluctant to classify first cross-cousins who are MBD but not simultaneously FZD as $ainkuin_1$ but even more reluctant to classify them as $ainkuinman_1$.)

[5] These include his actual M, MM, FZ, FFZ (if also MM), FM, Z, D, ZD, SD, DD. For female ego: her actual F, FB, FF, MMB (if also FF), MF, B, S, BS, SS, DS.

[6] These include the $kuin_1$ kinsmen of one's $kuin_1$ kinsmen. For example, father's brother is ego's $kayabi_3$ kinsman because he is a $kuin_1$ kinsman to ego's father. All of ego's $kayabi_3$ kinsmen are part of ego's $nabukuin_1$, which consists of the members of ego's families of orientation and procreation, that is, his $kuin_1$ kinsmen, and the members of the families of procreation and orientation of ego's lineal kinsmen, the $kuin_1$ kinsmen of ego's M, F, S, D, FF, FM, MM, MF, SS, SD, DS, DD, and so on.

[7] Under these circumstances, there is a good likelihood that one or more other pairs of competing focal males might emerge, leading to the development of political factions. Therefore, although the Cashinahua speak simply of village endogamy, I suspect that the more accurate phrasing of the rule should be that one should marry within one's political faction as well as within one's village (see chapters 10 and 14). My data are inconclusive on this point; I did not realize while in the field the potential significance of this distinction and so failed to follow up the clues contained in my notes.

[8] Her father is either her actual father or a step-father who raised her. It should be noted that although the wife's father is the pivotal figure in determining residence, Cashinahua males always speak of matrilocal residence as being with *achi*, FZ, a moiety mate, rather than with *kuka*, MB, a member of the opposite moiety.

[9] This ordering represents the sequence in which the options are considered.

[10] Although a man is under the authority of his father-in-law, his wife's mother (his *achi*) plays a significant role in the success of his marriage in the early years. If she is not satisfied with him as a worker, provider, and member of the household, she will agitate for termination of the marriage. She may either order him out of the house or make life so miserable for him that he will leave.

[11] I suspect that the addition of actual first cross-cousin as opposed to double first cross-cousin is a compromise necessitated by demographic realities because all informants agreed that a woman who was a FZD or MBD, but not both, was $ainkayabi_3$ but not $ainkuin_1$; in practice, many of them classified a FZD who was not also MBD, and vice versa, as their $ainkuin_1$.

[12] Many informants argued that marriage with an actual MM, FM, SD, or DD would be *chaka* but not *chakahaida*, since sexual activity with these persons is tolerated. For the perspective of the female ego, read F, MB, FF, MMB (if also FF), MF, B, S, BS, SS, or DS, respectively.

[13] Birth defects are not included in this list; the Cashinahua believe that birth defects and multiple births are caused by incubi.

[14] Like Goodenough, I am assuming that it is possible and desirable to attempt to develop a cross-culturally applicable definition of marriage; see also Leach (1961); Needham (1971a, 1971b); and Rivière (1971).

[15] I was reminded of this point by Robert F. Murphy, whose sage advice has been stimulating and helpful on other points in this paper as well.

[16] Marriage in the United States is defined by legal statute; all states require a license before marriage, and some require a religious ceremony. In addition, fourteen states (Alabama, Colorado, Florida, Georgia, Idaho, Iowa, Kansas, Montana, Ohio, Oklahoma, Pennsylvania, Rhode Island, South Carolina, and Texas) and the District of Columbia recognize common-law marriages, either by statute or on the basis of judicial decision (case law); the remainder do not, although, Delaware, Indiana, New Hampshire, and Wisconsin will grant exceptions under certain circumstances. (For legal sources, see Clark 1968: 45–46, especially nn. 9 and 11.) Thus in at least fifteen jurisdictions there are two kinds of marriage: legal-proper (regular) and legal-improper (irregular).

I gratefully acknowledge the legal research done by my former student, Sharon Jacobs, of the Miami law firm Chaykin, Karlan, and Jacobs, which made this note possible.

Chapter 10: Cashinahua Notions of Social Time and Social Space

An earlier version of this chapter was originally published in *Actes du XLIIe Congrès des Americanistes*, Vol. 2, 1976. (Paris: C.N.R.S. and Fondation Singer-Polignac): pp. 233–244. Comments and criticisms from Gertrude Dole, Rhoda Halperin, Jean Jackson, Waud Kracke, Hal Oringer, Kenneth L. Pike, Richard Smith, and David Thomas are gratefully acknowledged.

[1] I am not using the classification based on polarity 2 in this analysis because of its highly idiosyncratic and egocentric character, unlike classifications based on polarities 1 and 3, which are sociocentric and elicit a high degree of agreement among informants.

[2] Goodenough cogently demonstrates that the interplay between the categories of the ethnographer's folk and professional cultures on one hand and the concepts and categories of the society the ethnographer studies on the other can and should lead to the refinement of a genuine etics of culture.

Chapter 11: The Dialectics of Person and Self

This chapter was presented as part of the symposium, "The Body and the Self: The Concrete Philosophy of Person, Self, and Society in Lowland South America," at the 79th Annual Meeting of the American Anthropological Association, December 1980, Washington, DC.

Chapter 12: Dual Organization Reconsidered

An earlier version was presented at the South American Indian Caucus, Columbia University, October 1981. I am grateful to Bob Murphy and the members of the caucus for their helpful suggestions.

Chapter 13: Panoan Kinship Terminology and Social Organization

An earlier version of this chapter was presented in the symposium "Classic Panoan Topics in Light of Recent Research," 47th International Congress of Americanists, Tulane University, July 9 to 11, 1991, New Orleans, LA.

[1] Informants differ on whether or not persons who are not co-resident can be classified as *nabukuin*. Purists insist that once a *kuin* kinsman, always a *kuin* kinsman. Others argue that co-residence is an essential part of being *nabukuin*. They also differ on whether one's *nabukuin* includes the members of one's parents' *nabi*, that is, the entire nuclear family of orientation of each parent. Most agreed that FF, FM, MF and MM—one's *huchikuin*, *chichikuin*, *chaikuin/chaitakuin*, and *xanukuin*—are part of one's *nabukuin*, but they disagreed over whether the same sex siblings of one's parents—FB and MZ—could be part of one's *nabukuin*. Most insisted that only one's father and mother could be *epakuin* and *ewakuin* and thus *nabukuin*, whereas MB and FZ are always *kukakuin* and *achikuin*, even if not co-resident.

[2] Note that I am treating gender as the primary distinction made by the Cashinahua. In most earlier publications I indicated that the male moiety names are used to refer to both females and males. However, closer examination of my field notes show that only males use the male moiety names to include both sexes. Females consistently identify themselves with the female moieties and not with the male moieties. However, one could argue that the *inubake* and *duabake* are unmarked for gender and that *inanibake* and *banubake* are marked on the grounds that the marriage sections are not marked for gender. This argument is given some weight by the lack of gender distinction in the marriage sections where emphasis is placed on the fact that they are all *xutabu*, namesakes.

[3] A man names his firstborn son by each wife after his father; subsequent sons are named after his FBs. He names his firstborn daughter by each wife after his FZ/WM, that is, her MM; subsequent daughters are named after his WMZs, their MMZs. Spouse names are used by parents and siblings to address or call children until they have gone through the initiation rituals, after which only the appropriate vocative moiety term is used.

[4] Note that the Cashinahua talk about the members of the four marriage sections using the kin terms, that is, males refer to the members of their marriage section as their *xutabu*, siblings; to the members of their F's marriage section as their *epabu*; to the members of their MB's marriage section as their *kukabu*; and to the marriage section of their cross-cousins as their *chaibu*. Females refer to the members of their F's marriage section either as their *epabu* or *yayabu*; to the members of their MB's and M's marriage section as either *ewabu* or *kukabu*; to the members of their cross-cousins' marriage section as *tsabebu*.

[5] The Cashinahua relax in hammocks during the day and sleep in them during the night. Where a man hangs his hammock and who weaves it for him is indicative of his social status. When he is a child, he hangs the hammock made for him by his mother or MM near his mother's hammock. When he marries, he hangs the hammock made for him by his FZ (but usually not his WM) in the household of his new wife. Thereafter, his wife weaves and shares his hammock except while she is nursing a child. The hammocks of unmarried adult males are often threadbare, unless they are able to convince a sister to weave a new one for them.

Chapter 14: Leadership and Factionalism in Cashinahua Society

An earlier version of this chapter was originally presented in the symposium "Political Leadership in Lowland South America," American Anthropological Association, Mexico City, November 1974; published in Kracke, ed. (1993).

[1] Although Cashinahua males pride themselves on their extramarital affairs, they insist that such activities be carried out with the utmost discretion in order to avoid either embarrassing the aggrieved husband or provoking jealousy.
[2] I am using the term "arranged" very loosely. It would perhaps be more accurate to say that he encouraged and facilitated the marriage arrangements.
[3] I learned some years later that this move was precipitated by a desire to gain access to my trade goods and medicine.

Chapter 15: Invisible People
Ostracism in Cashinahua Society

An earlier version of this chapter was originally published in slightly different form in *Dialectics and Gender: A Festschrift for Robert and Yolanda Murphy*, edited by Richard Randolph, May Dias, and David Schneider. Boulder, Colorado: West View Press, 1988.

[1] This chapter reports on the only two cases of "full" ostracism I observed. Milder forms exist in which the person was not shunned by the entire community; such as children, who were shunned by their parents with some regularity. I became interested in this form of sanction after feeling its effects for having broken a taboo and failing to start the required month-long fast. I have never felt so totally isolated; the fast and the purification ritual, although most unpleasant, were a small price to pay in order to be restored to the good graces of the Cashinahua.
[2] In this event, the central figure, Dinis, is to a large extent offstage. However, it was his behavior during the preceding months that precipitated the drama. Over a period of nearly a year, Dinis, an immigrant to Xumuya, had systematically attempted to seduce most of the women with no little success.
[3] In 1993 Dinis was the successful headman of his own village and a highly respected member of Cashinahua society.

Chapter 16: Food Taboos as Markers of Age Categories in Cashinahua

An earlier version of this chapter was originally published in "Food Taboos in Lowland South America," *Working Papers on South American Indians*, vol. 3 (August, 1981): pp. 155–171 (Bennington, VT: Bennington College).

[1] For a discussion of the problem of etic and emic, see Fisher and Werner (1978) and Kensinger (1975b).

Chapter 17: Living with Spirits

An earlier version of this chapter was first presented as a lecture at Simons Rock College, February 13, 1990.

[1] Some speakers call this spirit *yuda baka yushin*, replacing the word *bake*, child, with *baka*. *Baka* can be translated as luster or glow, and in some contexts as shadow. Most of my older informants insisted that *yuda bake yushin* is the correct form, arguing that the spirit emerges from the body and therefore is the body's child. Other informants, particularly those who migrated from Brazil, prefer *yuda baka yushin*, arguing that it is this spirit that gives the body its aura of liveliness. Although both terms are currently in use, I prefer to use the term *yuda bake yushin*, because this aura can wax and wane depending on the state of a person's health. For discussion of the related concept of *dua*, see chapter 23.

Chapter 18: Cashinahua Medicine and Medicine Men

An earlier version of this chapter was originally published in Patricia J. Lyon, ed., *Native South Americans: Ethnology of the Least Known Continent*. (Prospect Heights, IL: Waveland Press, 1974. Reissued with changes 1985).

[1] Most of these data were obtained between May and August 1966 when I was working as an apprentice to Inkamatsi, the principal herbalist in the village of Xumuya. Additional data were gathered during eighty months of fieldwork in 1955–63. The 1966 study was supported by a grant from the joint committee for Latin American Studies of the Social Science Research Council and the American Council of Learned Societies. An earlier version of this paper was read at the 1969 Northeastern Anthropological Association meeting in Providence, RI. I greatly benefited from the criticisms and comments of Luis S. Kemnitzer, Bette Landman, Elmer S. Miller, Patricia J. Lyon, Paula Wineberg Sabloff, and John Szwed.

Chapter 19: Banisteriopsis Usage among the Cashinahua

An earlier version of this chapter was originally published in Harner 1973.

Chapter 20: "You Killed My Baby!" Dispensing Medicine in the Field

An earlier version of this chapter was first presented in the symposium "The Anthropologist as Healer," American Anthropological Association meetings, November 1990, New Orleans, LA.

Chapter 21: Disposing of the Dead

An earlier version of this chapter was first presented as part of the symposium "Death, Mourning and the Afterlife in Lowland South America," American Anthropological Association meetings, San Francisco, CA, December 1992.

[1] Awadetsati later gave a detailed text to Montag that was published as "Endocanibalismo Funebre de los Cashinahua" (Montag, Montag, and Torres 1975), portions of which (along with brief descriptions of several other funerals) are included in Montag (ms). This chapter is also based on texts from other informants and on fieldnotes about eight burials I observed. I also have drawn on Deshayes and Keifenheim (1982:240–249) that includes a description of Awadetsati's funeral in 1979 and from McCallum (1991). I am indebted to these fellow Cashinahua scholars for data that provide me with some perspectives on changes that have occurred since 1968.

[2] The description that follows applies only to adults and initiated youth. Infants and young children are mourned and buried by their immediate family and close kin.

Chapter 22: The Body Knows Cashinahua Perspectives on Knowledge

An earlier version of this chapter was first presented at the 48th International Congress of Americanists, Uppsala, Sweden, July 1994. It is an updated version of Kensinger (1992) based on my 1993–94 fieldwork.

[1] Chapter 15 provides an example of this story being used during the settlement of a dispute rather than as entertainment as in the present case.

[2] Currently 21 Cashinahua teachers provide primary education in thirteen villages on the Curanja and Purus Rivers. Two secondary schools, funded by the Peruvian Ministry of Education and staffed by three Cashinahua and eleven Spanish-speaking mestizo teachers, operate in two villages. Some Cashinahua, particularly the bilingual teachers, also attended secondary school at the Catholic mission in Esperanza or in a government-run school in Yarinacocha.

[3] Missionary linguists of the Summer Institute of Linguistics translated the New Testament into the Cashinahua language and taught Bible study classes throughout the 1970s; the New Testament translation was dedicated in 1983. Missionaries from Mision Suisa del Peru replaced the SIL missionary linguists in 1982. They selected several young men for training in Spanish at their Bible School in Pucallpa who now serve as pastors of churches in four of the villages. In 1993 approximately 15 percent of the Cashinahua were professing Christians, 15 percent were openly hostile toward Christian teaching, and the remaining 70 percent were basically indifferent.

Chapter 23: "Feathers Make Us Beautiful" The Meaning of Cashinahua Feather Headdresses

An earlier version of this chapter was originally published in *The Gift of Birds: Featherwork of Native South American Peoples*, edited by Ruben E. Reina and Kenneth M. Kensinger. Philadelphia: University Museum of Archaeology and Anthropology, 1991.

[1] In an earlier publication (Kensinger et al., pp. 69–83), I describe how the Cashinahua classify, manufacture, and use headdresses.

[2] My teacher, Ward H. Goodenough, used to tell us, "If you want to know why people do what they do, ask them! You don't have to believe what they tell you, but you better know what they mean by what they say if you don't believe their answer." This chapter is an attempt to put that advice to work.

Chapter 24: When a Turd Floats by Cashinahua Metaphors of Contact

An earlier version of this chapter was originally presented in the symposium "Cosmology, Values, and Inter-ethnic Contact in South America," American Anthropological Association, December 1986, and published in South American Indian Studies, no. 2.

[1] It should be noted that while male storytellers insist that the bird was male, his name is one presently given only to females. Several female informants insisted that the bird was female.

[2] For an update on Cashinahua relationships with the outsiders, see chapter 25.

Chapter 25: Twenty-five Years Later
Continuity and Change

I am most grateful to the Harry Frank Guggenheim Foundation whose generous support made it possible for me to return to the field in 1993 and 1994.

BIBLIOGRAPHY

Abelove, Joan M. 1978. "Preverbal learning of kinship behavior among Shipibo infants of eastern Peru." Ph.D. diss., City University of New York.

Aspelin, Paul. 1975. *External Articulation and Domestic Production: The Artifact Trade of the Maimande of Northwestern Mato Grosso, Brazil.* Latin American Studies Program Dissertation Series 58. Ithaca, NY: Cornell University Press.

Basso, Ellen. 1973 (reissued 1988). *The Kalapalo Indians of Central Brazil.* Prospect Heights, IL: Waveland Press.

Beckerman, Stephen. 1979. "The Abundance of Protein in Amazonia: A Reply to Gross." In *American Anthropologist* 81: 533–560.

Berlin, Elois Ann, and Edward Markell. 1977. "An Assessment of the Nutritional and Health Status of an Aguaruna Jivaro Community, Amazonas, Peru." *Ecology of Food and Nutrition* 6: 69–81.

Burling, Robbins. 1969. "Linguistics and Ethnographic Description." *American Anthropologist* 71: 817–827.

Capistrano de Abreu, J. 1941 (1914). *Rã-txa hu-ni ku-i. Grammatica, textos e vocabulario Caxinauas.* Rio de Janeiro: Edição da Sociedade Capistrano de Abreu.

Carneiro, Robert L. 1982. "Comment." In *Current Anthropology* 23: 418–419.

Chagnon, Napoleon A. 1983. *Yanomamö: The Fierce People*, 3d ed. New York: Holt, Rinehart and Winston.

Chagnon, Napoleon A., and Raymond B. Hames. 1979. "Protein Deficiency and Tribal Warfare in Amazonia: New Data." *Science* 203: 910–913.

Clark, Homer H., JR. 1968. *The Law of Domestic Relations in the United States*. Minneapolis-St. Paul: West Publishing Co.

Der Maarderosian, Ara H., Jew-Ming Chao, Frederick J. Goldstein, and Kenneth M. Kensinger. 1970. "The Use and Hallucinatory Principles of a Psychoactive Beverage of the Cashinahua Tribe Amazon Basin," *Drug Dependence* 5: 355–360.

Deshayes, Patrick, and Barbara Keifenheim. 1982. *La conception de l'autre chez les Kashinawa*. Doctorat de 3³ cycle, Université Paris VII.

Divale, William T., and Marvin Harris. 1976. "Population, Warfare, and the Male Supremacist Complex." *American Anthropologist* 78: 521–538.

Dole, Gertrude E. 1979. "Pattern and Variation in Amahuaca Kin Terminology." In David J. Thomas, ed. *Social Correlates of Kin Terminology*, Working Papers on South American Indians, no. 1: 13–36. Bennington, VT: Bennington College.

Erikson, Philippe. 1993. "A Onomastica Matis e Amazonica?" In Eduardo Viveiros de Castro e Manuela Carneiro da Cunha, editors, *Amazonia: Etnologia e Historia Indigena*. São Paulo: Nucleo de Historia Indigena e do Indigenismo, USP/APESP.

______. nd. "Mecanismos y estructuras de articulatión y reproducción social."

Fields, Harriet L., and William Merrifield. 1980. "Mayoruna (Panoan) Kinship." *Ethnology* 19, no. 1: 1–28.

Fisher, Lawrence E., and Oswald Werner. 1978. "Explaining Explanation: Tension in American Anthropology." *Journal of Anthropological Research*, 34: 194–218.

Goodenough, Ward H. 1970. *Description and Comparison in Cultural Anthropology*. Chicago: Aldine.

Gregor, Thomas. 1977. *Mehinaku*. Chicago: University of Chicago Press.

______. 1985. *Anxious Pleasures*. Chicago: University of Chicago Press.

Gross, Daniel R. 1975. "Protein Capture and Cultural Development in the Amazon Basin." *American Anthropologist* 77, no. 3: 526–549.

______. 1982. "Proteína y Cultura en la Amazonia: Una Segunda Revisión." *Amazonia Peruana* 3, no. 6: 127–144.

______. 1983. "Village Movement in Relation to Resources in Amazonia." In Raymond B. Hames and William T. Vickers, eds., *Adaptive Responses of Native Amazonians*, pp. 429–449. New York: Academic Press.

Hames, Raymond B., ed. 1980. *Studies in Hunting and Fishing in the Neotropics*. Working Papers on South American Indians, no. 2. Bennington, VT: Bennington College.

Hames, Raymond B., and William T. Vickers, eds. 1983. *Adaptive Responses of Native Amazonians*. New York: Academic Press.

Harner, Michael J., ed. 1973. *Hallucinogens and Shamanism*. New York: Oxford University Press.

Harris, Marvin. 1964. *The Nature of Cultural Things*. New York: Random House.

______. 1968. *The Rise of Anthropological Theory*. New York: Thomas Y. Crowell.

______. 1971. *Culture, Man and Nature: An Introduction to General Anthropology*. New York: Thomas Y. Crowell.

Harris, Marvín. 1974. *Cows, Pigs, Wars, and Witches: The Riddles of Culture*. New York: Random House.

______. 1979. *Cultural Materialism*. New York: Random House.

Headland, Thomas N., Kenneth L. Pike, and Marvin Harris. 1990. *Emics and Etics: The Insider/Outsider Debate, Frontiers of Anthropology*, Volume 7. Newbury Park: Sage Publications.

Henley, Paul. 1982. *The Panare: Tradition and Change on the Amazonian Frontier*. New Haven: Yale University Press.

Holmberg, Allan. 1969. *Nomads of the Long Bow—The Siriono of Eastern Bolivia*. Garden City, NY: Natural History Press.

Hornborg, Alf. 1988. *Dualism and Hierarchy in Lowland South America: Trajectories of Indigenous Social Organization*. Uppsala: Studies in Cultural Anthropology, no. 9.

______. 1991. "Panoan Marriage Sections: A Comparative Perspective." Presented in the symposium *Classic Panoan Topics in Light of Recent Research*. 47th International Congress of Americanists, New Orleans, LA.

Hurault, Jacques. 1972. *Français et Indiens en Guyane*. Paris: Union Générale d'Edition.

Johnson, Allen. 1982. "Reductionism in Cultural Ecology: The Amazon Case." *Current Anthropology* 23, no. 4: 413–428.

Johnson, Allen, and Clifford A. Behrens. 1982. "Nutritional Criteria in Machiguenga Food Production Decisions: A Linear Programming Analysis." *Human Ecology* 10, no. 2: 167–189.

Kay, Paul. 1970. "Some Theoretical Implications of Ethnographic Semantics." *Bulletin of the American Anthropological Association* (special issue) 3: 19–31.

Kensinger, Kenneth M. 1974. "Cashinua Medicine and Medicine Man." In Patricia J. Lyon, ed., *Native South Americans: Ethnology of the Least Known Continent*, pp. 283–288. Boston: Little, Brown.

______. 1975a. "Studying the Cashinahua." In Kensinger, Kenneth M., et al. *The Cashinahua of Eastern Peru*. Brown University Studies in Anthropology and Material Culture, Volume 1. Bristol, RI: The Haffenreffer Museum of Anthropology.

______. 1975b. "Data, Data, and More Yanomamo Data." *Reviews in Anthropology*, 2: 69–74.

______. 1977. "Cashinahua Notions of Social Time and Social Space." *Actes du 42ème Congrès International des Américanistes* 2: 233–244.

______. 1983. "On Meat and Hunting." *Current Anthropology* 24, no. 1: 128–129.

______. 1984. "Sex and Food: Reciprocity in Cashinahua Society?" In Kenneth M. Kensinger, ed., *Sexual Ideologies in Lowland South America*, pp. 1–3. Working Papers on South American Indians, no. 5. Bennington, VT: Bennington College.

______. 1985. "An Emic Model of Cashinahua Marriage." In Kenneth M. Kensinger, ed., *Marriage Practices in Lowland South America*, pp. 221–251. Urbana: University of Illinois Press.

Kensinger, Kenneth M. 1989. "Hunting and Male Domination in Cashinahua Society." In Susan Kent, ed., *Farmers and Hunters*, pp. 18–26. Cambridge: Cambridge University Press.

______. 1992. "A Body of Knowledge, or, the Body Knows." *Expedition* 33 no. 3: 37–45.

Kensinger, Kenneth M., et al. 1975. *The Cashinahua of Eastern Peru*. Brown University Studies in Anthropology and Material Culture, Volume 1. Bristol, RI: The Haffenreffer Museum of Anthropology.

Kracke, Waud H., ed. 1993. "Leadership in Lowland South America." *South American Indian Studies*, no 1. Bennington, VT: Bennington College.

Leach, Edmund R. 1961. "Rethinking Anthropology." In *Rethinking Anthropology*. London School of Economics Monographs on Social Anthropology, no. 22. London: Athlone Press.

______. 1968. *A Runaway World?* New York: Oxford University Press.

Lévi-Strauss, Claude. 1963. *Structural Anthropology*. New York: Basic Books.

______. 1969. *Elementary Structures of Kinship*. Translated by James Bell and John von Sturmer. Boston: Beacon Press.

Lizot, Jacques. 1977. "Population, Resources, and Warfare Among the Yanomami." *Man* 12, nos. 3/4: 497–517.

______. 1985. *Tales of the Yanomami: Daily Life in the Venezuelan Forest*. London: Cambridge University Press.

Loos, Eugene E. 1960. "Capanahua Patrilineality and Matrilocality." Unpublished manuscript.

Maybury-Lewis, David H. P. 1960. "The Analysis of Dual Organisations: A Methodological Critique." *Bijdragen tot de Tall-, Land-en Volkenkunde* 11: 617–44.

Maybury-Lewis, David, H. P., ed. 1979. *Dialectical Societies: The Gê and Bororo of Central Brazil*. Cambridge: Harvard University Press.

McCallum, Cecilia. 1989. *Gender, Personhood and Social Organization amongst the Cashinahua of Western Amazonia*. Ph.D. diss., University of London.

______. 1990. "Language, Kinship and Politics in Amazonia." *Man* (n.s.) 25: 412–433.

______. 1991. "Cashinahua (Huni Kuin) Death, Dying, and Personhood." Presented in the symposium *Classic Panoan Topics in Light of Recent Research*. 47th International Congress of Americanists, New Orleans, LA.

Melatti, Julio Cezar. 1977. "Estrutura social Marubo: um sistema australiano na Amazonia. *Anuario Antropologica*/76, pp. 83–120. Rio de Janeiro: Tempo Brasileiro.

Merrifield, William R. 1968. "Review of The Rise of Anthropological Theory by Marvin Harris." *Current Anthropology* 9: 526–527.

Montag, Richard. nd. "Funeral Practices Among the Cashinahua of Eastern Peru." Unpublished manuscript.

Montag, Richard, Susan Montag, and Pudichu Torres. 1975. "Endocanibalismo funebre de los Cashinahua." *Datos Etnolingüisticos*, No. 45. Yarinacocha: Instituto Lingüistico de Verano.

Murphy, Robert F. 1960. *Headhunter's Heritage: Social and Economic Change Among the Mundurucú*. Berkeley: University of California Press.

______. 1971. *The Dialectics of Social Life: Alarms and Excursions in Anthropological Theory*. New York: Basic Books.

______. 1974. "Deviance and Social Control I: What Makes Waru Run?" and "Deviance and Social Control II: Borai." In Patricia J. Lyon, ed. *Native South Americans*, pp.195–208. Boston: Little Brown and Co. (Originally 1961 and 1962.)

______. 1977. "Man's Culture and Woman's Nature." *Annals of the New York Academy of Sciences* 293: 15–24.

______. 1979. *An Overture to Social Anthropology*. Englewood Cliffs, NJ: Prentice-Hall, Inc.

Murphy, Yolanda, and Robert F. Murphy. 1974. *Women of the Forest*. New York: Columbia University Press.

Needham, Rodney. 1971a. "Introduction." In *Rethinking Kinship and Marriage*, Rodney Needham, ed., A.S.A. Monographs, no. 11. London and New York: Tavistock and Barnes & Noble.

______. 1971b. "Remarks on the Analysis of Kinship and Marriage." In Needham, ed. 1971a, pp. 1–34.

Overing Kaplan, Joanna. 1977. "Orientation for Paper Topics." *Actes du XLIIe Congres International des Américanistes*, vol. 2, pp. 9–11. Paris: C.N.R.S. et Fondation Singer-Polignac.

Pike, Kenneth L. 1967. *Language in Relation to a Unified Theory of the Structure of Human Behavior*. The Hague: Mouton.

Pollock, Donald K. 1985. "Food and Sexual Identity Among the Culina." *Food and Foodways* 1: 25–42.

Rivière, Peter G. 1971. "Marriage: A Reassessment." In Rodney Needham, ed., *Rethinking Kinship and Marriage*, A.S.A. Monographs, no. 11. London and New York: Tavistock and Barnes & Noble.

Romanoff, Steven. 1983. "Matses Adaptations in the Peruvian Amazon." Ph.D. diss., Columbia University.

Ross, Eric B. 1978. "Food Taboos, Diet, and Hunting Strategy: The Adaptation to Animals in Amazon Cultural Ecology." *Current Anthropology* 19, no. 1: 1–36.

Russell, Robert, and Delores Russell. 1959. *Vocabulario Amawaka*. Serie Linguistica Especial. Rio de Janeiro: Museu Nacional.

Salzman, Philip Carl. 1988. "Fads and Fashions in Anthropology." *Anthropology Newsletter* 29, no. 5: 1, 32–33.

Siskind, Janet. 1973a. "Tropical Forest Hunters and the Economy of Sex." In Daniel R. Gross, ed., *Peoples and Cultures of Native South America*, pp. 226–240. Garden City, NY: Natural History Press.

______. 1973b. *To Hunt in the Morning*. New York: Oxford University Press.

Speth, John D., and Katherine A. Spielmann. 1983. "Energy Source, Protein Metabolism, and Hunter-Gatherer Subsistence Strategies." *Journal of Anthropological Archaeology* 2: 1–31.

Vickers, William T. 1978. "Reply to Ross." *Current Anthropology* 19, no. 1: 27.

Wallace, Anthony F. C. 1980. "Review of Cultural Materialism, by Marvin Harris." *American Anthropologist* 82: 423–426.

Wistrand Robinson, Lila. 1968. "Cashibo Kinship System and Social Relationships." Unpublished manuscript.

INDEX

DATE DUE

Jan 3/06	